Socialism and Modernity

Peter B[eilharz]

*For Zygmunt
my advance copy, a
little avant-garde
with thanks
from Peter, 2009*

Contradictions

Craig Calhoun, Social Science Research Council, Series Editor

24   Peter Beilharz, *Socialism and Modernity*

23   Loïc Wacquant, *Prisons of Poverty*

22   Tariq Modood, *Multicultural Politics: Racism, Ethnicity, and Muslims in Britain*

21   Fuyuki Kurasawa, *The Ethnological Imagination: A Cross-Cultural Critique of Modernity*

20   Lawrence Peter King and Iván Szelényi, *Theories of the New Class: Intellectuals and Power*

19   Pier Carlo Bontempelli, *Knowledge, Power, and Discipline: German Studies and National Identity*

18   Elizabeth Jelin, *State Repression and the Labors of Memory*

17   Gil Eyal, *The Origins of Postcommunist Elites: From Prague Spring to the Breakup of Czechoslovakia*

16   Alan Milchman and Alan Rosenberg, editors, *Foucault and Heidegger: Critical Encounters*

15   Michael D. Kennedy, *Cultural Formations of Postcommunism: Emancipation, Transition, Nation, and War*

14   Michèle H. Richman, *Sacred Revolutions: Durkheim and the Collège de Sociologie*

13   Pierre-André Taguieff, *The Force of Prejudice: On Racism and Its Doubles*

12   Krishan Kumar, *1989: Revolutionary Ideas and Ideals*

11   Timothy Mitchell, editor, *Questions of Modernity*

(series page continued on page 227)

Socialism and Modernity

Peter Beilharz

Contradictions, Volume 24

 University of Minnesota Press
Minneapolis • London

Publication information about previously published material in this book is on pages 221–22.

Copyright 2009 by the Regents of the University of Minnesota

All rights reserved. No part of this publication may be reproduced, stored in a retrieval system, or transmitted, in any form or by any means, electronic, mechanical, photocopying, recording, or otherwise, without the prior written permission of the publisher.

Published by the University of Minnesota Press
111 Third Avenue South, Suite 290
Minneapolis, MN 55401-2520
http://www.upress.umn.edu

Library of Congress Cataloging-in-Publication Data

Beilharz, Peter.
   Socialism and modernity / Peter Beilharz.
      p. cm. — (Contradictions ; v. 24)
   Includes bibliographical references and index.
   ISBN 978-0-8166-6085-8 (hc : alk. paper) — ISBN 978-0-8166-6086-5 (pb : alk. paper)
   1. Socialism. 2. Social history—1970– I. Title.
   HX45.B45 2009
   335—dc22
                                            2009004569

Printed in the United States of America on acid-free paper

The University of Minnesota is an equal-opportunity educator and employer.

18 17 16 15 14 13 12 11 10 09   10 9 8 7 6 5 4 3 2 1

Contents

Acknowledgments	vii
Introduction: From Socialism to Modernity, via Americanism	ix
1. Socialism: Modern Hopes, Postmodern Shadows	1
2. Socialism by the Back Door	17
3. The Life and Times of Social Democracy	27
4. The Fabian Imagination	42
5. The Australian Left: Beyond Laborism?	50
6. Australian Laborism, Social Democracy, and Social Justice	72
7. The End of Australian Communism	87
8. Between Totalitarianism and Postmodernity	95
9. Socialism after Communism: Liberalism?	107
10. Socialism in Europe—after the Fall	116
11. Intellectuals and Utopians	142

12. Modernity and Communism: Zygmunt Bauman and the
    Other Totalitarianism   167

13. Looking Back: Marx and Bellamy   179

14. Socialism and America   189

Notes   201

Publication History   221

Index   223

Acknowledgments

The essays collected in this book cover twenty years of my life and the recent history of socialism. It is wonderful to publish an essay, to put a message in a bottle at all; to see this writing have a second life and a new and different audience is even more warming. The process of preparing these essays for republication is educative, because it confronts the author with the challenge of self-interpretation, of reading these earlier writings also as signs of times with their own histories and of watching these histories unfold after the fact.

Writing is a solitary act, but all its preconditions are profoundly social. Many people helped me on this path; many of their names appear across these pages. As I assembled the permissions for this book, I saw three recurrent licenses: David Lovell; Sage Publications and Chris Rojek; and *Thesis Eleven*. I thank them for encouraging me. The initial suggestion for this project came from Craig Calhoun, whose friendship and trust I value; I am proud to offer him this book in return. At the University of Minnesota Press, I worked with Carrie Mullen, Richard Morrison, and especially Jason Weidemann, who was always steadfast and fun, a real pleasure to work with. The editing work of Nancy Sauro and Marilyn Martin at Minnesota was amazing. I thank them.

Dor, Nikolai, and Rhea supported me across all these years, as has Bronwyn Bardsley. This book is dedicated to the memory of my father and my parents-in-law. Likely they never quite knew what I was up to, but it never really mattered: they were always there.

Introduction

From Socialism to Modernity, via Americanism

Over my lifetime the discourse of radicalism has shifted from socialism to modernity, from marxism to critical theory or whatever comes after. This volume gathers essays that cover a twenty-year span. Across that period there has been a significant historical shift and a conceptual semantic shift that reflects it. Twenty years ago there was still a Soviet world system; twenty years ago marxism was still a significant global influence, with or without reference to communism. The essays here track these shifts from socialism to modernity-talk or to what I called "postmodern socialism" in a book with this title published in 1994. Both of those terms have now dispersed as their objects have become diffused.[1]

When did the dominant radical discourse shift from "capitalism" to "modernity"? These days, we could well observe that capitalism (or at least its cognate global term, *empire*) has made a significant comeback. Karl Marx has been partly rehabilitated, not least in this global frame of reference, where the *Communist Manifesto* is now identified as the founding text of globalization-talk. But the prior issue, before we ask when the idea of "capitalism" gave way to that of "modernity," is where did the identification of modernity with capitalism come from in the first place?

For the left, the hero (or culprit) is apparent. It all began with Marx. Not socialism, which well preceded Marx both as theory and practice, but the identification of modernity with capitalism. The elegance and power of Marx's work can be condensed in a single image: Marx set out to establish the critique of political economy as the necessary ideology of capitalism. His most evocative works, *The Paris Manuscripts* (1844), the *Grundrisse* (1857–58), and *Capital* (1867), are successive installments of this project, which became Marx's lifework. The legacy of this work was historic. For subsequent marxists, from the Second to the Fourth International, there was one global problem, capitalism, and one solution, socialism. Problems of gender, race, religion, et al., became second-order problems that would be solved after the revolution. *Revolution* became the vital third term, the transit point between capitalism and socialism. Logically, for marxists its singularity was an effect of the singular nature of the problem. Capitalism: Revolution: Socialism. Revolution was the pivot; the overthrow of the bourgeoisie was the singular solution to the problem, though other factors such as the tendency of the profit rate to fall, capitalism's propensity to crisis and depression, and so on, could also help out. Marxism became monofocal, as pluralists were happy to point out. If there was any sense in which it could be claimed that there was a dispersal of power, the credibility of revolutionary marxism would collapse (Vladimir Lenin). Leon Trotsky knew not only how to advocate revolution but also how to do it: seize the post office and the centers of finance, close parliament. By the 1930s the marxists' Italian follower, Antonio Gramsci, decided that this revolution would not work, at least not in the West, where coercion was combined with consent and there was no single locus of power.

In the moment of myself and my associates, living in Melbourne, Australia, in the period when we started the journal *Thesis Eleven*, there was an essay that helped to crystallize this lack of a single locus of power. Ferenc Fehér and Agnes Heller, the Melbourne representatives of the Budapest School in exile, had made available to us in draft form a paper that eventually appeared as "Class, Democracy, Modernity" in *Theory and Society* in 1983.[2] Its object was to claim that modernity was characterized by three logics, those of capitalism, democracy, and bureaucratization. At this point the Hungarians had already done much to promote taking seriously the idea of the modern, as an aesthetic but also as a sociological category. Modernism and the modern mattered, but now, too, especially under the imperative of the postmodern, it became more pressing to interrogate the primary condition, that of the modern itself. Aesthetic modernism, of course, was connected with the period of cultural innovation before the Great War. Fehér and Heller had taken this impulse on variously, but not least from their teacher Georg (György) Lukács. Lukács had kept company with both Max Weber and Georg Simmel, as is made abundantly apparent in his most scintillating 1923 paper "Reification and the Consciousness of the Proletariat."[3] Lukács's essay already pioneered the idea of critical theory before the fact, for it synthesized Marxian and Weberian motifs in a way that fused them. Weber, of course, was always a sociological pluralist, one for whom the power of capitalism was indeed fateful but always to be weighed against the power of bureaucracy and the state. If for later American pluralists like Robert Dahl socialism was logically inconceivable because power was always dispersed, for Weber socialism could be only a nightmare because it threatened to replace one pole (capital) with another (the state). Weber had none of the faith of socialists in the civic or third sphere as a place where socialist currents might also dwell.

This kind of argument associated with the Budapest School in the period of their antipodean exile had very little effect on revolutionary marxists, who at this point were busy trading in their Louis Althusser for Michel Foucault. Foucault's work did eventually supply the kind of sensibility associated with Weber or pluralism, where power would be dispersed rather than monopolized by capital. Revolutionary marxism had no time for talk of modernity, which looked all too bourgeois, culturalist, smug, and indulgent. Nor were most revolutionary marxists very well equipped when it came to the challenge of beginning to make sense of Soviet-type societies.

Historically, three possible explanations of Soviet-type societies were logically available to marxists. The first was that these societies were some kind of socialism. The second was that they were some kind of capitalism, perhaps especially state capitalism. The third was that they represented a new form of society sui generis. Marxists generally went for one of the first two explanations because capitalism and socialism were viewed as exhaustive analytic categories.[4] Even Trotsky had anticipated the possibility that the Soviet Union was a qualitatively new social formation, but his followers, such as Ernest Mandel on the one side and Max Shachtman and Tony Cliff on the other, struck more closely to theories of the hybrid or degenerated workers' state versus state capitalism. Fehér and Heller, by now writing in collaboration with George Markus, wanted rather to advance the notion that the Soviet Union was best understood in the first instance as a political regime sui generis, a dictatorship over needs (as they called it in the title of one of their books), rather than as a political economy that could be assimilated to existing models or ideas of capitalism or socialism. This could in turn be connected to the argument concerning the three logics in "Class, Democracy, Modernity." The Soviet Union could then be viewed as a distinct combination of the logics of capitalism (or, strictly, industrialization), democracy, and bureaucracy.[5]

The question then emerges, was the Soviet Union another path to modernity, or was it another modernity? Triumphalist procapitalists after 1989 would of course announce that there was only one modernity, capitalism or more literally Americanism. In more recent years, the terms of argument have become not capitalism versus communism but America versus Europe.[6]

Responding among other things to *Dictatorship over Needs,* Johann Arnason developed the case for an alternative modernity in his study *The Future That Failed: Origins and Destinies of the Soviet Model*.[7] This, in turn, anticipated his later and significant contribution to the idea of multiple modernities.[8] Arnason's general sympathy was evidently with the sui generis approach.[9] His work was also sensitive to some of the more peculiar ideological crossovers involved. The reference to America in Stalin's 1924 definition of Leninism as a combination of "Russian Revolutionary Sweep" and "American efficiency" was, as Arnason observed, characteristic of postrevolutionary Bolshevik culture, as in the speculations about the new Soviet man as a "Russian American."[10] Yet the ideological enthusiasm and economic borrowing of the Soviets only substantively effected the logic of industrialization, perhaps bureaucracy; there was no democracy, not even in the formal sense.

While Lukács was shifting from sociology to culture into the 1930s, Antonio Gramsci was combining political economy and culture, not least in his prison writings on Americanism and Fordism.[11] Gramsci's great contribution was to understand Fordism as both culture and political economy. Fordism represented a new way of producing but also of consuming: it promised a whole new way of life, and indeed a New Man (women still had to wait). This promised a new civilization, a mass society based on closed national circuits of mass production and mass consumption—not just Detroit but Hollywood, later suburbia and Levittown. This promised, as Terry Smith puts it, to make the modern, to make modernity as a cultural order, a domestic regime, a design regime, and an advertising regime as well as an economy of conveyor belts run along the lines of scientific management. The Soviets loved this prospect at both the elite and mass levels. This was not a solo affair, however; the Germans also loved Fordism.[12]

As Alan Ball shows in his alignment of Russian and American modernism, in his study *Imagining America: Influence and Images in Twentieth Century Russia,* both ordinary Russians and their extraordinary Bolshevik leaders were infatuated with Americanism, whatever the ambivalences that complicated their reception of it.[13] Whatever the case, Ball retains a clear sense of focus on the vital fact that this Soviet enthusiasm was an example of mass modernism and not just a playful distraction for the avant-garde. All the motifs were there—speed, efficiency, the machine: locomotion, automation and automobile, progress and more progress, giganticism, growth at *Amerikanski tempo.* From aesthetics to everyday life, *Fordizatsia*—Fordization—saturated Soviet social life from the 1920s. Soviet publications called for the creation of "Russian Americans" and Soviet Americanism; Americanism was often viewed less as mechanical, in the repetitive sense, than as voluntaristic, possibilist; anything was possible.[14] Nikolai Bukharin called for marxism plus Americanism; Trotsky famously demanded Bolshevism in the form of Soviet shoes with American nails.[15] Lenin, in turn, demanded Soviet power plus Prussian railway order plus American technology and organization of trusts plus American public education and tractors.[16] Soviet Fordism took the particular form of Fordsonism; it was the truck and tractor rather than the passenger car that expressed Soviet institutional desire. Vladimir Mayakovsky loved the Brooklyn Bridge, and almost everyone admired Henry Ford. There were two cults of Ford, as Ball puts it—one popular, one at an elite level.[17] American technology and personnel played a key role in Soviet industrialization, not least in hydroelectrics. The plan for the Stalingrad tractor factory was made in America.[18] But these were socialist, not bourgeois, tractors. This was socialist steel, forged in the image of Stalin, the man of steel. The extent of this American and bourgeois support of socialism across the 1930s was extraordinary. As Ball puts it, for example, "no significant branch of Soviet industry developed in the 1930s without some assistance from the General Electric Company." Trotsky was in exile, but American nails arrived by the boatload. Stalin was happy to acknowledge that fully two-thirds of the nation's large industrial establishments had been built with American assistance.[19]

The Soviet Union and the United States were welded together by the enthusiasm for the new world and the technological futurism of the 1930s. Only the Soviets could not deliver consumer goods at the same time; this was a very different kind of Fordism to the consumption model of Detroit, where the producers of Model Ts and As were also potentially their buyers. In the Soviet Union the symbol of the future remained the tractor or truck, a collective good, rather than the passenger car.

Was this, then, a Soviet model of modernity, or merely another road to Americanism? One of the most profound of the state capitalist marxists, C. L. R. James, came to argue that the American case was indeed both exemplary and exceptional. He was not alone on the left in valuing what he called American civilization; others, such as Charles and Mary Beard and Max Lerner, argued the same.[20] For James, the American Dream mattered; it was not merely a bourgeois fantasy or a distraction from harder things such as class struggle.

James lived in the United States for fifteen years, during which time he became a "neighbourhood man," an observer of the ordinary intelligence and enthusiasm of Americans. He was a marxist, but unlike, say, Herbert Marcuse, into the 1960s he liked what he saw.[21] His sensibility was that the nineteenth century belonged to Europe, the twentieth to the United States. The American dialectic involved a "struggle for happiness," a tension between creative capacity and the modern trend to fragmentation and alienation. His older, European socialist sensibility told him that this was civilization compared to totalitarian barbarism but that the completion of civilization would be socialism itself. Democracy was a wonderful ideal, but it needed to be extended into the sphere of production. As he put it in the opening to *American Civilization,* "The American Civilization is identified in the consciousness of the world with two phases of the development of world history. The first is the Declaration of Independence. The second is mass production. Washington and Henry Ford are the symbols of American Civilization."[22] The puzzle, for James, was that Americanism could be so innovative as industry yet so derivative as high culture. Where it excelled in the latter sphere was in popular culture, which James applauded. It was *new.* In gangster films, radio dramas, and comic books were found the combination of frustration and violence that *was* period American culture. The cult of work led to a mechanized civilization and a standardization of everyday life that resulted in psychic anxiety, in the bizarre contrast between social prometheanism and personal powerlessness.[23]

James connected with Marx in all this, but also with Elton Mayo, Lloyd Warner, and Lewis Mumford. In their hands, the United States replaced the United Kingdom as the model for *Das Kapital.* The Soviet

Union became a dull bureaucratic version of state capitalism. Where Weber viewed the West as the universalizing culture, James gave that role to Americanism. "Yankee Go Home!" read the graffiti on third world walls, where in another hand there was added, "and take me with you." Americanism and Fordism indeed looked like the dominant postwar modernity. The American Dream became universal, and dispersed, as the Postwar Dream. In Australia this dream took the image of the Lucky Country, though it also spread through Europe in the 1950s and then into Asia.

But there are other modernities—Asian, Latin American, antipodean, and so on—and there are, or were, different socialisms, however they were internationally mediated. The essays collected in this book might be taken to address an Australasian exceptionalism or to defend alternative socialisms from orthodox, especially Soviet, forms. Like other socialist scholars, I have given much of my working life to the task of extricating early marxism and other socialisms from under the Soviet experience. In this my work has shadowed that of Zygmunt Bauman, whose footprints were always there before me.[24] It has also been much influenced by the antipodean scholar Bernard Smith, for whom peripheral culture also feeds the centers, for whom other people's modernities and modernisms are also exemplary.[25] As the focus shifts from socialism to modernity, it also shifts to socialisms and modernity. Whatever the asymmetry between their powers, it remains difficult to image one without the other.

What residual forms and presences does socialism take now? Bauman's work follows socialism into culture, though socialism also maintains a presence here as utopia, in the stronger sense of an imaginary state of affairs that guides thinking and desire but can never itself be actualized. Bernard Smith's work follows a similar logical path, where socialism, like any other significant cultural trend, becomes mainstreamed, lost into the broader flows from which it earlier emerged. But for me and my work, there is a great deal more than this to the contributions of Smith and Bauman. My encounters with them were transformative.

My earliest serious contribution to scholarship emerged from doctoral work with the great Gramsci scholar Alastair Davidson. It focused on the revolutionary tradition, Trotskyism in particular, which I wanted to get off the historic stage because of its fatal flaws, not least its Jacobinism.[26] Having cleared my stage, at least intellectually, it then became incumbent on me to replace these false idols with something more useful and ethically desirable. I have always, in a stronger or looser sense, been a marxist, but never a revolutionary. My natural attraction was to German and Scandinavian social democracy, to council communism, English ethical socialism, Western marxism, and Fabianism. My next major work, *Labour's Utopias,* compared Bolshevism, Fabianism, and social democracy with the obvious linear logic implied in their juxtaposition; Fabianism was far more interesting than most imagined, but German social democracy represented its richest inheritance, not least because of its foundational relationship to classical marxism.[27] Western marxism, in turn, definitionally opened the door for me to Weber via Lukács, though through these earlier years it was always Gramsci who appealed most, not least because Gramsci understood the importance of the Southern Question and not only of Fordism.

Being antipodean — in my case, living in Australia — also necessarily meant taking a position on laborism, on the dominant radical culture, and on its organizational form, represented by the Australian Labor Party. The ALP had a significant heritage, though intellectually this paled in contrast to the heritage of German social democracy or even English Fabianism. Laborism's limit was that it had always remained a producer's politics, strapped when it came to embracing wider conceptions of solidarity or citizenship. So far, so bad; but then it got worse, though definitely more interesting, as the ALP converted itself into Blair's New Labor *avant la lettre* from 1983. Together with Rob Watts, Julian Triado, and others around *Thesis Eleven,* I became a major critic of this New Labor, as documented in this volume. In retrospect it seems to me that our critique was often right, if for the wrong reasons. We took the easy path, in a sense, of comparing immediate Australian experience with images of the good society from Marx and others. Unsurprisingly, the ALP came out looking tawdry, though it did at the same time license the politics of globalization in Australia in a manner without precedent, except in the case of New Zealand, which went even further right.[28]

In 1994 I wrote two books, one on the ALP, called *Transforming Labor,* the other a set of second-order global reflections on this experience called *Postmodern Socialism.* Emotionally and intellectually I was in trouble. Socialism, the object of my desire and the subject of my life's work, was disappearing before my eyes. I faced a choice: I could either continue to work on socialism and risk getting bored or change, find a lifeline out.

My line out came with the realization that I should write about the work of Bernard Smith, then that of Zygmunt Bauman. Both gave me continuity, for they had also been lifelong socialists who shifted from politics to culture. More, they gave me an affirmative opportunity, for they are both exemplary individuals and intellectuals. More again, at that time, neither had yet gained the recognition that he so richly deserved. Smith was the leading Australian art historian, and well recognized as such, but the sociological import of his work, his views on the antipodes and cultural traffic, were barely recognized. Similarly, Bauman's work was widely represented in talk and footnotes, but there was, at the time of my writing, no single monograph interpreting his work. There was a certain logic of return in my path, too. After all, I had begun with the figure of Trotsky, with intellectual history though in a negative, critical register. Now I was able to interpret and to pursue the work of exemplary yet somehow marginal thinkers; to work and breathe with living, loving subjects; and to argue positively for their projects as exemplary. The personal had not become political for me so much as the intellectual had also become personal. Thus I was able to work continuously with my own past while simultaneously working out of and away from it.

The essays collected in this volume track some of this path. This Introduction and the last chapter, "Socialism and America," were written especially for this book. The first chapter, "Socialism: Modern Hopes, Postmodern Shadows," is used to open the volume in a panoramic way. It follows the broad sympathy of my work, where marxism is central to but never exhaustive of the socialist traditions that preceded and postdate marxism. The themes of romanticism and enlightenment also figure here, the former as a line to the postmodern, the latter as a central frame for the modernist hopes of marxism (though I also want to insist that romanticism remains central to marxism, especially to Marx's own thinking). Chapter 2, "Socialism by the Back Door," offers another kind of introductory optic, autobiographical rather than panoramic. The allusion is dual: by the back door might be where you stash yesterday's papers, pending further evaluation; it might also refer to my own point of arrival, for, given my modest origins, it was my good fortune to enter the house of socialist scholarship indirectly, never to be trumpeted as a new emperor.

The title of chapter 3, "The Life and Times of Social Democracy," is a pun on C. B. Macpherson's *The Life and Times of Liberal Democracy*. This chapter was preliminary to my later book *Labour's Utopias*. It tests the work of Eduard Bernstein and Karl Kautsky, seeking to save them from the dominant condescensions of posterity. "The Fabian Imagination," the next chapter, seeks to do the same for the Fabian tradition.

The dominant reception of Fabianism on the left has been to see Beatrice and Sidney Webb as "two typewriters clicking as one" and to overlook the extraordinary talents of thinkers like G. D. H. Cole. Marxists, in particular, have treated Fabians as idiots; the usual prerequisite of the encounter has been a refusal to read their work. My purpose here is simply to open another door, to let another tradition breathe.

At this point we take an antipodean turn. Chapter 5, "The Australian Left: Beyond Laborism?" was commissioned by Ralph Miliband for the *Socialist Register*. His doing so marked an important personal moment for me, for it involved trust on his part, sight unseen, and it gave me the opportunity to stretch out, intellectually, to tell the local story for outsiders, above and beyond the interventions and clashes of reviews and journalism in the immediately local debate about the prospects of Australian New Labor. The following chapter, "Australian Laborism, Social Democracy, and Social Justice," takes a step back to fill in some of the elements of the historical context of laborism and its conceptual and political limits. Chapter 7, "The End of Australian Communism," traces a different local history. As elsewhere, the Communist Party of Australia (CPA) combined the worst of tradition with some interesting innovations. As elsewhere, again, its orthodoxy did not prevent the CPA from attracting some of the best and most unorthodox of Australian minds. For better or worse, the CPA was also a little public sphere.

In the CPA's collapse, Australian communists also led. The CPA leadership in Melbourne dissolved itself into the Labor Party in 1984, five years before the global involution of communism. Some Australian journals also led, *Arena* (b. 1963) and *Intervention* (b. 1972) among them. Chapter 8, "Between Totalitarianism and Postmodernity," uses the themes of the *Thesis Eleven* reader of the same name published by MIT Press in 1992 to canvass some of these themes. It connects some of the signs of those times with the experience of *Thesis Eleven* (b. 1980) and the arguments developed in books I published in 1994, *Transforming Labor* and *Postmodern Socialism*, referring back to Gramsci and forward to Touraine.

Chapter 9, "Socialism after Communism: Liberalism?" addresses the paradox of liberalism and modernity. Every sociologist knows the limits of liberalism, the individualized perspective that indeed sociology set out to socialize. After socialism, liberalism has become a kind of universal default position. Yet in our everyday lives every little encounter or action is social and socialized, and this remains so even after socialism.

Chapter 10, "Socialism in Europe—after the Fall," was written at the invitation of Arthur Vidich, who wanted me to connect my own work to the magisterial 1996 volume of Donald Sassoon, *100 Years of Socialism*. Chapter 11, "Intellectuals and Utopians," enters the labyrinth of Zygmunt Bauman, tracking his particular concerns with socialism and what he calls the active utopia through to his ruptural work in *Legislators and Interpreters,* where socialism took a step back, from politics to interpretation. Bolshevism, which Bauman calls socialism's hot-headed younger brother, is the subject of "Modernity and Communism: Zygmunt Bauman and the Other Totalitarianism," the next chapter, where I seek to reconstruct Bauman's images of postwar Soviet and Polish modernity as a counterimage to Bauman's *Modernity and the Holocaust.*

In 1971, when I was in the final year of high school, my beloved teacher N. W. Saffin bid me to read Edward Bellamy's *Looking Backward*. It was an experience from which I never looked back. In 2002 I worked as William Dean Howells Fellow at the Houghton Library at Harvard, returning to Bellamy in an archival way. Some of the results are registered in the penultimate chapter of this book, on Marx and Bellamy. The final chapter, "Socialism and America," employs the Sombart Question as a way to trace and interpret some of the most significant views on American socialism, from Daniel Bell to Michael Mann. These encounters were supported by remarkable individuals such as Bernard Bailyn and Daniel Bell, with whom I became acquainted when I served as professor of Australian studies at Harvard from 1999 to 2000. I imagine that it was my work on Bernard Smith, *Imagining the Antipodes,* that persuaded the Committee on Australian Studies at Harvard that I was worthy. So I traveled to Cambridge to teach about Australia, but of course I learned a great deal more about America, though I also came to puzzle about what I really knew about my own place, in the antipodes. In any case, this is a confession that America came late for me; most of my earlier work was on Australia and Europe, and most of it was conducted in archives there rather than in the United States.

I came to America late as well; I first visited in 1993, at the invitation of Craig Calhoun, who also initiated the process that resulted in the book you are holding. My journeys stateside became at least annual, my friendships here some of my closest. I hope that writing this book might also be viewed as an act of reciprocity. For my journey from socialism to modernity has also been a trip via America, which itself expresses the best and worst of modernity and modernism. American dreams persist, as does dreaming in the antipodes.

One

Socialism: Modern Hopes, Postmodern Shadows

Today, socialism may seem to be part of the past; perhaps this is necessarily so. To begin to consider the arguments involved across various socialisms as social theory already means to begin to break up these firm, if imaginary, distinctions between past, present, and future. For if the socialist traditions often think back, they also necessarily reach forward. Socialism is one central trend in the critique of modernity, for socialism rests on the image of modernity as it is and as it might be. Its main strength has been its capacity to call out the critique of the present by comparing it with senses of pasts and distinct possible futures or else by comparing innovative experiences in some times and places with more routine achievements elsewhere. Socialism thus functions as critique, via utopia; and at the beginning of the twentieth-first century we might conclude that it works better in this critical register than as a politics aimed at the possession of state power. Socialism is, as Zygmunt Bauman puts it, the counterculture of modernity.[1] Well into this millennium, the presence of socialism may be more discernible as a culture than as a politics. In this broader sense, socialist argument replays various claims and counterclaims associated with modernity and critique via romanticism and enlightenment. Both rural and urban, modern and antimodern, socialist theory remains the alter ego of capitalism.[2] Thus socialism has run arguments parallel to many of capitalism's claims, including its obsession with economy and, into the middle of the twentieth century, with the state. Similarly, socialism runs a dialogue of its own with America and Americanism as the putative model and future of modernity.

To begin, it is important to register two historical facts. First, socialism has a history, a plurality of traditions across place and time. Second, the fact that marxism has come to dominate socialism does not mean that the two are identical. Socialism has a history; of which marxism is a part. Socialism preceded and postdates marxism.[3] These facts raise other issues, such as the extraordinary power of local cultures, to the extent that, for example, some communist traditions remain far more deeply marked by local stories than by the grand narratives of Soviet marxism.[4]

Socialism as a social theory coincided not only with the radical aspirations of the French Revolution but also with the earliest reactions against the industrial revolution. Arguably there are two streams of its development. Socialist argument has a local, practical current that emerged into the 1830s and emphasizes cooperation, contrasting socialism to individualism and hoping for a maintenance of the older orders and habits against modernization.[5] It also has an intellectual or middle-class stream that often incorporates these local insights into more ambitious schemes or hopes for the future. Robert Owen and Charles Fourier were earlier representatives of this intellectual stream, which really came into its own with Marx, where for the first time the socialist project became a property dispute between warring intellectuals. Marxism in a sense abducted socialism, but especially after 1917, when the Bolsheviks pinned the marxist flag to their own attempt to seize power and construct the socialist order in the Soviet Union. Socialism consequently is identified with marxism and with the Soviet and subsequent claimed socialist roads from China to Cuba and elsewhere into the third world. Marxism thus became an ideology itself and sacrificed its capacity to criticize the present.

Does this mean, however, that socialism can only ever be a negative or oppositional trend? The point for any consideration of socialism as social theory is that politics and critique do not get on well together, at least when it comes to state power. But this obsession with the state came late, discernibly in the interwar period of the twentieth century. Socialism is often identified with statism, but this is misleading. The earliest socialists, like Owen and Fourier, favored the local level of analysis and viewed cooperation or self-management as crucial, and Marx followed them in this; even Marx's greatest work, *Capital,* thinks its object at the level of the capitalist factory and thinks its alternative as the socialist regime of associated producers. Early socialists worked more at the level of the exemplary politics of the commune than at the level of large-scale organization, and again Marx followed them in this, for he failed to bridge intellectually the gap between the individual factory and the globalized world system. Local socialism thus has historically coincided with the idea that small is beautiful, and thus has revealed the power of its own romanticism or antimodernism. For it was only with the work of Max Weber, Georg Simmel, and Émile Durkheim in different ways that sociologists centered upon scale and complexity as irreversible features of modern social organization. Marx's social theory is still guided by the spirit of Rousseau, in that problems of scale and complexity are largely withered away. This is exactly what motivated later turns to market socialism in Eastern Europe, and marketism, say, with the later work of Alec Nove: the recognition that markets deal better with scale than do bureaucracies.[6]

From the beginning, then, socialists have been active in dispute as to whether socialism involves more progress or modernity or less. Some, like Henri de Saint Simon, anticipated Durkheim in presuming that socialism will be modern or it will not be at all, presuming therefore in this that socialism is a state of affairs to be achieved rather than an ethic or an attitude. Marx's own work indicates the shift from romanticism to modernism. Others dug in on different positions. Thus Ferdinand Tönnies' incredibly influential defense of community, *Gemeinschaft* versus association or *Gesellschaft*, was a leading example of the romantic socialist case, where socialism was the opposite of everything that capitalism indicated—size, mobility, speed, rootlessness, restlessness, dirt, promiscuous sex, legalism, money and contracts, and urban frenzy.[7] Tönnies' views in turn called out Durkheim's modernist socialism in *The Division of Labour in Society* (1893) and in his Bordeaux lectures on socialism (1894–95), where Durkheim sent Rousseau and Tönnies back to the eighteenth century and insisted instead that the idea of the whole romantic personality be replaced by the expanded solidarity afforded by industrialism.

Today we forget that Durkheim and Tönnies were both socialists, and this is one reason we fail sufficiently to think of socialism as a social theory. Perhaps the more explicitly recognized period dispute here was that between William Morris and Edward Bellamy, whose competing images of the socialist future clearly indicated corresponding critiques of the present and social theories appropriate to their understanding. Bellamy published his novel of the sleeper waking, *Looking Backward*, in 1888. Against the image of capitalist waste and disorganization, Bellamy posited the image of socialism as highly organized, without friction, and in effect militarized, nationalized, well-fed, fit, and, to our eyes, gray. Morris hit the roof at this philistine good news and wrote in return *News from Nowhere* (1890), depicting an explicitly rural, Thames Valley utopia where modernity was not celebrated but pushed away, small was beautiful, and beauty was central to the quality of living, as John Ruskin before him had insisted.

The history of socialisms since has worked this contradiction, among others, between the sense that the idea of socialism involved more modernity and the idea that it involved less. The significance of Marx's work here emerges most fully, for it covers both aspects, a fact that his followers generally avoided. Marx offered at least five images of utopia. To track them is to witness Marx's own embrace of modernity as industrialism, or his transition from green to gray. The Marx known to us in the English language from the 1960s was different from the Marx of the Soviets. The extraordinary efflorescence of marxism into the 1970s involved a humanist phase, maneuvered by the *1844 Manuscripts,* followed by a structuralist moment led by Louis Althusser. But in the 1960s the Marx for today was deeply romantic in spirit, more in tune with Schiller's lament for human fragmentation than with Lévi-Strauss's science of the human mind. The great Marx of the period was the Marx set against alienation, implying a wholeness and authenticity that capitalism had destroyed, making it necessary to destroy the destroyer in turn. The utopia implicit in Marx's *1844 Manuscripts* was one of guild labor, where the medieval connotations denied the very idea of the division of labor. Marx put a Fourier spin on this in the famous passage in *The German Ideology* where the good society, playfully pictured, would involve hunting, herding, fishing, and criticism—a horticultural life with not a smokestack in sight.[8] All this changed across the period in which Marx left the green of the Rhine for the dirt of Dean Street and the British Museum. His subsequent images of utopia evoke automation, the trade-off between boredom and free time in the *Grundrisse,* and the self-managed factory in the third volume of *Capital.* A fifth possible utopia is glimpsed in Marx's correspondence with his Russian admirers into the 1870s, where Marx allowed the dispensation that communal socialism might still be feasible in Russia.[9]

Marx, of course, denied utopia but dealt in it every day of his life— again, necessarily so. For his purpose was to show, at first, that capitalism was a blot on the natural landscape, then later, that it was not the only possible way to organize modernity or industrialism. Marx's social theory remains central not only because of its critical power and influence but because of its capacity to contain this contradiction as it coincides with the progressive entrenchment of industrialism. The young Marx, like Owen and Fourier, could still imagine that industrialism was reversible. By the time he wrote *Capital,* that realization had changed; already in *The Communist Manifesto* this other modernist stream was apparent, that the real challenge was to harness the forces of production to popular need. But there were other transformations across Marx's work as well. One is powerfully apparent in the 1859 preface to *A Contribution to the Critique of Political Economy,* where Marx made plain his substitution of political economy for the earlier Hegelian curiosity about civil society. This was a landmark in the history of marxism, for it plainly indicated that henceforth marxism's concern would be within political economy itself. Marx and subsequent marxists became the wizards of economic analysis, predicting capitalist breakdown, falling profit rates, and inevitable proletarian revolution. This logical turn away from politics or culture within marxism was not to be remedied until the later appearance of Antonio Gramsci. Culture and politics became epiphenomenal within marxism, the result of economics rather than realms in their own right. Socialism became a result of capitalism, because classes had their interests inscribed into them by the structural relationship of exploitation between bourgeoisie and proletariat. Marxists spent their lives trying to work out why the proletariat failed to live up to these projections rather than wondering about the logic or interests of the projectors themselves. As later critics such as Cornelius Castoriadis and Jean Baudrillard would put it, marxists were neither historical nor materialist and were not revolutionary but messianic; they had succumbed to their own mirrors of production.[10]

Marxisms proliferated after Marx, not least with the political victory of the Bolsheviks. The diversity of marxisms did not generally acknowledge the diversity in Marx's own work, partly because it was unknown and remained so until the Marx Renaissance of the 1960s. Marx's influence touched his contemporaries, but marxism did not take off as a political force until its institutionalization by the German social democrats closer to the turn of the century. Certainly Marx influenced those with whom he came into creative contact, such as William Morris, though the content of Morris's socialism, sometimes referred to as his marxism, was also thoroughly local. Romantic and technologically sensitive by turns, Morris was made to look like Marx because both insisted on the necessity of revolution. But revolution was not the property of marxism, even if gradualism or enthusiasm for reform was the more common attitude among English socialists.

Marxism emerged as the ideology and theory of the first mass political party, the German Social Democratic Party (SPD). The SPD became widely known as a kind of countersociety or state within the Prussian state. Its greatest strength also proved to be its greatest weakness; its ghetto nature made it vulnerable to the Nazis on their road to power after 1933, and its own messianism fed into the fatalistic slogan of the German communists, "first Hitler, then us." Marx's legacy had left unresolved the exact question of how socialism would emerge. Would it automatically follow the collapse of capitalism? Would it instead be the conscious result of self-organized activity? Or would it, as the 1859 preface to *A Contribution to the Critique of Political Economy* implied, involve some combination of these, where the correct economic conjuncture would call out the appropriate political intervention? Marx's inattention to the theory of politics left the question of the party unresolved, or absent. Marx's party, like Rosa Luxemburg's, looked like the whole working class. But classes did not act, as such, so political representation became necessary. Modernity caught Marx napping, together with Rousseau. The Bolsheviks closed this political hiatus by inserting themselves into it as the combatant, vanguard party. The German social democrats set out practically to make another culture, working in general on the sense of maturational reformism — sooner or later, socialism would come, whether out of crisis or a gradual growing over, whether by electoral means or collapse.

The larger political legacy of marxism left a dual possibility, reform or revolution. In *The Communist Manifesto* Marx and Engels had sketched out a ten-point program of minimum reforms; yet their tougher stance, outlined by Marx in the penultimate chapter of *Capital*, clearly indicated that socialism would arrive through revolutionary apocalypse. The German social democrats grew apart on the basis of this split. Some, like Eduard Bernstein, came to view socialism as a project of citizenship to be achieved by civilizing capitalism. Others, like Karl Kautsky, were happy to combine revolutionary rhetoric with reformist activity, while still others, such as Rosa Luxemburg, wanted to adjust reformist reality to fit revolutionary theory.[11]

The SPD turned marxism into catechism so that its rank-and-file members would have the revolutionary science at their fingertips. Marxist dogma insisted that the two basic classes, bourgeoisie and proletariat, would dichotomize until the vast majority of the working masses would bump off the capitalists. The "Bernstein Controversy" over reform versus revolution involved two distinct issues: one, whether reformism was to be preferred, and two, whether marxism must be revised in order to register this political recognition theoretically.[12] Was marxism a set of axioms, beyond challenge, or was it a method of analysis open to necessary revision? The process in which marxism became an ideology also involved its consolidation into scholastics. This is one of the clearest of historical cases in which a social theory intended to help explain and even change the world became an impediment to these processes. Marxism became, especially in the hands of Kautsky, a general theory of social evolution where each mode of production emerged triumphantly out of its precedent. Kautsky set out these formulae in *The Class Struggle* (1895), an unrepentantly modernist text where all that is missing from capitalism's industrial achievement is the crown of socialization. Kautsky therefore set out to prove that all would become proletarians, peasants included, before the bourgeoisie could simply be shown the door. At the same time, it was Kautsky who insisted that, left to their own resources, the workers would never achieve more than trade union or economistic consciousness, so they would always need good theoretical leaders like himself. Lenin agreed and built an ideology on this view in *What Is to Be Done* (1902). Kautsky eventually came to the opposite conclusion after 1917, arguing, like Bernstein, that history could not be forced.

In effect Bernstein and Kautsky formed a long-term intellectual alliance; Bernstein continued the marxian impulse of reforms in the ten-point program, while Kautsky carried on the revolutionary rhetoric of *Capital*. Bernstein's position was closer to the ethics of Kantianism or new liberalism, while Kautsky's sociology shifted in the direction of a Weberian marxism in his 1930 magnum opus, *The Materialist Conception of History*.

Max Weber had taken sides with Bernstein, however, in preferring revision as the normal attitude for social science and theory. Kautsky, for his part, agreed with Weber that specialization was our fate, and therefore that modernity would overdetermine socialism rather than the other way around. Lenin's utopia, best formally revealed in *State and Revolution* (1916), still sought a new world characterized by simplicity rather than adjusting to complexity, something of a contradiction given the driving modernism that otherwise characterizes his work. With regard to Bolshevism and the massive shadow that it cast over the twentieth century, it was Lenin who was dominant as actor but Trotsky who was the imposing theorist. What was Bolshevism as a social theory? Like other streams of socialism, Bolshevism was plural and its paths were many, though Lenin and Trotsky still stand out, together with Bukharin, to Lenin's right, and Preobrazhensky, to Trotsky's left. Lenin's theoretical writing was more occasional and less systematic than Trotsky's. Lenin in a sense combined Luxemburg's desire to radicalize practice with a kind of pragmatism that values political expediency above all else. Unlike Luxemburg, Lenin was always a Jacobin, for whom one wise man was worth a hundred fools. His ultra-utopia in *State and Revolution* combined the putative libertarianism of "all cooks can govern" with the grim insistence that the practical model for socialism would be the post office. This futuristic or modernizing scenario stood in contrast to Lenin's other views of the prospect of socialism, which tended to be populist and rural or at least based on the idea that Soviet socialism would remain agrarian and not only industrial. Lenin dreamed of extending direct democracy into Soviet experience, but the challenges of modernization without democracy became overwhelming.[13] While his final utopia looked more distinctly Maoist, accommodating Russian agrarian realities rather than forcing them, Lenin's high Bolshevik utopia was something more like the image of German capitalism, symbolized by Americanism ascendant. Lenin's belief, like Trotsky's, that the success of the Russian Revolution depended on the German Revolution was not merely strategic or even economic; Lenin viewed the "organized capitalism" analyzed by Rudolf Hilferding as the basic model for Soviet modernization.[14] Lenin's model of socialism as modernity was something like capitalism without democracy or with the lure of an impossible, direct democracy held over it by the Bolsheviks. Its political logic remained populist in that it pitted the people against their exploiters and rendered the alternative exploiters, the Bolsheviks, invisible in the process.

Lenin's response to various failures and setbacks was to introduce the New Economic Policy (NEP), which in 1921 recognized the status quo as the framework for future Soviet efforts. Trotsky, in contrast, accepted the NEP with hesitance, for his model of socialism had always been industrialist and modernizing. Trotsky's was a Faustian Bolshevism, one prepared even to risk life and limb for the thrill, the prospect of even glimpsing what men and technology could do. Trotsky hoped not merely to follow the Germans and Americans, but to outdo them, not least through developing enthusiasms for principles of Taylorism and scientific management. Americanized Bolshevism—that was the way forward for him.[15] Anything is possible—this was the motivation; the rational mastery of nature, and thereby of humanity itself—this was the canvas. Trotsky's impulse was a kind of developmental romanticism where the frenzy of creation reached out into the sublime.

The image of socialism in the Bolshevik tradition thus disperses across a spectrum, even if we consider Lenin and Trotsky alone, from a modest hope of feeding people on the one extreme to the project of endlessly reconstructing the world on the other. The futurism of Trotsky embodied something of the productivism, or obsession with technology, that became characteristic of marxism into the twentieth century. Socialism became a matter of harnessing the best of capitalist technology to what were claimed to be more benign ends. The line back to Marx was plain: if abundance was the practical precondition of socialism, socialism became another way of doing capitalism, or at least another form of organizing capitalist technology. The producer—or, more specifically, the proletarian—became not only the subject of history but also the citizen; and his incapacity to rule and to produce at the same time quietly kept the Bolsheviks in the business of "politics."

Russian radicals had long been divided into localists and Westernizers; the distinction was by no means peculiar to Russia. British socialism, too, divided between those who sought more willfully to return to or extend the past and those who sought to modernize it. The conflict between traditionalists and modernizers was acted out in various British sites, not least of them Fabianism. The Fabians became known into the 1930s as progressivists, reformers, and statists, sometime apologists for authoritarian regimes or at least for the principles of social engineering that underpinned them. Fabianism began as an alternative life movement, caught up as various European socialisms were in the 1880s with vegetarianism, alternative dress, and bicycling.[16] Its substantive theoretical impulse came not only from John Stuart Mill and Owen but from William Cobbett, Thomas Carlyle, John Ruskin, and indirectly William Morris, for whom the old image of England's green and pleasant land looked more interesting than the prospect of Coketown or the Satanic Mills. The opposition to modernity or civilization became a major theme of social criticism across socialisms and kindred positions such as distributism and Catholic ruralism. More recently these kinds of issues have been pursued with regard to broader questions of British industrial culture and the residual presence of romanticism even among the captains of industry.[17] British socialisms have long been more heavily influenced by medieval than by modernizing claims and motifs, at least until Harold Wilson and then Tony Blair.

The strongest English variant of medievalism was guild, or gild, socialism, associated with various theorists such as Sam Hobson, Alfred Orage, and Arthur Penty and with *The New Age* but defended most ably by G. D. H. Cole, who took its legacy into Fabianism, where it was lost as statism triumphed with the Beveridge Report into the 1940s. The guild socialists viewed utopia as a coalescence of local unions modeled on the medieval guilds, autonomous and capable of holding together the moments of conception and execution, or head and hand. The image of society involved would be based on direct democracy, but the producer would remain privileged; after all, Adam Smith's jibe against trade unions was more accurately addressed to guilds, charging that they were conspiracies against the public, closed and traditionalistic in the absolute sense. Cole's early hope was for the federation of these self-governing units, a veritable example of small is beautiful.[18] Different local English lineages also claimed that the way back opened the way forward; ethical or Christian socialism, based on the idea of fellowship among men and stewardship of nature led by R. H. Tawney, was a major contributor to the laborism associated with the British Labor Party into the 1930s.[19]

While Tawney worried about compassion and mutual responsibility and Cole echoed the early Marx's enthusiasm for the autonomy of labor, others, like Beatrice and Sidney Webb, puzzled over waste and inefficiency. The Webbs began from positions closer to liberalism or cooperation, with the added sense of evolutionism associated with the work of Beatrice's childhood tutor, Herbert Spencer. The idea of evolution alone—progress from lower forms to higher—plainly locates the Webbs on different terrain from that inhabited by the guildists. This point of their mentality was closer to Marx's, that the development of society made progress possible. But the Webbs' image of utopia lacked the monomaniacal developmentalism of Trotsky; their hope was rather to service such a minimum of provision as might enable all to flourish in their interdependence.[20] Revolutionaries have enjoyed the prospect of casting Fabianism as mere "gas and water socialism"; the problems of provision, of health, education, and housing, nevertheless remain fundamental. Socialism for the Webbs, then, consisted largely in practical terms of reorganizing the wealth that society already possessed. Social problems could be measured, their existence publicized, and appropriate reforms enacted to see to their resolution. Social solidarity could be developed on the emerging patterns of social evolution, so that, as in Durkheim's view, each would depend on all the rest. All citizens, in this view, would have a place in the division of labor; the middle classes, tempted by their location and tradition to social parasitism, would also need to find their social vocation.

The opposition to social parasitism motivated various kinds of socialism. Some, like Marx, viewed the bourgeoisie as implicitly parasitic or without social function. Others, like Lenin, viewed aristocrats, fat capitalists, or coupon clippers as parasites; for the Webbs it was middle-class folks lacking in social conscience who were parasites, at least until they took up the cause of reform. For yet others, like Lenin and Trotsky, the *kulaks* or rich peasants became the enemy. And for socialists and radicals of antisemitic bent, from Hilaire Belloc to Werner Sombart, it was finance capital that was parasitic.[21] Socialists had their distinct enemies, then, as well as their heroes, proletarians or mock proletarians for the Bolsheviks, factory inspectors for the Webbs, savants for Kautsky, scientists for H. G. Wells or Trotsky. But for Fabians the citizen would not be conceived as the proletarian, as in Bolshevism. Indeed, as the Webbs went on to suggest in their *Constitution for the Socialist Commonwealth of Great Britain* (1920), vocational electorates should be developed alongside geographical forms of representation in order fully to register the significance of work in political life.[22] The evident weakness in this, as in much else of socialist theory, is the failure to take seriously the private sphere and the gender consequences thereof. "Work," in this discourse as in most others, refers to paid public work rather than to the labors of the home. Not that socialists failed to address domestic labor, which they did from August Bebel through Wells; but they continued to presume its gendered nature, themselves reflecting the traditionalism of patriarchy, which itself violates the ethics of modernity and yet holds it up.

Fabianism in effect dissolved into the state, like British liberalism the victim of its own success, with the 1945–51 Labor Government. Fabianism had better articulated the common sense of the labor movement referred to historically as laborism, where the politics of socialism was constructed in terms of the defense and protection of workers and their families. Fabianism built on laborism an infrastructure of research, organization, and agitation, pushing an ethic that sought to tie together the gradual modernization of society and the solidarity imputed to its traditional forms. All this became fundamental to the postwar regimes of reconstruction until they were washed away by the processes of crisis and globalization that ran through the 1970s to the 1990s.

The idea of the Russian Revolution was exhausted by the 1940s, replaced in romantic Western imaginations by images of Chairman Mao or Che Guevara. Yet the image of the October Revolution excited many earlier, including George Bernard Shaw in England and in Italy the young Antonio Gramsci. The younger Gramsci was a council communist, taking up a position for the new proletarian, self-organized order, espousing a kind of social democratic syndicalism not unlike the view of G. D. H. Cole. Gramsci embraced the October Revolution as "The Revolution against Capital," by which he referred both to the power of capital and to the fatalistic influence of Marx's *Capital*. His view was that the marxism of Kautsky and his Russian equivalent, Georgi Plekhanov, had become a deadweight on marxists, who passively accepted Kautsky's maxim that their job was to wait for the revolution. Gramsci insisted on extending the voluntaristic and democratic element in Marx, that which indicated that socialism was possible only as a result of the action of self-organized masses of men and women. Gramsci insisted that marxism was a politics, not just a political economy—a statement of will, not only a recognition of constraint—and he was stubborn in this insistence until he was personally constrained within Mussolini's prison walls, where he wrote the famous (if thematically scattered) *Prison Notebooks*. Gramsci's *Prison Notebooks* reinstated the marxian formula of the 1859 preface to *A Contribution to the Critique of Political Economy*, that people make history but not just as they choose. The *Notebooks* also reconfigured marxist politics by placing Machiavelli at the fore and conceptualizing the Italian Communist Party as the New Prince. More significantly, the *Notebooks* foregrounded culture, ideology, and common sense as the practical field on which bourgeois societies ensure their self-reproduction. Hegemony, not only force, ensures social coherence; socialism, conceived as the practical project of a new class alliance or a new historic bloc, therefore depends on the possibility of counterhegemony.[23]

Gramsci was a revolutionary communist who was subsequently reinvented as a culturalist predecessor of the Birmingham School of Cultural Studies. He was not only Italian but, more specifically, Sardinian, a peripheral marxist who understood uneven development without falling for the hypermodern cosmopolitanism of a Trotsky. Vital to his legacy is not only *The Prison Notebooks* (1971) but also *The Southern Question*, where Gramsci opened the case that modernity would always ever be traditionalistic as well as progressive. Gramsci's contemporary, often grouped with him and the German philosopher Karl Korsch in the retrospective category of "Western marxism," was Georg Lukács. The Hungarian marxist Lukács not only founded the later Budapest School after 1956 but also was a central voice in the formation of the Frankfurt School into the 1920s, for Lukács was the pioneer of a kind of Weberian marxism, refracting together (as differently did Simmel) the themes of commodification (Marx) and instrumental reason (Weber) to develop the theme of reification.[24] The so-called Western marxists therefore developed the political and cultural spheres of analysis that had been neglected since Marx's call that vision lay in the analysis of political economy rather than civil society. In the case of Lukács's analysis, culture emerged only to show, by other means, the impossibility of socialism except at the hands of a magically endowed intellectual proletariat. The legacies of Gramsci and Lukács were either institutionalized or ignored by their respective communist parties. Korsch wrote one of the best books on Marx, *Karl Marx,* in 1936 before taking up exile in America, where his influence was negligible except for its impact on marginal local council communists such as Paul Mattick.

The critical theorists of the Frankfurt School, most notably Theodor Adorno, Max Horkheimer, and Herbert Marcuse, migrated to America to escape Nazism. There, among other things, they cultivated the antimodern or at least anti-American thread of the German tradition, viewing American culture as either candy floss or televisual totalitarianism.[25] The Frankfurt School, in common with Lukács, pursued a kind of aristocratic radicalism quite at odds with Gramsci's curiosity about popular culture and folk wisdom. The trajectory of critical theory, in contrast, was influenced not only by the failure of socialist revolution in the west, but also by the outcome of Nazism in the Holocaust. Western marxism, so called because of its guiding sense that Western cultures offered different challenges than those facing others like the Bolsheviks seeking socialism in the "East," was also deflated by those developments in the West, where the prospects of socialism gave way to the power of barbarism.

In the meantime, German Social Democracy became historically institutionalized as a form of social management into the 1960s, as did laborism in Britain. The extraordinary extent of the postwar boom and the arrival of mass consumerism through the 1950s, combined with the effects of the cold war, saw socialism lose impetus again until the 1960s, when critical theory and Western marxism were revived or reconstructed, especially by student radicals from Berkeley to the London School of Economics (the latter founded by the Webbs). Radicalism rode the wave, perhaps especially in the United States. American socialisms are long of lineage and rich in variety, though they have often been marginalized within scholarship by academics with short memories. The famous question put forth by Sombart in the title of his 1906 book was *Why Is There No Socialism in the United States?* which presumed that socialism was something necessarily to be measured by its presence or absence at the level of central state power rather than within civil society or as a countercurrent to modernity. Yet far from being absent in the United States, socialism has a rich American history, from the nineteenth-century utopian experiment through Bellamy and the Bellamy Clubs to the Industrial Workers of the World and various intellectual permutations from Lewis Mumford to the pragmatism of Max Eastman and Richard Rorty. If the answer to Sombart's question, rephrased as "Why was there not *more* socialism in the United States?" was material abundance, the real tease was yet to come, for more of that material abundance into the 1960s brought out the New Left with a vengeance. With Herbert Marcuse, Jürgen Habermas, André Gorz, and Serge Mallet, traffic increased both into English-speaking cultures and back to the centers as radicals struggled for equal rights and dreamed, still, of the end of alienation.

The Marx of the 1960s conjured up themes going back to alienation as well as commodification. Indeed, whether via Marcuse in *One Dimensional Man* or the newly translated Marx of the *1844 Manuscripts,* the essential message provided by radical social theory often seemed singular: the world needed to be changed all at once, which in effect, given the power of capital and its culture, meant not at all. Other socialisms were eclipsed by marxism, and marxist humanism was scorned by the rising star of structuralism, which also established an image of structure or history as unshiftable.[26] Reformisms could easily be made to look feeble by armchair revolutionaries who claimed a radical distance from the Soviet experience but whose vocabularies were basically Bolshevik.[27]

Marxism revived as a critical theory, perhaps for the last time before expiring, as state theory.[28] State theory was often caught up with the idea that a theory of politics could be derived from the analysis of capital. Thus, again, was Gramsci rediscovered as a political theorist.[29] For example,

Ernesto Laclau and Chantal Mouffe sought to use Gramsci as a way out of the impasse in *Hegemony and Socialist Strategy* (1985). The sticking point for Gramsci remained that of Bolshevism, or Jacobinism; was the party still the key agent of social transformation, or was it merely a collective noun naming the various related social movements that held it up?

The collapse of marxism as the key presence within socialist social theory at this point came in at least two different forms. The first involved the rediscovery of methodological pluralism, in principle available in Weber but politically accessible through the work of Michel Foucault. Foucault widely replaced Althusser, who had replaced Marx. Power was discovered to have existed throughout modernity, and not only in economy. The second point of erosion involved the rediscovery or renegotiation of democracy via liberalism as political theory in the reemergence of social movements and the reappraisal of civil society.[30] On both these accounts, marxism now appeared to be a regional theory rather than a general theory. The fact that liberalism could be seen as radical again gave a second chance to various nonmarxian socialist alternatives.

The general problem, inasmuch as it could be named, was now reidentified as the problem not of capitalism but of modernity. Working out of the Budapest School tradition of Weberian marxism, Agnes Heller and Ferenc Féher identified the field of modernity as at least threefold, characterized by the differing logics or dynamics of capitalism, industrialism, and democracy.[31] This was, in effect, to return to one of the earliest socialist sensibilities, that socialism was less a state of affairs to be achieved upon the negation of private property than a restatement of the priority of the social against individualism. The striking locational difference was that by the end of the twentieth century socialism lived in the academy perhaps more than anywhere else, for its claims to being taken seriously as a culture of social theory had outgrown its street credentials as a practical politics. After all that has happened in its name, socialism remains the kind of critique and utopia that it began as, diminished in its certainty just as its existence is warranted by what surrounds it, part of the past and thereby of our present.

Formally speaking, socialism might be said to have returned to the civil societies and social movements that originally called it forth. For as socialists have declared that the core of their utopia is democracy and not only equality, so have their ambitions returned to the horizons of social democracy and the radical liberal heritage that often informs it. If socialism began by claiming to pursue the ideals of the French Revolution, supporting the expansion of democracy against power or capitalism, its marxian claims to absolute difference may have been illusory. Socialism remains part of the critique of modernity; neither term seems possible without the other.

(2003)

Two

Socialism by the Back Door

"The story is one of the oldest forms of communication. It does not aim at transmitting the pure in-itself of the event, but anchors the event in the life of the person reporting, in order to pass it on as experience to those listening." Thus said Walter Benjamin.[1] Or, as the maxim sets it, *Geschichte ist Geschichte*—history is stories. These things seem to have some resonance for me, whether because they are German, I cannot say. But my own consistent sense is that we all have stories to tell, that we live in history, and that history is marked by contingency, twists and turns, coincidence, accident. That I should be here at all is an accident. My dad was born in Germany in 1923, the moment inflation reached wheelbarrow proportions, the moment, perhaps, that Weimar began to dissolve internally; my mum was born there in 1924. When I discovered the wonders of Weimar culture at a distance, I could not understand what she meant when she muttered that it was a *Scheisstheater,* a theater of shit. What I later encountered as magic, she had experienced as chaos. My father's path had gone through Palestine to Australia; having made the mistake of being a German national in a British protectorate when the Second World War broke out, he, like many others, had found himself on a boat, then in an internment camp overlooking the arid backblocks of Tatura.[2] My mother had remained in Germany throughout the war, worked in the land army in the south, and arrived in Australia in

1949 with her worldly goods—a promise of marriage, a suitcase, a five-pound note, and a salami. Customs confiscated and presumably ate the salami.

My parents' lives were formed by contingency more world-historic than mine. They ended up in Croydon, Australia, but they could equally have found themselves, and me, in Germany, in Palestine, in California, earlier even in Russia, where others of their people went. Their German-ness was not high German; they were from the south, spoke dialect, were modest folk. I inherited no stock of middle-class culture, although I suspect there was some subliminal pleasure for them in my discovery of Marx, a bad German but a German after all. Like others, I was an alien when young. I was beaten up at school for my origins; my enemies probably knew nothing of the crimes of Nazism but were simply pleased that the Huns again had lost. My family was then obliged to partake of something called cultural assimilation, a condition from which my parents have only now, on retirement, recovered.

But Croydon was a good place to grow up, a happy accident. I had one of those special teachers people sometimes have. He was a labor historian, a self-made intellectual, with two M.A.s and a Ph.D., teaching in the local high school. He opened the world of the mind to me at the same time as I entered the British migrant, part-bohemian, rock-and-roll culture of Croydon, a place where into the 1960s people painted, worked in metal and clay, read Kerouac and Camus, listened to the blues or to The Who and Pink Floyd, to the Mothers of Invention and Velvet Underground before they were popular, and made their own music in turn. So profoundly did my teacher, Norm Saffin, influence me that I decided late in sixth form that I could only be a teacher.

In the path of my life I have shown a modicum of competence at only one other practice, playing rock and roll, a life as precarious as the poet's. My musical career peaked on January 1, 1970, when my band, made up of Chris Finnen, my brother, and I, played the blues—"Crossroads" by Robert Johnson—with Billy Thorpe and the Aztecs at the Thumpin' Tum in Melbourne. The crossovers between music and the work I do now are still, for me, compelling. I learned a lot from the musicians I grew up with. They knew they were an underground, subaltern in a particular sense; they viewed their work as that of artisans. They had a sense of history, traditions too. They knew, and accepted, that talent and recognition were often distant partners. As in the throwaways of Marx and Trotsky, they were the Raphaels who would never be acknowledged; they ended up as storemen, working for Telecom, pumping gas or schoolteaching, bringing up their children, playing sometimes for fun. My brother, Fred, was the most extraordinary influence among them; he taught me a lot.

For years I pumped gas at Fred Gregory's Ampol station on weekends and watched the world go by. My enthusiasm for labor history and marxism were then drawn out by my history teachers at Rusden College of Advanced Education, especially Don Gibb, who gave me enough rope to swing on. At least I was now saved from the crisis-ridden identity politics of white boys who pretend to play the black man's blues and take on that genre's abominable gender politics. Secretly I still listen to the stuff, and I guess that if I had stayed a musician I would not care less. On Fridays, as an undergraduate, I would go across the way from Rusden to Monash University to catch the bands, but also to read journals like *Australian Left Review* and the *New Left Review*. I broke my studentship and transgressed the then actively policed binary divide between the college system and the universities. Herb Feith and Alastair Davidson held the door open for me. My project as an M.A. Prelim. student was to write a history of Australian Trotskyism, something Saffin had already set me on to. But now I began to read the young Leon Trotsky, the brilliant stuff on imperialism in 1905, and Alastair took me through Antonio Gramsci's equally brilliant text, *The Southern Question*. And so I wrote my Prelim. thesis not on Australian Trotskyism but on the relation between Marx's project and Bolshevism. For this project my supervisor was the extraordinarily talented Germanist Zawar Hanfi; Davidson was my examiner, together with Johann P. Arnason from across the city, at La Trobe. The attraction of Gramsci was powerful; he was peripheral, and he knew it and thought it a perspectival advantage. Trotskyism became more fascinating for me as a flawed but powerful political tradition; my capacity to monitor the shenanigans of the various Fourth Internationals was limited, and my flow charts of splits in the movement crawled erratically all over the wall. By now I was fellow-traveling with the Communist Party and had great hopes for the Political Economy Movement, which was formed in the mid-1970s in an attempt to connect again the politics and economics that modernity had sundered. I came increasingly to believe that it was necessary to maneuver theory and history, more explicitly to work across social theory and labor history.

Thesis Eleven was another pact of that moment that subsequently took on a life of its own. It is difficult for me in retrospect to sort out the relations between all these things, because my doctoral work and *Thesis Eleven* took form at the same time. My thesis and my later book sought to apply the cellular logic of Marx's *Capital* to Trotskyism, developing a logical chain from Trotsky's politics, economics, philosophy, and history through different thinkers such as Isaac Deutscher, C. L. R. James, and Ernest Mandel, who picked up particular but different clues from the Father and transmuted them into a third level, that of the various Trotskyist movements themselves, all of which also refract some aspect or other of Trotsky's own thinking.[3] At the same time, the concern with the transition to socialism crossed over into the original constellation of ideas that formed *Thesis Eleven*. *Thesis Eleven*, like other radical projects, expected to change the way journal life was lived, perhaps even to change more than that. It was interdisciplinary and thought that marxism mattered as the politics that Marx had never discussed, and it was, like Gramsci, proud to be peripheral and cosmopolitan at the same time. This came to be its greatest strength, particularly after 1990, when *Thesis Eleven* struck up a collaborative relationship with the MIT Press, projecting Australian argument into North America as well as continuing to introduce European and international ideas into Australia. While *Thesis Eleven* thus itself changed, as its left context in Australia collapsed along with the demise of the Communist Party and the rise of right-wing laborism in the Labor Decade, the project of the journal also consolidated as the metropolitan centers began more fully to recognize the significant insights that might be generated from the antipodes. The perspective from the edge is different, and it remains so.

Through another series of accidents I found myself teaching sociology, that happy refuge for misfits, first at Phillip Institute of Technology and then at La Trobe University. The last year I was at Phillip, 1986, my load was sixteen hours across five courses; my wife and I had a small child and hoped for another, but I could not cope, applied fruitlessly for postdoctoral fellowships, and was ready to give up writing and research. Another twist or accident, this time in the corporeal form of Stuart Macintyre, arrived, with Greg Dening in the shadows (Macintyre became my advocate, even though I was not his student; Dening, as professor, became my silent supporter). This was astonishing to me; we barely knew each other. I could not imagine what I had done to deserve the support of the research fellowship that opened for me. My project in the Department of History at the University of Melbourne was titled Bolshevism and Reformism; however, because I had time to read again, I read *everything*, and the project splayed out into two different books, one called *Labour's Utopias,* a comparative study of Russian, German, and British socialisms,[4] and another on the Australian Labor Party (ALP). The accident at Melbourne led in effect to another at La Trobe, where I was to take on Agnes Heller's job and course on the history of socialism and where travel funds enabled me to confirm my addiction to the use of the archives of socialism, not least of all at the legendary International Institute for Social History in Amsterdam.

My own work seems to me to take a form like that of a patchwork quilt, a series of contiguous plates that all add up to something that covers the same kinds of concerns, across socialism and politics, but also opens out or connects up in ways I cannot always anticipate. Trotskyism led to reformism via the question of transition. What did it mean actually to change the world? Whose world? Which change? Why, in the West, had reformists and social democrats done better? What did this say about the status of liberalism? *Labour's Utopias* emerged as an attempt to sort out the relation between Bolshevism and reformist utopias, arguing that these were different visions and not just different proposed paths to the same end. Bolshevism was a proletarian, premodern utopia; Fabianism and Social Democracy were less romantic, more modern, more useful. These kinds of concerns simultaneously connected to others about the Australian welfare state and the practice of social theory in general. Before I knew it, there were other books, *Social Theory, Arguing about the Welfare State, Between Totalitarianism and Postmodernity.*[5]

If this path suggests anything, it is the power of contingency. But it is also a path of ambivalence. I feel as though I have slipped into the back door of the academy when no one was looking; every other day I feel as though I do not belong. Part of this creative tension has to do with my roots and the postwar expansion of the tertiary system, shifts in class composition, and so on. Part of this probably has to do with the nature of the academic job market since the 1980s; I have always unpacked my books, in whatever office I have had, but have always expected to move on. My situation of unease, much more common than earlier, is one of concern about achieving an immediate sense of safety—sufficient to remain sane—together with a larger sense of discomfort about the world and the university. The university presents itself to me as still a world of privilege, a candy shop. Like others, I am still waiting to be found out.

This is more than I have ever been able to say about my path in public, and it is likely too much, given the culture of narcissism and not least of all because the traditions to which I am drawn—whether marxism or hermeneutics—tell us not to take seriously what subjects say about themselves. To refer to Benjamin again, one should never trust what an author says about his own work. So let me shift more directly to the story of labor history as I see it.

Becoming a marxist into the 1970s was a mixed blessing. It was theoretical—it may have been too theoretical—but it was also pluralizing. Extraordinarily, the efflorescence of marxism coincided with its dissolution. But marxism was only ever one set of traditions within those traditions called socialisms, and neither of those categories has ever owned labor history or the labor movement. The effect of marxism was mixed, partly because of its dubious claims to authority, to scientificity; yet at the same time, to read marxism was to discover its rich and plural traditions, its tensions, and—especially via Gramsci—to discover that its relation to national cultures was as complex as its internationalist pretensions. The core problem with contemporary marxism, I would argue, is one it shared with theory in general, or with the Western practice of philosophy: in modernity, especially, culture becomes too abstract and cerebral. As Marx and Georg Simmel argued, there were astonishing symmetries between modern forms of thought and the money economy. Both institutions chewed up difference and specificity. This is the other end of the dialectic between theory and history; history can be faulted for all kinds of reasons, but the major problem with theory is that it has become detached, turned into a formalistic and thin gruel of language games. We seem to forget, too readily, that whatever the various ways in which the classics can be criticized, at least Marx and Max Weber, Émile Durkheim, Ferdinand Tönnies, and Simmel worked up theoretical understanding as a part of substantive research projects on what they viewed as major social problems confronting them. They were also, in different ways, practitioners of history, and in this sense they were historicists.

This raises, indirectly, another problem, that of cultural cringe and the European social theorist as hero. Personally I take great umbrage at the kind of argument that suggests that Australians have hitherto had their heads in the sand; the problem is rather that we spend a great deal too much time worrying about what Europeans think this week. If we stand like idiots in a circle facing outward, there is a passing chance that one of us will catch a glimpse of Jacques Derrida's overcoat, but half of us will be watching penguins. If we look inward, relatively speaking, we will see each other, colonizer and colonized, and through the gaps we might still glimpse the heights and the underworld of New York, the delights and disasters called Paris, as well as something of Indonesia and New Zealand.

This much on theory. Determining the status we wish to ascribe to labor history is also less than straightforward. In an ordinary, archaeological sense, of course, there will *always* be labor history, even if in an imaginary time capsule. My hunch, however, is that there is a great deal more than this left. Labor history in Australia became caught up with marxism partly because peripheral marxists have been good at working on imperialism. Living on the other end of a colonial or imperial relationship usually generates some local insight: thus, for example, the Bolsheviks were better at explaining imperialism than the Germans. Globalization is in some ways just a new word for imperialism or the world system. As George Orwell understood, writing of the British colonies, this has long meant that parts of the British working-class movement in effect were elsewhere; trying simply to locate the "Australian" working class is now less than easy. Its future is in that sense elsewhere, so that the task of doing labor history in Australia transmutes; it does not simply close.

But then there are those who postulate rupture, saying that the "end" of modernity and the arrival of postmodernity or "post-industrialism," involves the end of the labor movement, of the project of labor history. This is one angle on the kind of issue raised elsewhere by Verity Burgmann and taken up now in *Australian Historical Studies* by Raelene Frances and Bruce Scates.[6] Is labor history dead? Starting from a different position, I would ask a different question: is the labor movement dead? This is a question best answered dialectically: yes and no. The historic project associated with the Australian labor movement, laborism itself, is dead; the Labor Decade, 1983–1993, witnessed the remarkable transformation of the ALP into a party of office at any price, leaving behind any sense of substantial historic vocation, usually identified with the signs of earlier moments—foundation, Chifley, or Whitlam; and the Australian Council of Trade Unions and the unions themselves have been modernized almost beyond recognition. Communists closed up shop from the mid-1980s on, many in order to enter the ALP to argue for industry policy, for a modernizing future for labor; the left, traditionally understood, has effectively disappeared, as is evident in the collapse of institutions such as *Australian Society,* the Communist Party, the old socialist left, *Modern Times, Australian Left Review, Broadside,* and the International Bookshop in Melbourne.

These kinds of issues flooded over me in writing *Transforming Labor: Labour Tradition and the Labor Decade in Australia*,[7] the local sequel to the European frame of *Labour's Utopias*. Here my initial intention, to try to explain the Labor Decade, shifted into a larger sense that the proper frame of reference was more like the century that opened with Labor's foundation in 1891, and its mythical reinvention under Ben Chifley and John Curtin and then Gough Whitlam. The theme of labor modernization again emerged as central, given the highly romantic rural, then suburban, inflection of the local labor tradition. A related brief, to write a book on socialism after postmodernism, led to another sensibility, that what had happened since the 1980s was that the social question, invented in the 1880s, had now been disaggregated into a series of social problems that we (and the poor) simply had to live with. The power of globalization, vigorously licensed by the deregulation of the 1980s, took us back to the world of two nations within, this with the remarkable difference by comparative standards, that Labor stood at the helm of this process.[8]

Viewed from one kind of political perspective, all this means is that the left is dead, but the New South Wales Right is alive and well and rewriting labor history from its own viewpoint. Thus, the socialist image of the labor movement may have collapsed, but the movement has achieved a pyrrhic victory or, better, has arrived in the house of power called the state and is stacking up the furniture in order to avoid future eviction. Labor history, by any criterion, then, still has its work cut out for it; laborism, à la Graham Freudenberg or Gerard Henderson, still has its work cut out for it. As I suggested earlier, the older, recovery work must still continue, regardless of whether socialism lives or not; we still desperately *need* a new history of the Communist Party of Australia, we need a great deal of excavation or construction on Catholicism and the labor movement, and there remains a great deal barely worked on, say the Victorian Socialist Party, the milieu of the New Age here and elsewhere, the cultures of individual unions, and work processes, male and female, public and private. And then there are all those fields that open when labor history is interpreted symbolically rather than parochially, as it was into the 1970s, when social history and women's history flourished. Filling in the gaps, establishing the records, digging out the archives, telling the stories, remains vital work, if only those of us who teach could persuade the youthful and faithful followers of Michel Foucault who wander through our classes that they, too, must use archives.

But the symbolic point is more suggestive, too. It is one thing to argue against the naysayers—those who charge that Western practices of knowledge making are impossible—by keeping at our work. It is another to rethink labor history as a moment in what, more generically, might be called the history of subalternity. Labor history developed as a part of the movement called social history against the old, conventional, narrowly political or diplomatic history. Labor history is part of a larger, modern interest in history from below. If marxism taught us anything in the 1970s, it was that class is *relational,* that all relations of power or domination are double-ended. Labor history is concerned with alterity, the other, the underground. Thus, it is part of a much wider intellectual trend that wants also to look at the other end of power. The key trope here is the idea of master and slave posited by Georg Wilhelm Friedrich Hegel in *The Phenomenology of Spirit* and then appropriated by Marx, who congratulated Hegel for privileging the idea of *process,* viewing substance also as *subject*. The metaphor traveled wide and far, especially into modern French philosophy through the work of Jean Hyppolite and Alexandre Kojève, percolating into the work of Simone de Beauvoir, Georges Bataille, and Frantz Fanon, and rendered into psychoanalytic register by Jessica Benjamin and others. Interest in the masters now necessitates interest in the slaves, and it is surely no accident that the image of slavery will not die. Carole Pateman extends it out of G. D. H. Cole, from guild socialism into feminism on the axis that the real problem we face is not poverty but slavery; Orlando Patterson's magisterial work *Freedom* argues so painfully that the couplet is always at work: we live, striving always for freedom not because we hope to "achieve" it but because we are forced to by the perpetual existence of slavery itself.[9]

It is not, then, simply a matter of arguing that labor historians need to get their acts together, themselves to modernize, to write about McDonald's workers as well as engineers or about sex workers as well as artisans. The ongoing dualization of labor markets will itself guarantee that there remains an underground, a subproletariat or underclass with numerous stories to tell. The more general issue, I suggest, is that labor history has been the name for a particular kind of inquiry into problems of alterity or subalternity. The practice of labor history in Australia has exemplified this kind of larger orientation in a particular set of orientations. It has called subalternity by a particular name and privileged particular sites of activity, and, like all particular activities, it has generalized its claims, centered on problems to do with laborism over other kinds of relations of domination. But to make such claims is not to say that the practice ought to cease but rather to request that it cultivate self-consciousness, that it place wageslavery back into the local and global frame within which forms of slavery proliferate. In his *Dream of John Ball*, William Morris says of socialism that "people fight to lose the battle, and the thing that they fought for comes about in spite of their defeat, and when it comes [it] turns out not to be what they meant, and other[s] have to fight for what they meant under another name."[10] This sensibility, I think, is entirely apposite to labor history: what matters is that it is continually practiced, not what it is called. Labor history, social history, women's history, history from below—all these are stories, a Babel of necessary stories about contingency, tradition, and modernity, about culture and power, about the human condition. *Pace* Morris, however, the picture at the moment suggests that the notion that socialism by any other name will smell as sweet is misleading; this was Marx's mistake and occasionally Hegel's—to imagine that the dialectics of master and slave would ever come to an end. But let that be my end.

(1994)

Three

The Life and Times of Social Democracy

Social democracy remains a major political current of modernity. Contrary to postmodernists and to certain marxists, modernity is not *all* about flux. We remain firmly stuck within modernity, and hence within social democracy. Recent events in Eastern Europe would seem to confirm rather than to deny this. Communism now is off the agenda; socialism remains on it. Or has socialism had its day as well? As C. B. Macpherson suggests in his *Life and Times of Liberal Democracy*, which I take here as my frame, the "life and times" approach is by nature suggestive of an obituary. Ideas, however, do not follow the life cycles of mere mortals. They merge into other ideas, recurring unpredictably and often simply refusing to go away. Socialism is one such idea, for as the alter ego of capitalism it changes forms without ever just expiring. All civilizations need their animating narratives; socialism remains one of the narratives of modernity. But with communism in decay, what of social democracy?

In this chapter I argue, in sympathy with Macpherson, that if the formal institutions associated with social democracy are more or less lifeless or decrepit, there nevertheless remains something alive in the project of social democracy. Like the Enlightenment, social democracy has let us down—or perhaps it is more accurate to say that we have let the project down, given that historic responsibility ultimately rests with actors and not ideas. The project, at least, remains to be realized.

In order to make my case, I need first to provide one definition, two premises, and one pretext. The core of the argument then takes up the theory of two dead dogs from the history of socialism, Eduard Bernstein and Karl Kautsky, in order to argue that far from being the idiots they are sometimes thought to have been, these central figures of social democracy were both theoretically sensitive and are socially useful today. The argument is staid rather than scintillating, worldly rather than wizardly, and I offer no apologies for this.

First, the definition. By *social democracy* I mean the political experience that preceded World War I. The point of this chapter is not to defend social democracy since World War II. Though revolutionary marxists would likely be loath to concede the point, social democracy was transformed by the events of the 1940s and 1950s: it was not always the gray cat that it came to be. The 1945–51 Labor Government, the Keynes-Beveridge consensus, and the ideological disputes over the socialist platform in the debates over Clause Four and Bad Godesberg all saw social democracy transformed from its earlier project, just as the events of the 1970s and 1980s again transformed social democracy, emptying it of all content save the thin gruel of "social justice" or socialist accounting. Thus I define *social democracy* as prewar because, unlike communism and relatively speaking, social democracy has been inconsistent, its historic path ruptural rather than entirely predictable. Where the experience of communism has been in some ways consistent—from the New Economic Policy to perestroika, from Kronstadt to Tiananmen Square—social democracy has been a more rapidly moving if simultaneously declining object. Where communism has been something of a piece—especially in the Soviet and Chinese cases—social democracy meant something completely different before the first war than it has since the second, and it will mean something still different again after the present economic crisis.

Second, the two premises. The argument in this chapter is built on the premise that all social and political theories contain utopias, or images of the good society. Here socialism differs from liberalism only in being more fully explicit or more wilfully utopian. But all arguments about how we ought to live rest on some utopic sense, however well or little elaborated, which looks romantically backward or futuristically forward (or both). A related premise on which this argument rests is that what we call modernity is in fact an amalgam of modern, premodern, and postmodern social forms, beliefs, and practices. The significance of this premise, in the present context, is simply that it highlights the way in which not all of our problems are "new." It follows that "old" social theory still speaks to us today.

My pretext for this case, as I have mentioned, is Macpherson's *Life and Times of Liberal Democracy*.[1] The essential message of Macpherson's essay is that liberal democracy is both alive and dead, simultaneously exhausted and yet capable of addressing the human condition in our times, especially with reference to classical hopes for active citizenship and individual-social self-development. Macpherson for his part thus speaks of the limits and possibilities of liberal democracy. The limits of social democracy are evident and will not be further discussed here: like other forms of political thinking, social democracy has become fundamentally implicated with the state and its paternalism, and it has refused to take its own professed principles seriously into the realm of policy, hoping rather that socialism might be worked out by others, by civil savants. The main concern of this chapter is rather with the discursive possibilities of social democracy, and this relates back to the earlier premise, that ideas matter, that "old" problems still confront us, and that consequently "old" ideas may be helpful in the process of attempting to develop a vocabulary for social change.

The central thinkers of social democracy, for this purpose, are the Germans Bernstein and Kautsky. Neither of these figures is taken sufficiently seriously by socialists, partly because of the tradition's own inclination to ridicule and caricature reformism. Bernstein is typically dismissed as a kind of Ramsay Macdonald in disguise; Kautsky is too frequently viewed as the pedantic pope of marxism, the crepuscular figure displayed by Trotsky, in his slippers, perpetually ready to retire. Bernstein and Kautsky deserve better than this, because they are arguably better sources for rethinking social democracy than the British figures who generate so much enthusiasm today, such as modern medievals R. H. Tawney and perhaps T. H. Marshall.[2] Bernstein and Kautsky are potentially useful because they provide better social theory than the British, partly because they descend from marxism and partly because they develop a kind of weberian marxism, and both dimensions are highly significant. My argument is that Bernstein and Kautsky offer modern socialist utopias—unlike Bolshevism, which, via Lenin, offers a premodern, one-class proletarian utopia, but also unlike Fabianism, which offers a modernist, functionalized utopia. Bernstein and Kautsky are significant because they accept the sober necessities of modern social organization without functionalizing them into necessities.[3]

Dead Dog I: Bernstein

Students of socialism from Belfort Bax to Helmut Hirsch have asked the question, Was not Bernstein merely a Fabian?[4] The answer to this question is no. Bernstein's wife may have translated the writings of Sidney Webb and Beatrice Potter Webb, but so did Lenin. The very idea that someone's cultural location should entirely form him or her ought to be thrown out together with Robert Owen's other enthusiasm, spade-husbandry. This is not to deny the significance of Bernstein's lengthy English sojourn, but it is to suggest that his incipient revisionism has its own roots as well. We could as well ask why Bernstein chose England as ask what England did to him. Reformism is not a disease, English or other; it is a legitimate socialist response to the problems thrown up by capitalist civilization. Against Fabianism, however, Bernstein had a different utopia, and he was a democrat, not a Democrat.

Part of the issue here is doubtless that Bernstein upset altogether too many good marxists by simultaneously advocating practical reformism and theoretical revisionism. But if this were the only problem, we might still expect today's radicals to take Bernstein's *Evolutionary Socialism* seriously, at least perhaps to read it. Bernstein, however, also wrote other things, even less recognized. Several distinct attributes become clear, for example, in his earlier articles in *Die Neue Zeit* and elsewhere. The first is that, opposed to Bax, Bernstein was a modern romantic. Bax viewed modernity and capitalism as coextensive and consequently conceived socialism as their negation. For Bernstein, by comparison, modernity contained capitalism, socialism, and civilization; the point was thus not to go backward, but to seek the fullest possible development of social individuals within modernity.[5] For Bax, modernity was all loss, no gain.[6] For Bernstein, capitalist civilization was for all its excesses still civilization, worth defending.[7] Civility thus mattered to Bernstein; unlike Rosa Luxemburg, he translated *Burgerliche Gesellschaft* as civil society, not bourgeois or capitalist society, because again he thought the practice of civility and the institution of civil society worth defending.[8]

The significance of civil society bears emphasizing here, not least of all because civil society was the primary arena of social democratic activity. When people spoke of the Social Democratic Party (SPD) as a "state within a state," their use of language was imprecise; the SPD was rather a matter of a society within a society. In contemporary language, the SPD was indeed a social movement, not a counterstate, and the bulk of SPD effort was expended within its voluntary cultural associations—bicycling clubs, libraries, singing clubs, smoking clubs, antismoking clubs, and so on.[9] For this reason I do not find Peter Murphy's particular view of the SPD in his provocative paper "Socialism and Democracy" convincing. The SPD viewed as a movement was incapable of the kind of oligarchy ascribed to it by Robert Michels in *Political Parties*. But more than this, the ordinary social democrats of Wilhelmine Germany knew something about democracy, and not just that they wanted to practice it in their cultural and associative lives; they also knew that Bismarck would not allow them to have it, long before Hitler was to deprive them of it. This does not mean, as Murphy rightly suggests, that the category *social democracy* can be used to resolve falsely, because semantically, the relationship between socialism and democracy. But it does suggest that social democracy became administrative; social democrats could just as well, in other circumstances, have chosen to become democrats. For democracy, like civility, is surely something not innate but something we in fact learn.

What attracted Bernstein to England, apart from his freedom from jailers there, was exactly the room to move, not simply to engineer socialism through the state. According to Bernstein, then, socialism grows not out of chaos but out of the "union of the organised creations of the workers in the domain of political economy with the creations and conquests of the fighting democracy in State and community."[10] In a striking anticipation of recent events in Eastern Europe, Bernstein wrote further:

> The socialistic theory of the bolshevists is, as much as it does not offhandishly recede behind Karl Marx, a marxism made coarse, its political doctrine is an overvaluation of the creative power of brute violence and its political ethics are not a criticism but a coarse misunderstanding of the liberal ideas that in the great French revolution of the eighteenth century have found their classical expression. But just as by the unbending language of facts they have already seen themselves compelled to subject their economic policy to a thorough revision, the time will not stay away when in the face of the rebellion/revolt of the ineradicable striving of the peoples to freedom and right they will also have to fundamentally revise their policy and their ethics.[11]

There are significant marxist critics, such as Guglielmo Carchedi, who would probably view this as further evidence of Bernstein's petit bourgeois socialism (i.e., not as socialism at all). In his important but relatively undiscussed study *Class Analysis and Social Research*, Carchedi analyzes the problem of revisionism via another sadly unnoticed book,

Hans Muller's 1892 study *Der Klassenkampf in der deutschen Sozialdemokratie*. Muller's case is that the SPD went rotten under Bismarck's antisocialist laws, as good working-class leaders literally became petit bourgeois, opening shops or workshops because their old employers blackballed them, denied them work as laborers.[12] The Carchedi-Muller case, somewhat like the Michels-Murphy argument, is effectively that the SPD lived out the contradiction of fighting for democracy by authoritarian means. The significant difference is that where Michels and Murphy view institutionalization or the state as the problem, for Muller and Carchedi class analysis explains the problem of class slippage; changes in class composition explain the change in or decline of the SPD.

The Muller case is indeed significant, and Carchedi is correct to observe that its forgetting is symptomatic—the implication is that the revisionism debate began a decade earlier than traditionally thought but was suppressed by Friedrich Engels's siding with the elders.[13] Muller emerges from this argument as possibly the primary sociologist of the party, writing as he was before Michels and Ostrogorsky and well before Antonio Gramsci. And yet there is something anthropologically or sociologically surprising about the sense of surprise in the case—as though the emergence of a division of labor in the party were atypical and as though class struggle were a legitimate meta-metaphor for social life as such. Unlike Muller, Bernstein and Kautsky saw something to defend in the institutions of socialism, an entirely understandable attitude. In this light, it is worth turning to Bernstein's (in)famous maxim that the goal of socialism is nothing, the movement everything. Contrary to received marxist wisdom about Bernstein, I want to suggest that this maxim is hermeneutically meaningful in a positive way. First of all, it should be said that Bernstein's maxim was deliberately hyperbolic; he was the first to qualify it when it was read as a sign of moral liquidationism.[14] Yet he had also, at the same time, chosen his terms cautiously. In proposing that the goal of socialism was "nothing," Bernstein's logic was that socialism was a norm and not a goal, a premise and not a telos, or, as he put it, a principle and not a plan of society.[15] For this reason Bernstein titled his work *Voraussetzungen des Sozialismus*, referring to principles from which we set out; it was only at Ramsay Macdonald's mischievous suggestion that the title was Anglicized as *Evolutionary Socialism* for the British edition. Clearly, then, Bernstein was committed to socialism; the argument from the left should have concerned the nature of this socialism, not its alleged nonexistence. Similarly, the idea that the movement was everything did not simply betray a monolithic institutional bias on Bernstein's part. He spoke of the movement, not the party, and used the category *movement* in the dual sense that we today associate with the work of Alain Touraine, referring both to the idea of the actor and to the fact of the process of movement itself: bourgeois civilization was not solid crystal; rather, it moved. Social progress resulted from social struggle, agitation, and organization. This process involved the slow transition to socialism, while the "final goal" emasculated such struggles, collapsing socialism into the utopia of dreamers.[16] This was Bernstein's view, in any case.

The society of the future, for Bernstein, ought thus to be complex and differentiated, dependent on social self-help, and given to the development of personality within the division of labor.[17] Moreover, he saw it as dependent on political obligation, a theme rarely discussed by socialists then or still now. Bernstein put emphasis not only on right but also on duty; he argued for an active rather than a merely passive or welfarist conception of citizenship.[18] Thus he thought civilization precedes and transcends capitalism, and citizenship precedes liberalism and contractualism. More than this, Bernstein had a sense of the past as well as of the future. He discussed the power of tradition and memory and argued for the centrality of the imaginary.[19] He agreed with Weber about the "centrality of interests vis-a-vis the ideal" and the "material" and proposed, Durkheimlike, that morality is even more durable than economic life.[20]

The novelty of Bernstein's thought is equally clear in the much maligned *Evolutionary Socialism*. Here Bernstein discussed socialism in specifically political terms having to do with the citizens of the future. Economy is to be subordinated to politics, not the other way around, as in the tradition of productivist socialism. Bernstein did not succumb to the instrumental conception of democracy, characteristic of social democracy after fascism. Socialism he understood as a movement toward a new order based on the principle of association.[21] He rejected the marxist-syndicalist proposition that unions are somehow the proletarian order *in statu nascendi*. He wrote: "The idea of democracy includes, in the conception of the present day, a notion of justice—an equality of rights for all members of the community."[22] Democracy, in short, is not the projection but the suspension of class government; class government is a bourgeois practice. The upshot was that "social democracy does not wish to break up this society and make all its members proletarians together; it labours rather incessantly at raising the worker from the social position of a proletarian to that of a citizen, and thus to make citizenship universal."[23] Its purpose is to set up not a proletarian society but rather a socialist one.[24] Socialism was in this specific regard best understood as the heir of liberalism, for the security of civil freedom is always a higher goal for social democracy than the fulfilment of some economic program.[25] Against Ferdinand Lassalle, and fully recognizing the constraints of his own native language, Bernstein declared that "we are all citizens *(Burger)*."[26] Yet in all this socialism is clearly an "ought," not an "is," Bernstein's maturational optimism notwithstanding.

Dead Dog II: Kautsky

It is Kautsky, of course, who is more often associated with "maturational reformism," the idea of the great day one day, made by itself and not by a party.[27] The theoretical issue at stake is probably more fundamental than we allow: all socialisms need a telos, a project, a sense of future, or a utopia. Doubtless Kautsky's real theoretical crime here was that he produced and subscribed to the most influential theory of automatic marxism, that of the Second International itself. But Kautsky was no fool. In fact, his views are interesting, I suggest, not only in their own right but also because they illustrate the difficulties of being an orthodox marxist with empirical sensitivities. What is interesting about Kautsky's theory is that he remained committed to a whole series of orthodox premises that Bernstein abandoned, but he did not defend these when they patently flew in the face of the problems confronting him as a social democrat.

There are two central texts here, both of them now, by happy coincidence, available in English, so that even Kautsky's local opponents may at last finally pay him the courtesy of reading his work. They are *The Agrarian Question* (1899) and *The Materialist Conception of History* (1927).

The Agrarian Question is an extremely interesting work because it shows Kautsky denying his orthodoxy where it stands to inhibit the analysis. If Kautsky was a shellback, it cannot be said that he never ventured out of his shell. Kautsky's task here was to illustrate the pertinence of Marx's claims about capitalism—the general trends toward the concentration of capital and the proletarianization of the mass—to agriculture itself. While Kautsky's own tedious defenses of scale now look dated in the face not only of ecological radicalism but also of postfordist flexibilities, we can nevertheless see him following the footsteps of Marx, freshly imprinted by Bernstein, regarding the so-called idiocy of rural life. Kautsky, like the Webbs and most other fin-de-siècle socialists, defended the ideas of culture and civilization; the task was not to abolish the galleries but rather to universalize access to them. Scale, of course, meant division of labor, and thus—and here he was perhaps more like Bernard Shaw than like the Webbs—Kautsky located the realm of freedom in leisure, the latter to be maximized while the working day was to be minimized.

Yet Kautsky's desire to prove the theses of *Capital* for agriculture was to come up against what sociologists respectfully call "the data." So Kautsky ended up, appropriately, explaining why Marx's theses were unhelpful and how the peasantry would continue to remain a permanent characteristic of modern class structure.[28] Consequently Kautsky even engaged in a half-hearted attempt to wax lyrical about a craft renaissance.[29] Certainly Kautsky's attitude toward William Morris was more positive than that of Bernstein toward his offsider Bax.[30] To mention their names in the same breath is also, however, to recognize that a word is in order prior to passing on the Bernstein-Kautsky pair itself.

If Kautsky was a pope, a theolog, Bernstein was by comparison an amateur, an artisan. Their approaches to the creation of knowledge were very different, Kautsky's still governed by some kind of pretense to the encyclopedic, Bernstein's more postmodern and fragmentary. But it is not at all clear that they ever disagreed that much. The oft-quoted quip of Ignaz Auer was that Bernstein had behaved stupidly by wanting to change the rules of marxism theoretically, not just in practice. As another contemporary saying had it, the SPD was keen on hanging onto the Sunday china even if it were never used. Certainly Bernstein's epistemology, like his politics, was pragmatic; he had no time for "dialectics" or for the kind of foundationalism characteristic of most marxism.[31] Yet, as I suggest, Kautsky's practical position did not differ excessively from this; we have to turn to someone like Georgi Plekhanov to see the stereotype of marxism more recognizably at work. So even Kautsky's authoritative chastizing of his friend in, for example, his anticritique *Bernstein und das Sozialdemokratische Programme*[32] is reminiscent of a teacher's reprimanding his wayward but preferred student. Their major difference here was simply over the social-democratic or more specifically proletarian telos that Bernstein had rejected. It was no accident that their views then merged after the first catastrophe of Bolshevism. What Lukács called Bernstein's triumph was no victory at all.

There is further evidence of these nuances in Kautsky's *Materialist Conception*. The first striking thing about this study is that it opens with a denunciation of materialism, conventionally defined. Historically, the problem has been that no one has read the book, particularly since Karl

Korsch sliced it up in doing pirouettes on sharpened skates in his 1929 critique of the same title. As one suspects is often otherwise the case, people seem to have read the critique and not the original text: case closed. But if the book is opened we find a defense not of any materialism but of classical marxism, tempered by an overriding concern with the "developmental history of mankind."[33] Perhaps Jürgen Habermas was less original than we were led to believe. Like Bernstein, Kautsky viewed modernity as formed by the past and saw the future as structured by it; the sense of history involved is fundamentally different from that, say, in H. G. Wells's *A Modern Utopia* or in Trotsky's *Literature and Revolution*, where it somehow becomes at least implicitly possible to step out of time, tradition, memory, biography, culture.

At the same time, however, Kautsky's work is also postmarxian in the literal sense that his utopic vision accepts and develops the distinction between freedom and necessity sketched out in the third volume of *Capital*. Kautsky here specifically rejected the hunter–fisher–cattleperson–critical critic utopia of the *German Ideology*, which had been published in 1926.[34] Moreover, he presumed a kind of skepticism in knowledge and in politics and argued about the limits to knowledge and to action, even though his frame was encyclopedic in breadth. He argued in detail, for example, about the weight of tradition and the conservative nature of the mind, balancing the romantic component of marxism with the sense that human beings seek self-development but also stability.[35] An important intellectual source that we find for this disposition in Kautsky is the study of anthropology, which serves as a useful artifact, reminding us that for all their modernism the social democrats did actually take anthropology seriously; probably there is still no better monument to this than the pages of Kautsky's own extraordinary journal, *Die Neue Zeit*, encyclopedic in interest and enthusiasms yet free of the sense of a governing or incipient synthesis.

Thus, for example, Kautsky discussed the Durkheim issue of the social construction of morality and the cultural autonomy of morality, and he rejected the Herbert Spencer argument central to *The Agrarian Question*, that society is an organism (it is *not*, Kautsky says, because it consists of individuals, each of whom is not only sentient but possessed of consciousness).[36] Given that he took social differentiation seriously, what we end up with is the image of socialism as a society based on differentiation, based practically on production but not on the image of production. Kautsky saw socialism rather as based on variable forms of activity that work against the syndicalist identity of the tradition; work is central but diverse and is viewed as a responsibility. These kinds of arguments occur in the context of a discussion that is explicitly sympathetic to Weber and critical of Engels, with whom Kautsky is typically guilt-associated.

The Weber connection is significant here because Kautsky took up both Weber's political "realism" and his methodological "idealism." Unlike a generation of marxists more recently, Kautsky duly engaged Weber's thought, and not just in the footnotes. Kautsky referred to *Economy and Society* and to the *General Economic History* and presented the thesis of *The Protestant Ethic* as a complement to that of *Capital*. Kautsky does not seem fully to have understood the argument about rationalization as a social trend.[37] What may perhaps be more of a surprise to the marxist shellbacks of my generation is Kautsky's attempt to address the question of politics as a vocation. Here, again, Kautsky seems to have understood the modernizing moment of Weber's thought, not the fears of cages iron or regulative.[38] His discussion of the limits of charisma is jarring, composed as it was only five years before the rise of the charismatic leader in Germany.[39]

More fruitful, however, are his theoretical affinities with Gramsci. If Kautsky's reading of Weber is one-sided, his comments on intellectuals are more positively reminiscent of *The Prison Notebooks*. Here, like Gramsci, he discussed the universality of intellectual life. The autodidact, the organizer, is as much an intellectual as is the critic of opera,[40] Kautsky said, and here he repeated an argument from the *Agrarian Question*, that there is no reason to believe that the possession of academic knowledge elevates the modern citizen over the populace of "primitive" society.[41] There are further parallels in the shared sense that state and society must be transformed via democracy and that socialism emerges from order, not crisis—if at all.[42] However, where Bernstein would place democracy, still, as the central premise of socialism, Kautsky persisted in giving this place to the proletariat.[43] Kautsky added, though, that the theoretical possibility that the needs of the proletariat could be met within capitalism would necessitate the renunciation of socialism, the implicit liquidation indicating one basis of his reunification with the spirit of Bernstein's project. For as he put it, the final goal of the proletariat is not a final goal for the development of humanity. "An enduringly perfect society is as little possible as an absolute truth," he wrote. "And both the one and the other would mean nothing other than social stagnation and death."[44]

This is not, I think, the figure of Kautsky loosely portrayed by Trotsky, a man in a smoking jacket, cosy but terminal both theoretically and practically. Conversely, I do not mean to turn Kautsky (or anyone else) into some kind of new hero for the 90s of our own century. He would have looked ridiculous in hair gel, with a flat top and in black. My argument rather is that notwithstanding idiosyncrasies to do with Darwin and whoever else, Kautsky and Bernstein still talk to us, and in language that is more alike than we might at first think. For Kautsky and Bernstein seem to have understood something of the limits on the future (if not its propensity to generate degeneracy and barbarism) and yet to argue for human possibilities within it. My case is not that we should all become Kautskyists so much as that those who still identify with the aims and traditions of socialism should actually attempt to clarify what those aims are and where those traditions speak or are silent.

This is not to say, then, that Kautsky (in particular) was not a shellback (though even Rosa Luxemburg was equally crustacean in political economy). It is striking, however, that even when Kautsky ventured out, no one noticed, and then we had to suffer the slings and arrows of Althusserian political economy or Poulantzian class analysis in the 1970s as a dull replay of some of these earlier, forgotten events. We then received the discovery that socialism has something to do with democracy as a great surprise, too great a surprise, as though it was actually invented by Eurocommunists, although Bernstein had already argued the case in *Evolutionary Socialism* and Kautsky had taken it further in 1918, in *The Dictatorship of the Proletariat*. The case presented here, then, is that the social democratic project, in contrast to Bolshevism, at least provides a place to start, for it possesses a concrete utopia. Thus, in Weber's sense, social democracy presents itself as one of the warring gods between whom we must choose.

We return here to the idea that the German social democrats engage a kind of Weberian marxism, by which I mean a kind of marxism that is politically realistic, takes ideas seriously, and embraces the postfaustian future. This may be a heavy-handed way of describing a marxism come of age, for certainly I refer to something different than the Weberianized marxism that has frequented sociology since Frank Parkin's "bourgeois critique" and something more pragmatic than Maurice Merleau-Ponty's tracing of Weberian marxism via Georg Lukács in *Adventures of the Dialectic*. I refer back, rather, to the effective location of social democracy in the heart of classical social theory, the theory that sits on the cusp of modernity and tells us so much of the spirit, hopes, and woes of our time.[45] This locus offers us a view of sober optimism and a modern sobriety rather than the implicitly medieval sobriety of R. H. Tawney's worldview. It reminds us, as well, that as Martin Jay puts it, the fin of our siècle somehow compels us to reconsider the fin of the previous siècle, its hopes and dreams, failures and nightmares.[46]

There are myriad possible objections that could be put against this case. The most powerful, I suspect, is that asking West Europeans to revive social democracy is about as futile as hoping that East Europeans might care to revive the imaginary of communism. It is almost certainly true that the persuasiveness of my case will be weak for denizens of cultures that have in any way recognizably been "social democratic" since the Second World War. *Weltgeschichte ist Weltgericht,* as Castoriadis reminds us; if people take the postwar experience to be social democracy, we have to accept this and find a new language. These are real claims, which have to be taken seriously, but they in turn raise others, apparently insoluble, about how we transcend liberalism from within a liberal or post-liberal culture. My response is that the reception of the present case is likely to be better in Anglo cultures, where social democracy persists in representing a project and tradition superior to those of the local tradition of laborism.[47] Laborism, as feminists such as Marilyn Lake have shown, is in its genesis in fact a *rural* utopia that cannot have adequate purchase on everyday lives lived mainly in the cities of modernity.[48] Until recently, with the miraculous arrival of the Australian Labor Party–Australian Council of Trade Unions Accord and particularly *Australia Reconstructed,* so tellingly criticized in *Thesis Eleven* by Kevin McDonald,[49] the Australian labor movement has, with certain syndicalist exceptions, sought the utopia of yeomen, first in the bush, then in the suburbs. Perhaps because the German social democrats pitted themselves against the miseries of peasant life, theirs was a utopian vision that was never to reach this far back into history in search of inspiration—or escape (for men).

Social democracy matters, I would argue, because it mediates between social theory and politics and, moreover, it bridges premodern and modern. Durkheim was not the only one to recognize that communism was premodern, while socialism was modern; so did the dead dogs of social democracy. The issue is significant because while communism's utopia was premodern, so too was that of ethical socialism. The problem in the latter connection is that while medieval ethics may be extraordinarily valuable—a theme actually suggested by Macpherson himself[50]—medieval social theory will not do. Arguments for the romantic, English-style "simple life" do not adequately address the needs structures of modern citizens or the peculiarities of postmodern culture, and while these phenomena are obviously socially constructed, we do need some sense of the difference between the way forward and the way back. Moreover, arguments for reviving the past, literally, produce what Michael Ignatieff calls moral narcissism, a sort of middle-class version of the "prolier-than-thou" attitude governed by the misty nostalgia for better days bygone, for 1945–51 in Britain or 1972–75 in Australia.[51] These may have been better days, but they are no future.

Dead Dogs, Slumbering Hopes

I conclude by returning to Macpherson and to *The Life and Times of Liberal Democracy*. In this chapter I have resisted Macpherson's attraction to model building with reference to the idea of a social democratic utopia. This is consistent with Bernstein's sense that socialism has to do with norms, not with plans. I leave it to other colleagues and friends to indicate economic directions for the future of Australia. As regards models, however, I share Macpherson's sense that one-class models, whether those of proletarian socialism (Bolshevism) or freeborn Englishpersons with or without spade husbandry (Tawney, Owen), are past, perhaps even dangerous. The vital point in connection with Macpherson is the idea of uncoupling citizenship and functional status or labor market status. With reference to the future, however, a possible socialism based on difference as well as on differentiation need not fetishize democracy any more than it need universalize politics. "Democracy" needs "responsibility," just as "rights" call forth "duties."

Of course, other issues are involved. As Beatrice Potter sensibly if wickedly put it, democracy has limits of other sorts; the slogan "the factories to the workers" misses the point that the workers may possibly not want the factories any more than the sewer workers want absolute sovereignty over their own vocational domain.[52] Democracy is a problem as well as a "solution."

The logic of my case has been that social democracy runs a line between romanticism and realism, between Bax and the Webbs, between anarchism and bureaucracy, between Morris and Bellamy, between moral and mechanical socialism, between the possible dichotomy of the values of freedom and life. This is so because social democracy is simultaneously sociological and ethical. Because it is sociological, it has developed a sense of some of the ambivalences that characterize modernity. Because it is ethical, it is able to address some very ordinary questions about our own existence. Among other things, it opens a discourse that perhaps helps us better to see that part of our predicament today lies not in the institutions upon which we frequently blame the present impasse but in our own failure to become more fully human. With that, however, I accept the view—as did Bernstein and Kautsky—that new social institutions will always be necessary, even if we do not yet know what they are. Pierre Rosanvallon may be right to suggest that this project be called post–social democratic.[53] However, this reinforces the sense that we ought to take social democracy seriously, especially if post–social democratic means anything like "postmodern" or "postmarxist"—new, yet continuous—for these are still the tracks within which we work.

(1990)

Four

The Fabian Imagination

Why discuss Fabianism today? If socialism is over, the problems to which it was a response persist. Socialisms are traditions, and we are all, still, creatures of tradition. Ours, of course, is a moment in world history when to speak of socialism is to risk looking distinctly dated, if not downright unfashionable. So be it. For ours is also a moment when melancholy and misery are more widespread than in recent memory, when paid work is increasingly casualized and a dual labor market calls up, once again, images of the underworld that holds up the world we inhabit, where peoples long for freedom and identity and struggle still in pursuit of them.[1] Ours is, in short, a moment when the old debate about continuity versus change has a much greater than academic importance.

The traditions we call socialist emerged in response to these social problems and others concerning freedom, subjection, life in the cities, the repression of sexuality, and aesthetics, locality, and so on. Socialism is the generic name given to these reactions to capitalism and industrialism; it is the alter ego of modernity.[2] The present impasse of socialism is unlikely to be eternal, but its terms of reference, its norms and values, will very likely again find a place in public debate as the more corrosive effects of deregulation and global development are registered.[3] Radicals still have their work cut out for them.

The maelstrom that we feel about us also has a name: it has been encountered before and named as such. One vital flag here is that of the fin de siècle. The term seems to exhibit a wonderful capacity to capture that simultaneous sense of the sublime and the terrible. Postmodernism is, in one sense, an extension of romanticism, but it is also a revival of fin-de-siècle enthusiasms and fears.[4] But if the fin de siècle puts us on the precipice, there is also the longer cycle now upon us—the millennium itself, its notions of apocalypse on a scale more civilizational than cultural, its resonances of judgment and even retribution.[5] My sense is that socialist ideas remain a potential source of argument today because so many of the problems that were controversial then remain unresolved. Here I want, especially, to defend Fabianism even as gas and water socialism, for the basic provision of services in cities will remain a fundamental problem into the new millennium. The sense of continuity is for me pervasive.

I

David Lovell correctly identifies marxism as the most apparently rigorous of all socialist claims to social scientific understanding.[6] Elsewhere I have argued that it is, however, a dangerous arrogance for marxists to assume, as they long have, that those who do not kneel before their own claims to science are simply stupid or ignorant. The Fabians, in particular, clearly understood marxism and rejected it. They read *Capital* and remained unpersuaded.[7] But if Marx remains an inspirational thinker,[8] there are all manner of other thinkers who can now—after communism— more readily be recognized and heard. The hegemony of the Bolshevik tradition after October meant that leading social democrats such as Karl Kautsky and Eduard Bernstein were subjected to calumny, their major works left unread.[9] Fabianism arguably suffered even more, as Sidney and Beatrice Webb in particular were subjected to ridicule by H. G. Wells in *The New Machiavelli,* setting a precedent rerun with cheer into the 1970s by the able staff of the *New Left Review.*[10]

Like Social Democracy, Fabianism was transformed by world history: by the wars, by fascism and Stalinism, but also, in the British case, by its affiliation with the British Labor Party and the heroic period of welfare statism. But just as the various plural socialisms have been submerged by marxism, so have the various Fabianisms been blotted into a single, glutinous image redolent of bureaucracy, statism, centralization, and Eastern Europe's spreading somehow across the channel. Scholars such as Alan McBriar and Ian Britain have shown that Fabianism has always been a deeper and richer tradition than that.[11]

In recent times G. D. H. Cole has been revived, with guild socialism rather than Fabianism the emblem of enthusiasm.[12] Paul Hirst has identified the pluralist stream rather than that of direct democracy as the motif worthy of extension.[13] The Fabian Women's Group, which pioneered investigative research in the context of British sociology, still has adequately to be analyzed or appraised.[14] The probing intellectual curiosity of Leonard Woolf has still to be acknowledged. Some, like the Woolfs, can be said to have embodied their images in their practices. Others, like Cole, drew directly from William Morris and John Ruskin, defending the guilds but with a practical edge, seeking less to return to the past than somehow to extend that residue of medieval logic into the hostile environment, cash nexus of the present. Wells, for his part, more famously advocated social scientific utopias, whereas Bernard Shaw sang praise of dictators—they did things—pulled legs about eugenics, and worried over leisure time and what we might do with it (his answer: be active). There were, then, various Fabian imaginations, some more romantic, some more given to modernization.

II

The core concern of this chapter, however, is not so much the different specific practical projects pursued by particular intellectuals as it is the proposition that in a post-Bolshevik world Fabian ideas still have purchase. The Webbs, in particular, gave great effort to thinking of the future as an extension of the present. Sidney Webb was obsessed with what Max Weber called an ethic of responsibility: his socialism commenced from admittedly pragmatic points of reference, but these were also deeply moral in motivation. His ethics were like Émile Durkheim's: his sense was that individuals could come to fruition only in the context of social relations, that mutual service ought be the norm rather than the exception in social life. There is, however, a sense of urgency in his writings: "The first thing and the greatest connected with the sin and pain on earth is to do what we can to remedy it; to discover its cause is but an after amusement."[15] Though Sidney Webb is typically cast as a philistine in comparison to his scheming yet romantic wife, Beatrice, there are striking parallels between their early work—critical enthusiasms for Marx, positive interest in cooperation—and across their work there are echoes between Sidney's early spiritualism and Beatrice's famous premodern longings for lost community in *My Apprenticeship*.

Notwithstanding his own formal refusal of utopia, Sidney Webb subsequently penned a utopia, *The London Program*, in 1891. There is an ecological impulse in his program that has obvious utility for radicals today, in that his pitch is for the importance of urban ecology, that moment when the romantic emblems of nature intersect with problems of everyday life. For Webb, then, ordinary social reform had an anthropological and civilizational dimension and was not merely the instrumental fantasy or will to power of the would-be Samurai caricatured by but also enthused about by Wells.[16]

Were the Webbs centralists, then? Local stalinists in British drag? They fell badly for the image of the Soviet Union in the 1930s, that is true, but they also shared the enthusiasm of Joseph Chamberlain and others for municipal activity. And they enthused over cooperation, but especially consumer cooperatives: Beatrice Potter published her first non-children's book, *The Co-operative Movement in Great Britain*, in 1891. Here Robert Owen was her guiding light, but with an urban twist. Moreover, she identified Owen's utopia as premodern in its essential characteristics, evidenced not least of all in the absence of Democracy from his new view.[17]

Beatrice Potter elaborated on these claims in a paper presented at a conference of trade unionists and cooperators in 1892. Here she identified the experience of the Rochdale cooperators as a microcosm of the good society.[18] A cooperative society, she suggested, was impossible: the state was obliged to organize railways and communications. Unionists and cooperators represented necessary and necessarily different interests in economic life—each had its proper sphere.[19] The Webbs, together and separately, favored consumer cooperatives because they favored the view of the consumer. But at the same time they never identified with Lenin's utopia in *State and Revolution;* they analyzed syndicalism sympathetically but viewed the interest of the producer as one social interest among others.[20] Theirs was a multiclass, functional utopia. For the Webbs worked with a conception of social contribution that was not narrowly economic or governed by calculations to do with GDP. Here it is worth locating their socialism not so much against Robert Owen as with William Cobbett, for the vital critical impulse in their work is against parasitism at both extremities of the social scale.

Questions of social contribution and social reward thus persist, even though they may also remain beyond resolution. The domination of politics by economics is evidently one of the major features of modernity. Fabianism—at least in the hands of the Webbs—rejected the labor theory of value and viewed value in broader terms of social contribution or service. Sidney Webb's sense was not that the middle class was an evil historical excrescence that refused to push off but that it had a duty that it all too often failed to discharge.[21] The middle classes were functionally necessary but careless, presuming their privilege as a right, while the working class and their children expired young and without pleasure. Reward without service was "simply—robbery."[22]

III

The most significant text for our purposes, however, is the utopian frame constructed together by the Webbs in their 1920 book *A Constitution for the Socialist Commonwealth of Great Britain*. Crowley has identified a certain symmetry between this great work and their worst, the mid-1930s *Soviet Communism—A New Civilization*,[23] though Leonard Woolf pioneered this observation.[24] Notwithstanding their interest in structures of power, the Webbs were a little too enchanted with the idea of a constitution itself. Yet utopias, or arguments for the good society, themselves also need constitutions, and there is an important intersection between the tradition of utopian speculation and the necessity of constructing the constitutions that might imaginably frame good societies. The Webbs' particular enthusiasm was arguably less that of the lawyer and more that suggested by the semantics of constitution, as that notion has been revived, say, by Anthony Giddens or more creatively by Cornelius Castoriadis in his kindred notion of institution.[25] How can we imagine the spheres of society, their interaction, independence, and interdependence? The Webbs' utopia is that of a differentiated, functional, multiclass society. For them, division of labor generated interdependence. This symbol of function is followed to the extent that democracy, too, must be functionalized. Thus the Webbs proposed that there be separate realms of consumers' democracy, producers' democracy, and political democracy.

For the Webbs, democracy meant representative democracy, though they were also able to accommodate some of Cole's insistence on direct democracy. Even the younger, more radical Cole was obliged to concede that guilds would need some kind of representation in a council of guilds in cases of dispute or national policy.[26] The Webbs' counterargument was equally obvious: such a council was indistinguishable from a parliament, so why not call it by its name? Cole, more than the Webbs, warmed to the idea of the Russian Revolution. Citizens, in Cole's conception, would be identified as members of specific occupational groups, and electoral divisions, so to speak, would be vocational rather than geographical.[27] In the view of the Webbs, by comparison, vocational groups would galvanize professional and public identity in the workplace and the public sphere, but not as political units.[28] The sphere in which the Webbs finally made peace with Lenin, however, was that other world in which the legacy of Henri de Saint-Simon lives on, that musty realm where politics is identified with administration.

The Webbs thus suggested a formal and functional differentiation of political purposes. Political functions, they thought, could be disaggregated into a separate organizational sphere addressing law and order, diplomacy and defense. A separate parliament would deal with social functions, issues of welfare, and national "housekeeping," following the example of the London City Council. The national parliament could thus be split into two departments within the House of Commons, one to follow police and external functions, the other to pursue domestic and welfare purposes.[29] The logic at work here resembles that in Beatrice Webb's *Minority Report of the Poor Law Commission*. This is itself an extremely important document, partly because it anticipates the Beveridge Report but also because it is, as Pease suggested, in effect a concrete utopia: it presumes that not all citizens will or can be healthy, sane, effective, or autonomous.[30] The *Minority Report* introduced the sense that provision for health, education, and so on was not essentially related to the imaginary of the Poor Laws, nor could these functions properly be facilitated except through departments that had distinct and particular purposes. The notion of undifferentiated pauperism led to unspecialized management.[31] The Poor Law regime thus generated mindless regimentation and undifferentiated order. Here the Webbs shared the concern of Durkheim, Weber, and Alfred Marshall that none of this could be expected to build character.[32] Yet it still approved and provided enthusiasm for voluntary agencies and their work.[33] Locality was viewed as the most appropriate basis upon which to proceed with the extensive process of necessary social reform.[34]

The clear message across the welfare writings of the Webbs is that destitution involves the loss of human potential and spirit. But what happened to politics in all this? Modified by functional disaggregation, parliament could more readily become vulnerable to the power of research methods of measurement and publicity; the public agenda would henceforth be set by the *"searchlight of published knowledge."*[35] Surely the Webbs' conception of politics would be comic were it not so dangerous. This fatal flaw in the constitution of politics, however, was not to be duplicated in the Webbs' thinking about economics. For the Webbs imagined an economy of mixed property forms. The economy in their long view might consist of three major sectors—nationalized leading sectors, municipal and local property, and cooperatives. There are significant echoes here in the work of Karl Kautsky.[36] The essential difference between Kautsky and the Webbs was that for Kautsky big alone was beautiful, and Kautsky's defense of democracy escalated in the face of the Bolshevik experience.[37] For the Webbs, by comparison, small was sweatshop, and Democracy had its proper place.

My concern here is not to defend the manifest content of the Webbs' utopia so much as to show the plurality evident in its logic. The Webbs defended the image of socialism as one with a mixture of political and economic forms. They were insufficiently sympathetic to notions of democratic participation, and they failed to argue in the way we would for the centrality of markets. Soon they were to pen a study unambiguously entitled *The Decay of Capitalist Civilization,* with no question mark. Their skepticism about the capacity of markets to deliver was as much a hallmark of their own times as the sense that markets rule is a hallmark of the present. Socialisms, then, already offered a storehouse of possibilities that we might now, in good conscience, recycle, rediscover, rethink: for these were traditions that had pushed aside the shadow of Marx and discussed many of the problems that still confront us.

For the Webbs it remained the case that "a constitution based exclusively on wealth production seems as lop-sided as a constitution based exclusively on wealth possession. Surely we shall not fight," they wrote, "for any ideal smaller than Humanity itself; and that not only as it exists at present, but also as it may arise in the future."[38] Notwithstanding the contempt of postmodernists for such grand categories, there will likely remain those who choose to hope that humanity can do better even as it muddles through. The Webbs' approach to social policy was consistently governed by an image of the good society with which specific practices ought to be congruent.[39] Like Durkheim's project, theirs was motivated by a sense of the importance of moral and social regulation. The very idea of a national minimum was oriented to this social end, reinforcing the sense that individuals were always only ever social beings.

The contemporary attack on the social and its accompanying dismissal of socialism suggest a future of increasing individualism. To engage this future we need to know our pasts, our traditions, to defend the centrality of the social if not the dominant images of socialism. If we seem, on occasion, to be incapable of transcending the culture within which we find ourselves, some of the sensibilities of these traditions may nevertheless enable us less than blindly to retread the path of the past.

(1994)

Five

The Australian Left: Beyond Laborism?

A decade ago it was popular to argue that the two major parties in Australia were no more different than Tweedle Dum and Tweedle Dee. This kind of thinking, if it can be so called, fed on a traditional refusal among those on the Australian left to take seriously the problem of laborism. This refusal has now, in the 1980s, returned with a vengeance, as farce. Many on the left are now subservient to the very Labor Party they had earlier derided. Labor itself has developed in particular corporatist directions. Many on the left have seized on these developments as offering a new beginning, beyond dogmatism, beyond clichéd militancy, beyond ultraleftist rhetoric and head banging. But there is little prospect that any of this will lead beyond laborism. In the Australian case as in the English, laborism encompasses a pragmatic politics in which the essential focus is on concrete demands of immediate advantage to the working class and organized labor. Laborist politics in Australia, as in England, of course takes place on, and accepts, the terrain of capitalist social relations.[1] Yet laborism has a magnetic effect on the Australian left, and this tendency has been strengthened during the past ten years.

In 1972 the government of Gough Whitlam came into office. The conservative ice age was ended: this was the first federal labor government to be elected in Australia since the postwar reconstruction period. The response on the left was euphoric, even among those who were less than enthusiastic at the prospect of what came to be called "technocratic laborism." The common argument on the extra–labor left was that this government had effectively been summoned by capital to do its bidding, to do what the conservatives had been unable to do: to rationalize the economy, modernize the polity, and regulate and control the union movement. The Whitlam experience was, however, cut short by vice-regal intervention; the left was now forced to reevaluate its often cavalier detachment from the world of labor politics. By the time the conservative government of Malcolm Fraser was ousted by the government of Robert Hawke in 1983, many leftists had shifted their perspectives to the extent that they were prepared to become willing servants of this labor movement. The Labor Party and laborism itself have long provided the central focus for the Australian left; much of the left had thus returned to its historic home, in and around the Labor Party. The Hawke government was elected on the basis of the Australian Labor Party (ALP)–Australian Council of Trade Unions (ACTU) Accord, a pact on prices and incomes that had been formed in 1981. Many on the left have enthusiastically embraced this new situation as one offering great potential for change in a socialist direction. Guilt produced by an earlier abstentionism seems to have resulted in an overwhelming desire to be where the action is. Yet socialist politics in Australia seems thereby to have become ultimately little more than defensive of laborist tenets.

Ten years ago it seemed plausible enough to argue, as Winton Higgins did in the *Socialist Register* 1974, that the Australian left and indeed the Communist Party of Australia (CPA) were shaping up for a great future. The Labor Party has since changed; as the mark has shifted, so has the left around it. Today the influence of the Communist Party is at an ebb; it has just experienced its third major split since 1963. Having disgorged its Maoists in that year and its pro-Soviets in 1971, the CPA split again in 1984, this time at least in part over the question of where the action was—with the ALP or independent of it? Ironically, then, those who railed bitterly against technocratic laborism under Whitlam are now busily embracing its corporatist extension in the Hawke regime. Others who were arguing for a coalition of the left in the 1970s have not changed their tune; their political positions have been structured by the dominance of laborism across these years, the difference now being that the ALP is given a more central place in this "coalition." Some points of continuity emerge, then, though clearly much has also changed. Political discourse in Australia, as elsewhere, has shifted right, and the left has followed this shift. In this context the question to be asked of Australian socialism is whether it can indeed pass beyond laborism, or even fulfil its aims. Some would argue that it can, or perhaps already has, passed from laborism to social democracy, however interpreted. Others might argue that in these times, the problem is rather even to achieve laborism in order to surpass it. For although the record suggests that many of labor's victories in Australia have been pyrrhic, laborism still dominates political life for those who are committed to the struggle for socialism. This chapter begins to survey some of these problems.

The Context: Australian Politics Shifts Right

The aura of reform still adheres to the Whitlam years. Whitlam's government had some striking motifs: it had a cosmopolitan disposition, by Australian standards; it had a European ambiance in the sense that its policies and image were urbane, meritocratic in social policy, expansionist in economic policy. It introduced a major social reform in Medibank, a compulsory and universal national health insurance scheme. It encouraged the growth of the welfare state, and it specifically encouraged the public service to be a pacesetter in wage levels. Unemployment rather than inflation was now regarded as the primary problem facing the Australian economy; the containment of prices rather than labor costs was seen as the policy priority in the early Whitlam years. Although no real social contracts of any substance were negotiated between the ALP and the ACTU in these years, the Whitlam government did seek control over prices and incomes through referenda that were unsuccessful. This program of gentle reform was disrupted not once but twice by conservative refusals to pass labor's supply bills in the Senate (a prerogative peculiar to the Australian rendition of Westminster). The first refusal in 1974 prompted a double dissolution of Parliament and a joint sitting of both houses of Parliament that momentarily overcame the Liberal program of obstructionism. On the second occasion, in 1975, the governor general, Sir John Kerr, circumvented the problem by precipitating a constitutional crisis, sacking Whitlam and his government and installing Fraser, the leader of the Liberal Party, as caretaker prime minister pending a yet further election. The atmosphere of incompetence and sundry scandals surrounding the Whitlam government, together with the conservative conspiracy to eject it from office, resulted in Whitlam's final defeat at the polls. The experience left indelible marks on many in the ALP; it seemed to confirm the popular slogan of the time that they had gone "too far, too fast."

Since the dismissal some on the left have produced a kind of mythology around these events and its central labor characters; as Peter Wilenski has argued, the Whitlam period was the closest Australia had come to an experience like that of 1945 in England.[2] Certainly some Labor supporters, such as Patrick White and Manning Clark, look back on the period with moist eyes; as Xavier Herbert put it in less nostalgic prose, the events had proved what bastards Australians really were. The extra–party left shared this distress, and not only because of its hostility to vice-regal relics like Kerr or haughty graziers like Fraser; there were mass demonstrations, even arguments for a general strike. The representatives of technocratic labor emerged, after all, as being superior to the forces of Australian conservatism. This was indeed a judgment well based. Certainly the Whitlam experience was something less than flawless; that its last budget had already initiated the process of spending cuts to be extended by the incoming Fraser government ought to have been edifying for the left. The Whitlam government had made some preliminary gestures in the direction of gradualist reform at the very moment when the present economic crisis was making its first real effects felt; the Whitlam project thus accentuated the fiscal crisis of the Australian state, prompting the slide away from Keynesianism toward monetarism in economic policy.[3] The Fraser government substantiated this shift, if unevenly: it established a Razor Gang to extend further spending cuts; it elevated the issue of inflation as the most urgent policy priority; it highlighted labor costs over price increases; and it introduced punitive industrial relations legislation. It restored the *status quo ante* in social policy, eroding Medibank, the symbolic core of the Whitlam era. Its program of cuts, however, was less radical in some sectors than parts of the left may have imagined; the parallel with Thatcherism here was more rhetorical than real.[4]

Bob Hawke, former leader of the ACTU, had in the meantime entered Parliament and replaced Bill Hayden as leader of the labor opposition. The unceremonious dumping of Hayden in favor of the charismatic leader was symptomatic of the growing importance of electoralism in the party. Hawke had for some time possessed an image of national reconciliation and consensus.[5] His populist credentials stood him in good stead: he led the ALP back into office in 1983. Fraser stepped down as leader of the Liberal Party; the party conducted a postmortem of its second defeat in eight years, coming to the conclusion that they had not been sufficiently conservative. The report of the Commission of Inquiry,

Facing the Future, argued that the liberals had a credibility problem: they spoke the language of monetarism, but the policy basis of their practice was insufficiently different from that of Labor. The solution was self-evident—Liberal policy had to be more consistently aligned with its conservative or reactionary rhetoric.[6] The Liberal opposition since has developed a policy advocating further cuts in government spending, large-scale privatization, cuts in real wages, and so on. At the same time, however, the Hawke government has been stealing its thunder, so that the shadow treasurer, John Howard, a leader of the Liberal "dries," has been obliged to express a begrudging admiration for the achievements of Hawke's treasurer, Paul Keating. The Liberal Party, then, has clearly moved to the right and has expressed its wish to move further in that direction in the near future. The bipartisan commitment to Keynesianism characteristic of the postwar period has been decisively rejected; thus the spectacle in which marxists, in Australia as elsewhere, have become Keynesians. But labor has also shifted right, and taken the broader left with it.

Labor Shifts Right: The Hawke Era

Whereas the imagery drawn on by Whitlam was Fabian or social democratic in nature, Hawke's identity draws more on images of the laborist past, garnished with the ideology of consensus. In particular, Hawke claims an affinity with John Curtin, Labor leader during the war.[7] The choice of association is less than apposite; Herbert C. Coombs, for example, has argued that the parallel is concocted, that Curtin was a real reformer,[8] while Rob Watts has shown that even this reformism was somewhat less than thoroughly committed to principles such as equity.[9] The Curtin government operated very much within the field established by "new liberalism,"[10] and this in itself would seem to be suggestive of the distance between Hawke and Curtin. The left, in any case, has seen the election of the Hawke government on the basis of the Accord as representing a new beginning,[11] opening new opportunities, formalizing, as it allegedly does, the rights of unions in political decision-making processes. The argument over the Accord is essentially one about potential; many leftists would argue that although the Hawke government is up to the same old tricks, the Accord itself offers new and real possibilities for socialist politics.

The Accord is essentially a deal regarding incomes and prices in conception, though it has in fact functioned in such a way as to actually involve wage restraint in exchange for tax cuts and social wage increases. As a political document, the Accord is a masterpiece of ambiguity: it offers all things, effectively, to all men (women still do not register much on the instruments of laborist politics). The Accord is a document that facilitates several quite distinct interpretations, and it is this that explains the diversity of argument over the question of its potential. The pragmatic subtext of the Accord rests on its bottom line, a commitment to centralized indexation. The introduction to the Accord, in comparison, offers a rather more ambitious project, vitiating this bottom line in its conception of the objective of full employment as a long-term goal.[12] The most ambitious subtext of the Accord is yet more ethereal, manifest in its claim that poverty can be abolished[13] (via mechanisms unseen; the implicit and mistaken presupposition is presumably that poverty and unemployment are coextensive). The Accord also claims to address the question of equity,[14] yet this problem is clearly beyond the scope of a wages deal based on indexation, which leaves the question of income distribution and relativities untouched. A further problem emerges: the different subtexts of the Accord bear no necessary relation to each other and are written in without guarantee; for example, the Accord's proposition to restructure taxation progressively and to shift away from indirect taxation, a clause clearly inserted at the behest of the ACTU, floats freely in the text, unsecured by mechanisms that might guarantee its implementation. The document called the Accord, then, contains at least three largely independent subtexts—a bottom line, concerning wages; an intermediate level, addressing issues such as taxation and health and safety; and a maximum program, involving claims such as that regarding the abolition of poverty. All these claims are constructed within one central project: economic recovery. Rather than specifying conditions of interrelation between these programmatic levels, the Accord issues merely a pretentiously titled list of "mechanics of implementation" that reduces to the construction of an Economic Planning Advisory Council (EPAC) and a Prices Surveillance Authority and a commitment to extending the current information base.[15]

In terms of practical results, it has been the lowest common denominator—the incomes-and-prices deal—that has become the effective reality of the Accord. Yet the fact that the Accord contains other claims and projections allows some socialists to argue that this is a deal to which the labor leadership can be held, and not only in its minimum requirements. The most significant arguments here relate to the provisions in the Accord for industry development policy and long-range planning arrangements, which have been picked up both by major unions like the Metalworkers and enthused over by left labor academics. This is one crucial source of debate on the Australian Left, which I shall return to later.

The Accord, this incomes-and-prices deal between the ALP and the ACTU, was broadened into a de facto tripartite deal at the National Economic Summit held in April 1983. The summit was a brilliantly orchestrated and televised public relations coup that effectively developed the Accord into the basis of a tripartite deal by extracting capital's consent to the arrangement. The summit brought together a massive cast of representatives from the three major power blocs in Australian society—business, labor, and government—as well as a smattering of others who spoke from positions less powerful and influential. Welfare, for example, was represented at the summit, but its voice was ignored; its pleas for recognition of the pressing needs of those who were suffering most in society fell on deaf ears.[16] The central motif of the Accord—that economic recovery could best be facilitated by an incomes-and-prices deal—now emerged again as the central motif of the summit. Treasurer Keating, speaking immediately after Bruce McKenzie, the welfare representative, set the agenda for the summit by returning the focus to the *real* issues—the relationship between business and unions, prices and incomes, and the size of the deficit.[17] The summit finally culminated in the issuing of a communiqué that consolidated the Accord by securing the post facto consent of business to its basic proposals.

The simple point is that such radical potential as might arguably exist within the Accord has not been realized.[18] This is so partly because of the very nature of corporatist or tripartite arrangements. The net effect of the Accord has been that profits have been increased while the wages of better-placed workers have been more or less maintained via indexation. Some stronger unions—for example, those in oil and in construction—have managed to make deals outside of indexation, while smaller unions, such as those representing the food preservers and the furnishing trades, have been bludgeoned into accepting its limits. Lower-paid public servants have highlighted the internal contradictions within the Accord by arguing for increases outside indexation in order to maintain the parity between the public and private sectors that the Accord also claims to provide. The Hawke government has seen this general pattern of events as accurately representing the potential of the Accord; its object, as we are frequently told, is to bring Australians together, to soothe away the contradictions of class relations and difference (at the expense of those excluded from its arrangements).

The Accord has been implemented within a process that has seen the consolidation of the right-wing economic program foreshadowed but barely enacted by the Fraser government. The Hawke government has actually initiated policies of economic deregulation the likes of which Fraser had only contemplated: it has deregulated the banking system, allowing foreign banks into the domestic economy; it has also floated the dollar,[19] prompting speculation, both of the monetary kind and of the political kind, that Australia's economic path is leading toward "third worldization."[20] Meanwhile, the Hawke government has been revealed to have a foreign policy well to the right of those of previous Labor governments[21] and has drawn little substantial inspiration from the policies of its sibling in New Zealand. While it has established Medicare, the child of Medibank, it has funded it in an anything but adequate way; it has refused to actually restructure the health care system or to confront the power of the Australian Medical Association, and it is driving those who can afford not to queue into the arms of the private insurers.[22] It has argued for the reintroduction of the tertiary education fees abolished by Whitlam, and it has privileged the private school system over the public, contrary to Labor policy. It has developed an obsession with the size of the government deficit and with being seen to please business. It has argued very forcefully for retrogressive changes in the taxation system and has moderated these arguments only in the face of overwhelming opposition from the labor state governments, the unions, and other non–business interest groups (this was one occasion on which the union movement argued that preferred Labor policy would jeopardize the Accord). It has used Labor's own 1984 National Conference in order to override branch-level opposition to uranium mining and to further marginalize the left within the ALP (though some would argue that the left's marginality is self-inflicted). It has at this same conference formally shifted its own economic platform further to the right.[23] It has reneged on its somewhat less than radical proposal to increase welfare benefits to 25 percent of average weekly earnings. It has systematically avoided addressing the fact that at least three million of the fifteen million Australians live in poverty or on benefits. Both Hawke and Treasurer Keating have publicly tongue lashed welfare lobbyists who have sought to draw public attention to these issues, substantiating the worst fears that there is now to be an authorized representative of the public interest—the Hawke government—that cannot, in principle, be disagreed with. This Caesarist touch has prompted some to draw analogies between the regimes and personalities of Mussolini and Hawke.[24] Such analogies are bent: the problems are different, and contemporary arguments about corporatism throw more light on them than such fanciful parallels.[25] But these are issues that have barely been registered by those on the Australian left, many of whom have fallen into either celebratory or antagonistic positions on fairly predictable grounds.

The Left Shifts Right or Consolidates

How could the left draw inspiration from any of this? The answer can best be rendered in terms of arguments about the potential embodied in Labor governments in general and in the Accord in particular. The left within the ALP has drifted with this tide, arguing typically in terms of the "potential" of the Accord, as has that part of the CPA that split off in 1984, eventually to form the Socialist Forum. Some left Labor politicians have argued that the Accord could function even as an Alternative Economic Strategy (AES) of sorts;[26] at the same time, other Labor politicians have argued that the present government would do best to return to the socialist tradition within laborism.[27] These responses in different ways raise questions about what laborism in Australia traditionally has stood for and what it means today. The problem is essentially the same one, for the laborist tradition still dominates left labor thinking today.

Different parts of the ALP have of course struck up rather different positions over the question of socialism and labor. Until recently, the most radical faction, the socialist left, was dominated by old socialists whose views were often indistinguishable from those of older communists and whose influence rarely extended into the Parliamentary Labor Party. They had a clearer set of policy priorities over questions in the Middle East than within Australia; it is now generally conceded that their arguments helped establish the irrelevance of socialism in Australia. New blood within the socialist left has produced a fairly dramatic change over the past two years. These newer, younger socialist leftists are less given to Stalinoid dogmatism and more predisposed to technocracy. They now have cabinet representatives in state Labor governments like John Cain's in Victoria but remain more marginal within the federal government.[28] Like those who remain in the CPA, the members of the new socialist left are given to supporting the Accord and simultaneously arguing for the extension of welfare. But their views hold relatively little sway within the inner sanctums.

The centrist or Fabian current in the ALP, its guiding theoretical "conscience," has now mobilized in the newly formed center left faction,[29] which claims to function as a moderator between the left and Hawke's power base in the right (largely to the latter's advantage, apparently). Given the dominance of the laborist tradition in Australia, it would seem reasonable to expect that it has been the gradualist politics of social justice that has held the theoretical roost. The hegemony of this position can be detected in the ongoing, if somewhat less than enthusiastic, debate about Labor's socialist objective. The ALP's formal commitment to the socialist objective has never been as forthright as that in Clause Four of the British Labor Party's Constitution. Since 1921 the socialist objective has been qualified by the rider that socialization was appropriate only where necessary to prevent exploitation or the antisocial use of the instruments of production.[30] Clearly the presupposition here is that exploitation is accidental to capitalist production, the result of bad will on the part of evil men; the argument indicates the fundamentally populist nature of labor thinking in Australia.[31] This imprecision notwithstanding, attempts have been made to dilute the objective yet further; the arguments that have been put forth in this direction are reminiscent of Hugh Gaitskell's, for the primary motivation is that even "socialist" rhetoric is an electoral liability, that language can easily be "modernized," that the old connotations can still be sloughed off and social democratic intentions adhered to.[32] Some party socialists merely negate this case; other socialists, like Bob Connell within the party and Agnes Heller from outside it, have put forth stronger cases for the maintenance of a socialist identity.[33] While socialists like Heller have made much of the idea that socialist arguments *must* be democratic, indeed that socialism ought best be canvased as radicalized democracy,[34] other defenders of socialism have often tended to manipulate murkier arguments about an allegedly strong distinction between the social democratic tradition and that of democratic socialism. Some unreformed reformists within the party argue that Labor ought to see itself as social democratic, in the Bad Godesberg sense, and argue that the Whitlam experience can best be understood in this light.[35] Others, more concerned with maintaining socialist credentials, insist that *democratic socialism* is a more powerful nomenclature; this is the terminology used by the center left of the party in its odd ideological moments. The argument reduces to the proposal for parliamentary socialism, with the caveat that the process of transition "of course" involves more than that.[36]

The language of socialism, however contrived, has little to do with Labor practice, and when it is used it is often inauthentic. The socialist objective, even as it stands, is light years away from present government concerns. Socialist argument within the ALP is typically rhetorical and usually private. And when it comes to a socialist program rather than a socialist objective, the result is again either posturing and irrelevant or pragmatic and ill considered.[37] Yet people persist in expecting great and indeed socialist things of the ALP, arguing, for example, that the Accord could somehow lead forward to socialism. The fundamental issue here, oft avoided, is the difference between the Labor Party and labor governments. It may be possible to argue that the Labor Party is wedded to *some* conception of socialism, but the record of labor governments suggests a different story. And yet those who enthuse over the socialist potential of the Accord always seem ultimately to presume that labor governments will, at the very least, be well disposed to union-led initiatives in the direction of socialism. The will to socialism does not inhere in the ALP, yet those who argue for the Accord as an AES-type strategy must ultimately presume that Labor can become a vehicle for a committed left-wing parliamentary majority with such a will and an appropriately revolutionary policy package.[38]

It is this situation that has in the past led Australian socialists into "independent" left parties like the Communist Party. Yet given the ineffectiveness of marginal politics in Australia and the hegemony of laborism, the smaller left parties have always been to some degree structured by laborism. The Communist Party is probably the best example here, for despite its occasional fits of sectarianism, it has often tended to function as though it were the left wing of the Labor Party. Frontism is a strong current in its history; indeed popular frontism and social fascism are expressive of its two basic moods, reflecting its fundamental ambivalence toward laborism: we need the Labor Party, but it spurns us yet; we support it, yet it betrays us.

Winton Higgins has indicated, if unwittingly, the enthusiasm for Althusserian marxism among the young revolutionaries who came to the Communist Party in the early 1970s. The Althusserians arrived from the desert, so to speak, and they were armed with theory. In some ways their arrival was timely, for apart from an early entente with Antonio Gramsci the CPA was not oversupplied with the theory that was gripping European intellectuals.[39] This was the period before the recognition that there was a crisis in marxism, so it could easily be argued that the theory-practice relation had lain undeveloped because of an absence of good theory. It followed that an immense theoretical revolution was a necessary prerequisite to good practice. This is not the place to offer a general assessment of the effect of Althusser in Australia; suffice it to say that the results were mixed, that some young marxists around the journal *Intervention* put Althusser to good use in developing a political economy of Australian capitalism,[40] while elsewhere the effect was foreclosure, sclerosis, and involution, culminating in the identification of marxism with Althusser and prompting, in the 1980s, disappearance into Francophilic antimarxism.[41] In his *Socialist Register* essay, however, Higgins radically overstated the impact of Althusserian marxism,[42] to the extent of suggesting general CPA leadership sympathy with these arguments.[43] What Higgins's case overlooked—and the point is of course made easily in hindsight—was that outside radical intellectual circles, the new arguments, if accepted at all, were assimilated into the existing communist wisdom of frontism. The fact that Nicos Poulantzas, for example, had directed much of his energy against the frontist tradition was of no import within the rank and file of the Communist Party. It was the Eurocommunist element in Althusserianism that took seed, for it complemented an ongoing tradition; its revolutionary element found no ground, particularly after the defeat of Whitlam. The "coalition of the Left" policy developed in the late 1960s may have fed on radical sources, but it came to depend ultimately, again, on the Labor Party. The reception of André Gorz's "revolutionary reforms" and Stuart Holland's AES-type strategy likewise needs to be located in this context; these arguments, regardless of their own potential, were read through the frontist grid that was necessarily laborist. Thus, for example, major communist unionists such as Laurie Carmichael could enthuse about Holland's arguments knowing but not acknowledging that in the absence of a vital Communist Party in Australia, the role of vanguard would fall by default into the lap of the Labor Party.[44]

Within the CPA, then, the revolutionary rhetoric of the late 1960s and early 1970s has finally given way to a sensible pragmatism. The change can indeed be seen in its rhetoric. John Sendy has observed, for example, that the period of "ultraleftism" was so fulsome that the CPA's 1974 Congress political document used the words *revolution* and *revolutionary* no fewer than fifty-four times in nine pages.[45] Even during this period, however, central figures in the Melbourne leadership were making much ado about Friedrich Engels's aside concerning the obsolescence of barricades in order to promote the cause of parliamentary socialism.[46] The argument was drifting toward social democracy, if in the traditional sense; it is now very likely the case that *democracy* is the magic word, the associations again being traditional rather than innovative.[47] Eurocommunist arguments were well received in this environment, particularly in Melbourne, because they facilitated this process of pragmatizing socialism. Leading communists in Melbourne had been heading in this direction at least since the early 1970s; viewed retrospectively, what is surprising about the 1984 split is that these liquidationist tendencies took so long to surface. In April 1984, twenty-three leading members of the Victorian CPA announced their collective departure, at least partially in response to what they viewed as abstentionist tendencies over developments like the Accord.[48] Some who stayed within the CPA clearly saw the split as premature, for the "prospects for socialism" debate canvased within the party since 1982 had already produced strong arguments for liquidation of the party. The most recent communist manifesto, *Towards Socialist Renewal in Australia,* indicates a general commitment to the idea of a new socialist party.[49] What all this seems to suggest is that the dispute between the CPA and those who departed reduces to the terms and conditions of fellow-traveling with the Labor Party. Although the CPA remains committed to an alliance of independents, those who now form the Socialist Forum eschew independent party forms and policy and avoid the proscription clause of the ALP by refusing themselves party identity. The forum's *Statement of Identity* could be said to read like an argument for social democratic *agitprop,* though it also suggests an openness that has not generally characterized the communist tradition in the past. The forum's generalized endorsement of the Accord is suggestive of something else.

Unfortunately the animosities between those who left and those who have stayed in the CPA seem to be sufficient to prevent a debate of the kind that has occurred in Britain in, around, and over *Marxism Today*. The CPA's equivalent, *Australian Left Review,* has become, on occasions at least, so pluralist as to be almost meaningless, or at least self-contradictory, combining new-look graphics and sometimes punky arguments with the views of old-timers, side by side. The CPA can, for example, simultaneously publish feminist antimarxism in *Australian Left Review*[50] and punctuate the letters columns of its weekly *Tribune* with complaints from its pro-Soviet elders. Although today feminism has a strength and attraction that marxism cannot rival, its new hegemony has been achieved largely through displacement rather than an open exchange of ideas about, say, class and social movements. Debates over strategy or policy have thus barely begun within the *Australian Left Review*. While the members of the Sydney CPA have produced usefully temporal arguments about the reform of the taxation system[51] and argued that the Accord itself needs reforming,[52] the Socialist Alternative Melbourne Collective associated with the Melbourne CP has furthered debate by producing a pamphlet on Socialist Melbourne as it could be in 2000 CE.[53] It can be observed, with some irony, that these arguments about a marvelous socialist Melbourne not only seem to reflect classical utopian views but also retread the path of local communist utopianism; Ralph Gibson, for example, had already anticipated a socialist Melbourne in a 1951 CPA pamphlet. Clearly the dates needed adjusting. Those whose memories reach back this far could also observe that the Socialist Forum is a kind of second coming and wonder whether the new forum might follow the direction of its namesake, into the mainstream of the Labor Party.[54] Here, then, can be witnessed the limits of a process of returning to local traditions, or recalling the ghosts of the Australian past.

Some attempts have also been made to stimulate argument on the left by highlighting ongoing debates in England. Clearly the arguments advanced in *Marxism Today* have a strong attraction for younger sections of the Communist Party. Unfortunately, however, some of these arguments have been derivative in a crippling way. In the document *Socialism in Australia: Toward Renewal?* a dossier including Australian communist arguments and those of Stuart Hall and Beatrix Campbell, David McKnight, for example, argues in effect that Australian problems *are* English problems. While drawing attention to some very real problems facing the Australian left—such as the growth of social movements largely outside the left—McKnight argues as though the real problem centers on developing "Thatcherist" tendencies in the Liberal Party, as though the ALP leadership has been unaffected by such tendencies.[55] The argument is that Margaret Thatcher is novel, as though Hawke were not; Hawke, indeed, on this view, is John Callaghan.[56] The liberal shadow treasurer is castigated for free market rhetoric, while Labor's Keating somehow remains immune. The Accord is dealt with only in terms of its allegedly socialist potential. The specific differences between Britain and Australia are here eclipsed; the arguments raging in Britain are applied mechanically rather than creatively. The specific nature of laborism, as a major concern, once more eludes scrutiny.

Beyond the mainstream left, sects like the Spartacists of course vehemently oppose laborism.[57] The International Socialists, lacking the strength of their British counterparts, are still waiting for world revolution to beat a path to their door.[58] The Socialist Labor League, in Australia as elsewhere, relies on catastrophist economics and exclusivist dialectics for its mass appeal.[59] More significant but still peripheral parties like the Trotskyist Socialist Workers Party (SWP) and the pro-Moscow Socialist Party of Australia have struck up an unprecedented alliance against the Accord: they have swum through the proverbial river of blood separating Stalinists from Trotskyists to clasp hands, midstream, against class collaborationism.[60] This collaboration itself raises controversial issues about the precise relationship between Stalinism and Trotskyism; it is clear that on this occasion, at least, the two are united in their pro-Sovietism.[61] The SWP's pro-Sovietism has also been manifest in its role in the peace movement, where its centrism helped to precipitate a major split within the newly founded Nuclear Disarmament Party.[62] In any case, these newfound allies in the SPA and the SWP have together argued that the Accord is to be understood in traditional terms as a capitalist attack on the working-class movement, which they of course offer to lead, now in tandem, to the barricades. Yet, simultaneously, both parties must still acknowledge the centrality of the ALP, as they do.[63] It is of course quite possible to be allied to Sovietism and laborism at the same time. The question of the status of the Soviet Union remains largely undebated on the left; rather, the stock positions are merely struck up. In the mid-1970s arguments within the CPA had divided the party, with some like Eric Aarons arguing a position similar to that of Isaac Deutscher, that the Soviet Union was "socialist based," while those allied with *Intervention* had argued for the "transitional" category in the manner of Ernest Mandel.[64] Today there seems to be an unstated consensus that Eastern Europe functions as bad publicity for the left, but there is no real debate over the nature or lessons of the experience of Soviet-type societies. This remains a major limit on the peace movement in Australia.[65] It seems to be reflective of a residual Sovietism in terms of images of the future, one that is entirely compatible with the populist and Fabian traditions.

The trade union movement remains closely allied to leftist laborism and communism. With the exception of a few unions allied with the SWP-SPA or with the remnants of Maoism, most unions and indeed the ACTU are locked into the Accord, arguing simultaneously that the Accord can have a minimum function of preventing further ALP leadership perfidy and a maximum function of opening new possibilities, especially with reference to saving jobs via the development of industry policy. Traditionally militant unions like the Metal Trades Unions have taken on and developed the notion of industry development policy from the Accord in their document *Policy for Industry Development and More Jobs*.[66] In the foreword to the Metal Trades Unions plan, Laurie Carmichael argues that full employment can be restored through, first, a program of expansionary macroeconomic strategies; second, a program of redistribution of tax and wealth; and third, effective industry strategies including modernization, expansion via increased exports, and tripartite decision making. Nixon Apple's introduction to the plan then clarifies its basis in the ideology of endless growth, the logic of economic recovery being one in which, first, nominated industries would be developed for local consumption, and, second, industries would be developed, sequentially, for export; the third step in the process would involve the withdrawal of government support from successful firms and the reallocation of resources to the next set of industries selected for development.[67] The logic at work in the plan itself is Keynesian and masculinist. Full employment is not problematized as full (male breadwinner) employment; feminists could readily make the charge that the proposal is one of jobs for the boys. Problems like poverty and welfare are given summary treatment;[68] as the essential motor here is the "trickle-down" economics of reluctant collectivism, structured on the logical chain that industry policies produce growth, which in turn produces increased employment, which produces decreased inequality.

The Metal Trades Unions plan is an impressive indicator of the union shift away from the old combination of revolutionary rhetoric and wages-and-conditions militancy. It arguably provides a policy for economic recovery, which Australian capital itself has sought but been unable to achieve. Yet, in a sense like the Lucas Combine Plan, it has simultaneously inspired outsiders but has achieved no substantial results in its own terms. Perhaps there is a pattern here; Sweden also seems to attract more admiration outside its own boundaries. In Australia, business, in any case, has offered a rather less interventionist view of industry policy,[69] and it seems to be the case that this view is rather closer to that of the present government. As with the Accord, policies like those articulated by the Metal Trades Unions have been identified as a focal point for intervention. In the absence of a vigorous labor government, neither would seem likely to have any visible impact on the socialist agenda; despite these policy initiatives, laborism in Australia remains largely inert.

Arguments over the Accord and Corporatism

All these developments have served to elicit theoretical debate over corporatism and the future of socialism. Regrettably, relatively little such debate has occurred within or between groups on the left. So much of the left is complicit in the Accord that it seems unable to argue reasonably over its nature. Obviously people are likely to be defensive of a project they have sponsored, argued for, and defended against opponents on the right. And the argument can always be put forth, and sometimes is, that the Accord is better than nothing, that a system of ongoing wage indexation must be more reliable than an erratic mess of collective bargaining arrangements, and so on. Yet the left's complicity ultimately seems to be more awkward than this; as the *Australasian Spartacist* observed, the CPA is likely to be less than critical of an arrangement that it helped plan,[70] while other groups, such as the Political Economy Movement, have also acknowledged the difficulty of critically assessing proposals that they have played no small part in forming.[71] Similarly, there is no shortage of ALP members who are privately critical of the Accord and what it symbolizes but who cannot speak out for fear of being construed as antilabor. What this has meant is that such debate as has occurred has taken place between academics on the left. Two broad positions have emerged in the debate over corporatism in Australia. Some, like Stewart Clegg, Geoff Dow, Paul Boreham, and Winton Higgins, have argued that the Accord offers new directions for socialists, particularly in the direction of what they call political trade unionism; others, associated with the journal *Thesis Eleven,* have argued that recent developments not only foreclose the possibilities for socialism in Australia but must also serve to foreclose the scope of discourse about the future of socialism.

The central source of dispute here, in a sense, is the question of whether Sweden offers a possible road to socialism in Australia. Clegg, Dow, and Boreham argue that corporatist arrangements facilitate socialist development by allowing union politics to shift generally economic interests to specifically political ones, such as the claim to participate in the planning process. They argue that a robust capitalist economy with high growth rates and high standards of living is *incompatible* with capitalist social relations. Displacement of decision-making procedures to tripartite bodies is therefore potentially progressive: trade union energies can thus be progressively channeled into political unionism, facilitating the process of democratic class struggle.[72] Clegg et al. thus argue with Walter Korpi[73] and with Higgins and Apple[74] that the class representation of labor and capital is necessary both for economic recovery *and* for the transition to socialism: the premise is that recovery can be managed in such a way as to shift power decisively to the working people and their families. Social contracts, then, can in a sense be turned against themselves; a "war of position" can be waged from within the bastions of bourgeois society. The process of democratic class struggle can allow unions to use tripartite mechanisms to prevent the losses inflicted on them by previous social contracts. Clegg et al. argue that, in the Australian case, these principles or possibilities are obscured by the rhetoric of consensus; the important point, for their case, is that the EPAC can open up the hitherto privatized decision-making processes of capital, indeed that tripartite mechanisms like the EPAC can benefit *all*, including those who are excluded from the labor-capital relationship, even if they do not know it.[75]

Higgins has argued a similar position, though in a more cautious manner; his arguments in defense of political trade unionism are less explicitly related to the Australian situation. Higgins puts forth a very strong case for the view that the real potential of Accord-type arrangements is that they provide openings for outside voices in the development of industry policy. His is a pragmatism of a sensible rather than sniveling sort: the argument is that historically the left in Australia has always lost the credibility stakes because it has too often fallen victim to the temptation of empty sloganizing when it could have been developing an independent alternative policy of its own. The way forward for socialists is to produce more concrete and credible—and therefore radical—policies to deal with immediate electoral problems, to win more votes, and then to educate "public opinion" and win it around.[76] Higgins and Clegg et al. alike, acknowledge the poverty of parliamentary socialism; in common, they effectively shift primary political responsibility for social change onto the shoulders of the trade union movement, though the argument remains Swedish inasmuch as it presumes an at least well-disposed leftist government. Theoretically, John Maynard Keynes and Michal Kalecki are summoned here as approving authorities.[77] The essential proposal, then, is that political trade unionism can allow the left ultimately to pass through laborism and enter a social democratic phase, in the Swedish rather than the German sense. As Higgins puts it, the Labor Party has been trapped for too long in laborism; the extraparty left can help push it further, not into becoming a socialist party but into becoming a party with some credible socialist policies.[78]

Robert Watts and I have contested this case and its practical logic in defending the Accord. We pick up the argument of Julian Triado, that the problem with corporatist arrangements is that they represent producer groups at the expense of the citizenship principle; consequently, the Accord necessarily results in the political exclusion and disenfranchisement of those who are already economically powerless.[79] In this way, tripartite arrangements may be held to benefit those who actually enter into them, but they cannot be presumed to have universally beneficial effects. On this view, then, the rhetoric of consensus is no mere tactical accretion on corporatism but is rather a significant part of its baggage. As Triado argues, the novelty of corporatism is that it furnishes the institutional means to mediate the demands of functional interest groups in capitalist society, with the aim of developing an administrative consensus over resource allocation, investment planning, industry restructuring, and so on within an overriding conception of the "national interest."[80] Inasmuch as it involves the incorporation of dominant class interests or interest groups, corporatism has no socialist telos; it emerges as a form of crisis management, the limited strategic potential of which reflects the general balance of social forces. The general balance of forces, for these critics, is something less than favorable: business is not yet a force for socialism, and neither is the Hawke government, but trade unions cannot reasonably be expected to function as political vanguards. Historically, trade unions in Australia have been immersed in the culture of laborism;[81] experiences like the New South Wales Builders Laborers' foray into ecological politics in the 1970s are the exception to the laborist norm. As Stephen Frenkel and Alice Coolican have shown, trade union militancy in Australia has no specifically political base;[82] consequently, it is unreasonable to expect Australian unions simply to break out of this mold and emerge as fluent speakers of Swedish. It can reasonably be expected, rather, that the Australian labor movement will be somewhat selective in what it partakes of from this smorgasbord; for while unionism in Australia is political, its politics are those of laborism. This is not to say that we ought not to hope for better but rather to ask for realistic hopes. It is also to ask that arguments for alternative policy be viewed within the real constraints that surround them.

As Triado observes, it is worrying that corporatism has elicited so little debate on the Australian left, given its pertinence to recent events.[83] Some have argued as though the use of the category *corporatism* is itself a device of foreclosure, that others wish to sidestep the nature of the problem simply by naming it.[84] The major arguments outlined earlier would seem to suggest the contrary—that the problem remains to explain the nature of recent developments and their potential. What seems to be occurring, rather, is that debate has not progressed far because those politically or organizationally close to the Accord do not really want to talk about it. It is in this regard that we may speak of the negative political consequences of corporatist arrangements, for these arrangements not only disenfranchise the powerless but also effectively silence parts of the left involved in their formation and threaten to vaporize their critics. This is the sense in which critics of corporatism would advance the view that rather than repoliticizing social arrangements, corporatism *depoliticizes* Australian society in general and the Australian left in particular. No longer, for example, are cases advanced for even an AES; the Accord has filled its place. Most of the left seems, in fact, to have bought into the "politics" of consensus. But the enthusiasm for strategy cannot of itself generate socialism.

Laborism and the Impasse of the Left

Into the eighties, then, laborism has consolidated its hold on the politics of Australian socialism within this rightward ambit. Within the Labor Party arguments about socialism are rarely heard unless in the guise of arguments about the Accord. The Fabians do not seem to argue much, not even among themselves. The Communist Party, which historically has vacillated between foreign inspirations and local sources, has largely left behind its Soviet and Chinese residues, through the *via Italiana* drawing closer to the laborist tradition itself. As Alastair Davidson noted in closing his history of the Communist Party, the vicissitudes of CPA history were largely due to the fact that it thought the Russian Revolution was entirely relevant to Australian history—but it was not.[85] The traditions of the later Comintern did become assimilated to some extent with local traditions; but, looking outward, because of internal failures, the search for the holy grail continued. If it can be argued that the CPA and the Socialist Forum have now returned, more or less, to an Australian orbit, it ought also be acknowledged that this has been achieved at a high cost: the dependence on imported overseas arguments has been transcended at the cost of finally *declaring* the CPA's faustian pact with laborism in Australia. Further, this shift "into the mainstream" has been consolidated at the very moment when the mainstream itself is shifting right. Australian Trotskyism, which has always been derivative,[86] has also been drawn practically toward laborism, even if it claims publicly to be repulsed by it. Maoism is in tatters, and the smaller left groups remain essentially irrelevant and aggressive in proportion to their irrelevance. The old new left that emerged in the late 1950s has dispersed,[87] in some cases into the Labor Party; its main legacy lives on in Melbourne in the journal *Arena*, which has become a major independent institution on the left. There are no comparable filiations in Sydney, where marxism is now distinctly unfashionable and radical politics has been beaten from pillar to post; the Althusserians, who may have been off the track but who *did* contribute to the improvement and vitality of debate in the 1970s, have disappeared. The theoretical debates that raged between humanists and Althusserians over Marx and over Chile have long since dried up; the differences that brought about the 1984 split in the Communist Party remain essentially unaired. The debate over corporatism has barely taken off, presumably because too many on the left are too closely involved to engage in self-criticism. Yet the debate around corporatism ought to be central, not for its own sake but because it raises for consideration a whole series of central issues that need to be analyzed about the future of socialism, about the nature of trade unions and parties, about the adequacy of class analysis, about the necessity and nature of alliances, about masculinity and left strategy, about the future of the welfare state, and so on. But these are of course bad times; disillusion is rampant on the left, or illusion; nihilism is fashionable, as are narcissism and privatization; and the dull compulsion of everyday life of course affects leftists, too.

The broader dimensions of theoretical argument in Australian leftism reflect these facets of life in the 1980s; they might also be said to reflect the cleavage in theoretical interests that informs the left. Two major tendencies can be identified. The first, formed around labor history and revived in the 1970s by political economy, hovers around laborism as its immediate focus. Ironically, perhaps, the renewed crisis tendencies of capitalism in the 1970s represent a double blessing for many Leftists: their arguments, apparently suspended by the postwar boom, emerged again, correct, and improved through the use of Althusserian theory, thereby saving these people from the task of addressing politics in anything other than a revolutionary way. The second tendency, which is often more marginal, has fixed on ideology and culture as primary interests, again often at the expense of politics other than the personal. Certainly the left has been much drawn to the idea of a dominant ideology, and class analysis here intersects with culturalism, to the extent that radical Australian sociology has only just begun to address the questions raised earlier and elsewhere about the same.[88] It can also be observed that the left has long labored under the delusions of populist ideology, identifying conservative figures such as B. A. Santamaria or Malcolm Fraser or Rupert Murdoch as the source of the problem or blaming the local or American secret police for ongoing conspiracies rather than considering the question of why most Australians might be indifferent to arguments about socialism. Certainly there can be no space for arguments about magical political solutions to the impasse of the Australian left; but the legacies of economism and ideologism remain inhibitors as far as the process of developing a specifically political discourse is concerned. Indeed, it would seem reasonable to argue that a more specifically political discourse might have the function of mediating between existing discourses. But in Australia, as elsewhere, there seems to be a proliferation of more or less hermetic radical languages that has continued unabated since the 1970s.[89] This is not to suggest that there can or ought to be a unitary discourse or master language; indeed, the principle of difference and the separation between strategic and theoretical interests is in some ways vital.

What this means is that although both theoretical and strategic renewal has begun, Australian socialists are not yet facing a new beginning in any generalized sense. There is no clear sense of a socialist project on the left. The Accord may or may not last; it is quite possible that the Hawke government will lose office before the Accord might come to grief. The left would seem likely to remain structured by recent developments. The Accord would seem now to be a labor motif; like Whitlam's Medibank, it will be ready for a comeback as labor's generative framework for crisis management. Whether corporatist arrangements lead in the direction of social democracy or merely consolidate laborism, the future represents a sobering challenge for socialists in Australia. A generalized recognition of this situation and the responsibilities it raises would itself pose a first step in the direction of its resolution.

(1985)

Six

Australian Laborism, Social Democracy, and Social Justice

The experience of the Australian labor movement, from the outside, has always seemed different from labor movements elsewhere. Since its inception, Australian labor has been happy to promote the image of its own exceptionalism. From its earlier strengths through its tepid, near-British postwar period and the real excitement—and disappointment—provided by the Whitlam years, the Australian Labor Party (ALP) arrived in the 1980s as a force that has indeed been exceptional.[1] Where the new right has taken distinctly traditional forms across the Atlantic, the current ALP government of Robert Hawke has managed the apparently impossible, coalescing into something like a laborist Thatcherism.[2]

Thatcherism, of course, it is not. But neither is it laborism, at least not in its postwar or Whitlamist senses (i.e., along the lines of European social democracy). Its friends are in business. Its modernized labor leaders share the concerns of austerity economics, tax cuts, and balance-of-payments reports. Its Accord—the social contract binding the labor movement to the ALP government—has seen a dramatic erosion in standards of living, a declining social wage, and welfare cuts across the board. Its voice is still that of social justice, but its hand is that of austerity. Its social justice strategy has explicitly shifted from the universalism of Whitlam to the particularism of "targeting." And above all, its heightened sense is that justice is delivered by the market.

Many problems confront those concerned with social justice in Australia. Plainly, those who would use the idea of social justice as a bludgeon or a beacon against the labor government find themselves compromised, for Hawke too claims that slogan of social justice as his own. Moreover, those who would criticize present tendencies are then faced with the problem of explaining past performance. "Are they defending Whitlam against Hawke or the 1940s against both?" bluster supporters of the present regime, who presume, in postmodern manner, that history begins with them.

Those who would understand these problems need to take a further step back from the noise and flying dust of the ALP's bazaar. The larger problem that confronts Australian radicals is that their own tradition—laborism itself—has always been particularistic, and thus removed from the universalism of social democracy. The core issue is that laborism could not deliver social justice even if it were completely successful in its own terms. Today all socialist traditions find themselves in the dark. Social democracy can at least be viewed as a project that has yet to be fulfilled: its present degeneration by no means denotes the end of the story. Laborism is another issue altogether. It is here that any genealogy of social justice in Australia must start.

Laborism in Australia

Laborism, as a category, refers to the experience common to Britain, New Zealand, and Australia, whereby the labor movement sought out specifically political representation of its interests. Whereas social democracy in Europe was socialist first, laborist second, or at least held the two principles in some tension, the Australian labor movement historically has read the socialist project as being coextensive with the defense and extension of its own interests. The peculiarly Australian laborist strategy was to defend these interests through the market, and hence to develop only a residual welfare state, as Castles terms it, a *wage-earners' welfare state*. Social justice has in consequence been defined narrowly rather than broadly, and this is where the problem begins.[3]

Laborism, or "labor socialism," in Australia has traditionally allowed for argument crossing two distinct interpretations of the theory of value. The more radical stream has argued the old, premarxist view that labor deserves to receive the full rewards of its exertions. The central figure in this discourse is that of the proletarian, not the citizen, and the image of socialism behind it is a utopia peopled exclusively by proletarians, male, usually white, frequently skilled. In this purview, the masculinism and racism of the Australian labor movement becomes more intelligible, as does its preference for a slender liberalism rather than the social liberalism that was on occasions, at least in principle, available to the British movement.[4] Here the Australian labor movement's populism also takes on more discernible features, for its thinking becomes more evidently given to the dualism characteristic of myth making—good-bad, us-them, us-Shylock, us-capital, the worker versus the fat capitalist, the peace of hearth against international militarism, and so on.[5]

Alongside this more radical stream was another closer in affinity to Fabianism.[6] This more moderate view seeks the adequate recompense of labor's exertions alongside those of both capital and talent. In this broader yet still emasculated view, social desserts go to those who are deemed *productive* by this cross-class definition. Just as the more "radical" view leaves nonproletarians off the social agenda, so does the more moderate view sidestep the problems of those whom it has defined as beyond productivity and effectively without rights.

The labor movement in Australia has failed to get beyond the assertion of economic rights, however defined. One central reason for this failure can be located in its historically ambivalent relationship to liberalism. The liberal tradition is especially significant in Australia, not least of all because the labor movement has often been its unwitting bearer. Liberalism provides a kind of binding medium in modern Australian history.[7] Because liberalism rests on the axis of private property, it allows an ambivalence of outcome in political terms: economic or classical liberalism can render liberty negatively, as the freedom of property from (state) coercion, while social or new liberalism views social property rather as the precondition of positive freedom, interpreting social development positively, as the sum total of individual human developments. Liberalism is a pivotal tradition because it is capable of providing a grammar for both more innovative and more conservative policies.

The particular variant of this grammar that the labor movement in Australia was to draw on was new liberalism. Liberty in the "new liberalism" became closely identified with individual welfare, the maintenance of civic freedom with class harmony and consent, and laborism sat quite comfortably with this doctrine. The idea of new liberalism had emerged in the mid-1890s to describe the ideology associated with economic intervention, welfare measures, and a redistribution of wealth to remedy the unemployment and poverty that composed the "social question." Its initial dominant voice was that of Thomas Hill Green (1836–82). Green was prepared to argue that property ought to be subordinate to the free life and the common good. Leonard T. Hobhouse (1864–1929), like the German revisionist Eduard Bernstein, saw liberalism as providing the original values from which socialism could flow. Bernstein's views undoubtedly were related to his practical and biographical proximity to English reformism and Fabianism in particular. New liberals such as Hobhouse were critical of what they called the "official" socialism of the English labor movement. Indeed, Fabianism came to be identified as an elitist and technocratic view of socialism understood as a capitalist society, reformed gradually from above. But not in Australia.

The Motifs of Laborism

If the Australian labor tradition was never really socialist, in any universalistic way, what was it? We have already noted the elementary distinction between laborism and social democracy. Laborism identifies its political subject as the organized male working class and develops a strategy directed toward the defense and protection of the interests of that "class." Laborism is above all concerned with the advancement of concrete demands of immediate advantage to the working class and organized labor: wages and conditions of work; trade union rights; the better state provision of services and benefits in the fields of health, education, housing, transport, family allowances, unemployment benefits, pensions; and so on.[8]

Laborism in Australia, even more so than in Britain, has long had a special relationship with the state, yet one that has maintained a sense that the market has primary responsibility for the delivery of social justice. It is often observed that Australia has a statist tradition; this is hardly surprising given that Australian society was the product of the (British) state. There is now a growing recognition that the capitalist state was part of the formation process of the capitalist economy, that the state was no mere supplementary apparatus tacked onto the capitalist accumulation process in the twentieth century. What we witness in Australian history is the exact opposite of the old, now discredited commonsense view, for the colonial state formed capitalist social relations in Australia. The colonial state formed the market, and the labor market, in a process that has been referred to as "colonial socialism" (more properly, "colonial liberalism"), and the state has been ever present ever since as the protector of these markets.[9] Thus the market remains the track along which laborism slides.

From the late nineteenth century, Australia and New Zealand became widely publicized as "social laboratories" of progressive legislation and experiment, the keystone of which came to be the development of conciliation and arbitration and the notion of the basic wage. Rather than merely supplying the conventional infrastructure and assistance, the Australian state had a primary role in social development, and the labor movement has long danced a special tango with this state. The relationship between the Australian labor movement and the state was consolidated between 1890 and 1920.[10] In the period before that, labor and its liberal political representatives had sought the protection of workers from "sweating." The major strikes of the 1890s, the maritime and shearers' strikes, saw the defeated unions form the Labor Party but without any particular independent ideology of its own. Laborism, rather, drew on the elements of social or new liberalism developed by the likes of Henry Bourne Higgins and Alfred Deakin and argued for earlier by David Syme and George Higinbotham.[11] The slogan of the turn-of-the-century Federation era was "New Protection"—a shift beyond the simple manipulation of trade barriers to the development of a shared "lib-lab" social policy that was to ensure that workers also benefited from tariff protection of domestic capital. Laborism as an ideology, then, was formed by colonial liberalism, by the progressive ideology forged by the alliance of local manufacturers and workers. Indeed a "social compact" was formed here, one that endured until its rupture in the Great Depression.[12]

The more radical ideological currents characteristic of earlier Australian laborism were likewise derivative of other experiences. William Lane had developed a laborist argument for socialism, drawing on Edward Bellamy's industrialist fantasy of a highly technologized economy. W. G. Spence drew inspiration from Henry George to produce a protocorporatist populism. The shared motif across such arguments was a common workerism. This was not, then, a "socialism without doctrines," as the visiting French socialist Métin supposed, but a "socialism with economistic doctrines."[13] "A dollar a day" was the real symbol of the working man's paradise. The more pragmatic ethos of this paradise was meanwhile articulated by the liberals, who were effectively purveyors of social policy to the labor movement. Their New Protection envisaged the use of economic protection mechanisms as the basis for the social protection of the working class. A political trade-off, New Protection had the characteristics of a social contract. As Deakin explained it,

The "Old" Protection contented itself with making good wages possible. The "New" Protection seeks to make them actual. It aims at according to the manufacturer that degree of exemption from unfair outside competition which will enable him to pay fair and reasonable wages without impairing the maintenance and extension of his industry, or its capacity to supply the local market. . . . Having put the manufacturer in a position to pay good wages it goes on to assure the public that he does pay them.[14]

State as guarantor, market as distributor—fairness and reasonability within capitalist relations—such were the key categories of the new liberalism.

This was the immediate social context for Justice Henry Bourne Higgins's momentous 1907 Harvester judgment. The 1906 Excise Tariff Act had stipulated that the Australian employer would benefit from economic protection only if his workers were paid "fair and reasonable wages." Higgins's 1907 judgment established the principle of a basic or living wage for the unskilled laborer, his wife, and his children on this basis. The outcome was of considerable ideological importance, even if it was less immediately effective in wage terms than is often thought, for it solidified the pact between labor and the state, consolidating a corporatist bias or tendency that was later to be seen in the Accord.

The Higgins judgment was radical in that it elevated the criterion of proletarian need over that of the capacity of industry to pay as a wage-fixing principle. At the same time it was retrogressive in that it was fixed on male wage rates; Higgins himself was later to formally decide in favor of lower rates for females, necessarily given his family focus, in the 1912 Mildura Fruit Pickers Case. As Macintyre observes, Higgins's 1907 judgment was suggestive of backward-looking medieval values of community responsibility—values that the capitalist market had already mauled. Moreover, the judgment institutionalized the value of *equity* rather than *equality* in its guiding notion of "fairness."[15]

Higgins's values, widely shared among those in the labor movement, were set on the notion of equity between the unequal and relied on reason as the flux of social harmony. Higgins indeed sought a "new province for law and order" in which "reason is to displace force: the might of the state is to enforce peace between industrial combatants, and all in the interests of the public."[16] Higgins's utopia also drew on the specifically Catholic themes of protocorporatists such as Pope Leo XIII, who had argued in his encyclical *Rerum Novarum* that "reasonable and frugal comfort" was the right of every working man.[17] Seeking harmony within the existing social arrangements, then, the Harvester judgment embodied the interventionist but masculinist principles of new liberalism, while Protection itself (along with White Australia) maintained the racist current of laborism. The market was to be regulated; substantial alternatives in state or society, however, were foreclosed. The early new liberal enthusiasm for the development of human potential had gone.

If the Great Depression saw the revival of the case for "capacity to pay" in parliamentary labor and conservative circles alike, the consolidation of the welfare state in the 1940s saw a renewed enthusiasm for arguments about regulation and equity. Even in the 1930s, it could be argued, the commitment to state activity was suspended on tactical rather than substantive grounds. As leading liberals such as W. K. Hancock and Frederic Eggleston had acknowledged, the state had a central role in economic and social policy, and it could not simply close up shop. As Hancock put it in 1929, "Australian democracy has come to look upon the State as a vast public utility whose duty is to provide the greatest happiness of the greatest number."[18] The same utilitarian sentiment had earlier been well expressed, in laborist timbre, by C. J. Don, the first working man to sit in the Victorian state parliament: "How is the problem of the greatest possible amount of happiness for the greatest number to be affected? I will tell you; by regulating the number of hours that a man shall work in a day, sufficient to feed, clothe, and educate the population."[19] Here spoke John Stuart Mill, with a statist twist: regulation could facilitate fair arrangement of the benefits that the market produced. It was only a slightly more intense desire for harmony that had led William Roylance to argue at the First International Trades Union Congress that via cooperation there could be achieved "an indissoluble solidarity of interest [that] would unite employer and employed; one would belong to the other, as limbs to the head, each being . . . essential to the other."[20] All this together produced less "state socialism" than a paternalist statism, with the working class sitting on the state's avuncular knee.[21] As Spence had it, the state here was merely protecting the people (understood as workers and others of more independent means) against the parasites.[22]

What emerged from the 1940s did not violate this tendency, though it did confirm the niggardly welfarism and begrudging Keynesianism of parliamentary labor. That John Maynard Keynes had corporatist inclinations is well recognized. The mission of the ALP governments of John

Curtin and Ben Chifley in the 1940s was compatible with Keynes's mission in that it sought to revive the sense of social contract between labor and the state. What the labor movement claimed for itself was more ambitious. It celebrated loudly the arrival of labor's alleged "Golden Age."[23] Having marched through the valley of death in European and Pacific war theaters, the labor movement was now urged to set its sights on a new beacon, to march further toward the "light on the hill"[24] — a cloudy evangelical mirage projected by the labor government, evocative of equality but barely even capable of delivering equity. For what was delivered was a thinly strung welfare safety net rather than a set of arrangements recognizing citizens as the active subjects rather than the passive objects of welfare.

Despite the euphoria for this "Golden Age" now revived by some on the left, it is clear that Australia experienced a somewhat milder version of the reformist fervor than that which had struck Britain during and after the war. Postwar reconstruction in Australia saw the pursuit of equity and rationalization — the values of new liberalism given a parliamentary face. The centerpiece of the local welfare legislation was an insurance package introducing, among other things, a cash unemployment benefit. Child endowment had earlier been introduced by the conservative government of Robert Menzies, indicating something of the breadth and durability of liberalism's appeal and something of the ambivalence of the Australian reform process. There had been much controversy over whether such an endowment might be used to undercut male wages or whether it might rather potentially extend the citizenship principle by defining women and their children as independent beneficiaries and therefore as subjects in their own rights. The general results of the reform process were begrudging. Although William Beveridge's plan for Britain institutionalized the idea of contributory but universal welfare, Chifley had argued against the insurance principle yet followed this progressive welfare principle in a retrogressive manner, which meant that the working class paid, quite literally, for the reform package through increased taxation.[25]

Yet the reconstruction period was conspicuously one of reforms and of arguments for reform. Nowhere can this be better seen than in the arguments of Chifley about the limits of the capitalist market. In 1944 Chifley told Parliament that if "regimentation" were necessary for the achievement of basic socialist goals, he would indeed prefer it to the "economic individualism that we had under the old order."[26] And while the Labor government's defeated attempt at bank nationalization in 1947 was still representative of the old labor populist demonology about "money power," it nevertheless symbolized something of the interventionist reforming resolve that activated Labor.

Ironically enough, these aggressive intonations in Labor's postwar economic and social policy were eventually to be supplanted by the greatest expansion in capital accumulation and mass consumption imaginable. It was this explosive development in the economy rather than these changes in state policy that was responsible for the boom. The slogan "Full Employment" became the equivalent of the earlier "New Protection"; the fundamental premise was still that the market could see Jack and his master look after themselves, while welfare, rather than the devil, might take the hindmost. These arrangements continued largely unaltered through the long years of the conservative "Menzies Millennium"; indeed, these sympathies were also claimed by Menzies, at least in rhetoric. Throughout the 1950s and 1960s parliamentary labor remained entrapped within the racist and conservative currents of the laborist tradition epitomized in its leader, Arthur Calwell. It is these elements of continuity that help make sense of the combination of the elements within the party that were to come into violent antagonism only with the ALP split. Although the split was electorally disastrous for the ALP, it set the scene for the later modernization of the party by Whitlam.[27]

Whitlam: Reform and Tradition

The Whitlam experience represents the high point of what Stuart Macintyre has termed "the short history of social democracy in Australia."[28] Macintyre's catchphrase is appropriately hyperbolic: it suggests something of the contrast between the 1970s and the earlier provenance of labor, alluding to the impact of a reformism that in a sense had more aura than it had substance. Social democratic the Whitlam government was not, if by that term we mean to invoke the fuller-blooded Swedish program or the reformist vision of German social democracy before the Great War. Whitlam stood rather for the civility and progress that had earlier been claimed by the likes of George Higinbotham, Alfred Deakin, Henry Bourne Higgins, and Herbert Vere Evatt. His arguments were more often aligned with those of John Stuart Mill than with the stronger demands of the new liberals like Hobhouse. Whitlam argued for, and his government to some extent realized, the extension (or application) of the elements of social liberalism to which the labor movement has so long been formally attached. Whitlam stood for the view that citizens had to be taken seriously as citizens, a view resting still on the principle of equity rather than equality but with this increased franchise. Whitlam called this position the "doctrine of positive equality." As he wrote: "This concept does not have as its primary goal equality of personal income. Its goal is greater equality of the services which the community provides. This approach . . . positively requires private affluence to prevent public squalor." According to Whitlam, the "citizen's real standard of living, the health of himself and his family . . . [and so on] are determined not so much by his income but by the availability and accessibility of the services which the community alone can provide and ensure."[29] In his argument the citizens remained linguistically masculine, but the argument was better: it was that of enlightened liberalism. Equality was not in any meaningful definition the object of such a doctrine as much as was equity or meritocracy, for the strategy produced aimed at that elusive Fabian goal, equality of opportunity in a society of unequals. This is not to say that the Whitlam regime produced no real reforms in theory or practice: Medibank finally arrived, having long waited notionally in the antechamber of reform; tertiary education fees were abolished, resulting in substantial increases in the number of women attending tertiary institutions; the Australian Assistance Plan offered new power to the local community; and so on.

Whitlam's views were consonant with those of the tradition of British reform that ran from John Stuart Mill via Thomas Hill Green—at least as far as concerns about citizenship are concerned—to Anthony Crosland. This would seem to be an affinity far clearer than that with postwar German social democracy or the "Swedish miracle," though ideological parallels occur here as well. For the notion of "positive equality" remains essentially meritocratic liberalism recast in rosy hue. The focus on health and education as preconditions of individual achievement and social performance is enough to suggest that. Education and health policy under Whitlam reflected the presence of what C. B. Macpherson (1977) has called "developmental" liberalism. For Whitlam this meant—in a view naive yet reflecting a touching pathos—that every child should have a desk, a lamp, and privacy in which to study. As he put it, in his characteristically grandiloquent public inflection, "What we aim at is the achievement of the classical liberal idea of the career open to the talents—equality of opportunity—in a vastly expanded form." Whitlam argued that, beyond the classical conception for which education alone was central, his program rested on the idea of the development of community services as such.[30]

Closer, on occasion, to the new liberals, Whitlam argued that security was not a goal in itself—security was merely a precondition of participation. Chifley's "light on the hill" was the way out of despair for those who had suffered the "shafts of fate, which leave them helpless and without hope." Whitlam imagined that his task was of a higher order; this is manifest nowhere more clearly than in his 1972 election speech, in which he exhorted citizens to support a labor program based on the promotion of equality, popular involvement in decision making, and the liberation of popular talents, uplifting the horizons of the Australian people.[31]

The rhetoric of 1972 is certainly important in making sense of Macintyre's hyperbole. Yet there was more to the Whitlam experience, and it was reminiscent of less inspiring lineages in the reforming traditions. Clearly, Whitlam's vision was that of a "social democracy" of prosperity that, like Crosland's, was likely to be speechless before the opening economic crisis. For it was Whitlam who had argued, but ten years earlier, that "socialists should not be content with nationalising where necessary; they should be intent on competing where possible and initiating where desirable. . . . The sins of capitalism in Australia are ones of omission rather than commission and of not being sufficiently enterprising and independent."[32] The parallels in postwar reformism are abundant. Like Beveridge, Whitlam was happy to spur growth by entrepreneurial means rather than state activity, except in areas such as health. Like the fact-gathering Fabians, he saw urban services, "gas and water socialism," as a still necessary priority. Like Crosland, he argued as though the economic necessity of socialism had simply been made redundant by capitalist boom. Like Hugh Gaitskell and others in the British Labor Party, along with those in the dominant stream of the German social democrats, particularly after 1959, he viewed socialism as an electoral liability. He did on occasion summon social democracy, in statesmanlike rhetoric, as calling for "redistribution in wealth and incomes and social benefits"; but the essential message was about *opportunities* within the existing social relations.[33]

The Whitlam government was thankfully distant from the dull sort of logic now associated retrospectively with postwar labor governments in Britain and Australia. In its hands, modernization and constitutionalism became the two major themes. The central shift in the 1970s from the would-be nationalizers of the 1940s was one in which traditional suspicions of the market were cast off in favor of the rhetoric of competition. In the 25 percent tariff cuts of July 1973, as in much else, Whitlam sought planning as the active facilitation of competitive market forces. In Whitlam's insurance legislation, the activating principle was no longer state monopoly but rather competitive public enterprise. Here the point of continuity from the 1940s to the 1970s is the opposition to the reign of monopoly capital, but the response was modified, from statist to competitive. In this, however, Whitlam was challenging business to perform, and it is this that has maintained the distance between the 1970s and the deregulationism of the 1980s.[34]

Looking back on this period, Whitlam himself identified the absence of an actual social contract between the ALP and the Australian Council of Trade Unions (ACTU) as a major drawback. A coherent and systematic project of social justice, beyond positive inequality, was also lacking. His government had delivered dramatic increases in the social wage but lacked any contractual mechanism to prevent wage breakouts.[35] The result was an increase in labor's proportion of national wealth, which federal governments of both persuasions have been concerned to reverse ever since. The first round of wage cuts was instigated not by the government of Malcolm Fraser, the conservative regime that displaced that of Whitlam, but rather by Treasurer Bill Hayden in the Whitlam government's last budgetary stand. Despite its vocal penchant for monetarist rhetoric, the Fraser government did rather less by way of dismantling the welfare state than has often been thought.[36] If any recent government has turned the welfarist tide, this dubious distinction must go to the Hawke socialist government, particularly after the creation of its 1986 budget. The ACTU-ALP Accord was at least to resuscitate equity for the working class; its more ambitious advocates also hoped that it would do rather more. Its actual performance was another matter, for the Accord has not only eroded the living standards of ordinary workers but also frozen out laborism's dispossessed.

How is this decline to be explained? It is evident enough that the context was set for the rightward slide by Whitlam's economic policies but not by his social policies. Some defenders of the Hawke government have been keen to argue that the earlier precedents were sounder. Certainly Treasurer Paul Keating has claimed some continuity with the labor governments of the 1940s.[37] Curtin is hailed as providing support for this case, though the austerity regime of James Scullin would probably serve as stronger support; apparently, restraint with equity means never having to say one is sorry. This atmosphere of social siege, the evocation of Curtin's wartime crisis, may merely be suggestive of the fact that war has been declared this time not on an external enemy but on an internal one—the poor. For although the "Swedish miracle" still inspires economic and social admiration in different quarters of the labor movement, the Hawke government seems to be committed to the pursuit of economic "competition" with the compensatory welfare mechanisms so central to the Swedish experiment.[38]

This is not to say that Australian Labor governments (federal and state) in the 1980s are nothing but callous capitalist machines. Some among them remain committed to the idea of social justice;[39] this and Mr. Hawke's belated rediscovery of poverty in the 1987 election campaign can hopefully be put to good use by those who would argue, once again, about poverty and unemployment within the vocabulary of the "new" liberalism. Even parts of the Fabian tradition may be usefully revived in this process, though Hawke has also attempted to circumvent such potential by claiming the consensual and corporative themes of that lineage.[40] Into the 1980s, the lofty images of citizenship associated with the new liberalism seem fully to have succumbed to the pecuniary aspirations of those who are financially well off. What remains is a labor government claiming affinity with the begrudging welfarism of the 1940s and an ACTU that is still animated by the progressive parts of the laborist ethos which that government has vacated.

Conclusions

Viewed synthetically, the contours of Australian laborism emerge with some clarity. The new liberalism was the informing impulse of the ideology of laborism, blended with its local features, the populist conception of society and mechanical or instrumental conceptions of politics as a means to further self-interest. This vision of politics effectively forecloses the possibility of the social democratic strategy and all kindred arguments that democracy and citizenship need to be core values of socialism rather than strategic devices for it. Liberalism has moved on its pivot since the 1880s, to the left with Whitlam and ultimately to the right in the 1980s with Keating's and Hawke's economic liberalism (now mystically called economic "rationalism"). Laborism as a tradition has always manifested some tendency or bias to corporatism—from the "New Protection" to the Harvester judgment, from the "light on the hill" to Whitlam's "doctrine of positive equality," culminating, for the present, in the Accord. The historic pact between manufacturers and unions has weakened with the present recession, just as it was suspended in the 1930s, and today labor governments are again seen as crisis managers, as the best administrators of popular austerity.

In all of this it remains true that Australian politics is an economistic politics; its political history is the history of producer groups, primarily those of business, labor, and agriculture, seeking collaboration with the state in order to protect and extend their own interests. Labor has certainly been party to this process, both in parliamentary and in industrial terms. What this means is that social justice strategy has shifted across the field dominated by liberalism and laborism, has been viewed variously as a kind of electoral pork barrelling or as a larger priority, but has never been pursued with any seriousness of intent or thoroughness of purpose outside market premises.

If we view social justice as a matter of citizenship rights, including the right to well-being as a necessary prerequisite to social and political participation, the Australian experience is less than inspiring, and also something less than exceptional. What is striking about the Australian case, rather, is the history of lost opportunities for social reform. Labor is certainly the victim of its own thought traditions in this regard. Clearly even its most adventurous thinkers remain within these traditions. The most ambitious recent attempt at left intervention, the industry development policy argued for in the ACTU's *Australia Reconstructed,* effectively manages to avoid issues of welfare and social justice, arguing that justice can still be accomplished via universalizing participation in the labor market; social justice becomes essentially a matter of refloating the local manufacturing sector.[41] Certainly such a strategy can be defended, for it at least indirectly makes the point that social justice ought be defined in terms of the national political agenda and not dictated by the wiles of the world system.[42] Yet the industrial intervention strategy simultaneously revives one of Keynesianism's most pernicious myths by posing the terms of full employment and social justice as synonyms and by subsuming social policy to economic policy once again.

And yet, amid these apparent ruins there remain spaces for argument, and somehow living with Hawke's Labor government does not seem to have produced the sense of profound demoralization characteristic among radicals elsewhere. So long as space for argument exists, there remain hope for discussion of these issues and possibilities that there might emerge a more muscular discourse concerning rights and social justice. Looking backward, now, can better enable us to view the way forward. Better understanding of the discourse of laborism is one prerequisite step forward.[43] Reconsideration of the values of socialism — including the idea of social justice — might hopefully be another.

(1989)

Seven

The End of Australian Communism

In 1952 a young man named Frank Hardy published his second major book. Still surrounded by the controversy over *Power without Glory*, he titled his new venture *Journey into the Future*. It was, of course, a defense of the workers' paradise. Hardy claimed that most of the stories told about the Soviet experience were bourgeois lies, and probably they were; his own response, to replace them with "proletarian" lies, offered no great improvement.

Hardy's motif was that of so much writing in this now dead genre — Lincoln Steffens's "I have seen the future and it works!" But his book was also the stuff of high Stalinism. Hardy defended the proletariat on the grounds that it alone was the "useful class, the decent and progressive class."[1] This bizarre amalgam of Jeremy Bentham, George Orwell, and Henri de Saint-Simon set the stage for the usual litany of Soviet miracles. For Hardy proposed that not only proletarian labor, but even the labor of childbirth, was conducted in the workers' paradise, *without pain*.[2] He painted the usual picture, where bubbling Soviet youth, simultaneously engaged in gymnastics and dialectics, provided a wholesome contrast to the dissipated youth of the West, transfixed by the decadent culture of Hollywood. He discovered, to his evident delight, that even horseracing was organized on socialist lines (though one cannot feel from the narrative whether all the punters win or they all lose).[3]

Like other pilgrims, Hardy waxed lyrical about the Moscow metro and the cars that sped along its roads; he embraced the imagery of modernism to which the Soviets aspired but that even Leon Trotsky viewed as chimeral; as Trotsky commented in *The Revolution Betrayed,* one could not send trousers to the cleaners without having them return sans buttons, and automobiles could barely manage ten kilometers per hour on the highways to Soviet socialism.[4]

Here it was Hardy who took his readers to the cleaners, for his argument culminated in the period hymns to Marshal Stalin: "one cannot find a major error that he has made in thirty years";[5] crime and mental illness are rapidly fading away;[6] the Soviet Union is the most democratic state in the world; and so on.[7] Little wonder that there were also Australian Trotskyists. But the Trotskyists were out of step. The cult of the Soviet Union affected Australian life in an emphatic way. Trotskyists, too, embraced Stalinism.[8] Stalin made the cover of the *Women's Weekly.* Peaking at 23,000 members, the Communist Party of Australia (CPA) even had a bookshop in the middle-class suburb of Camberwell. And writers like Hardy were not alone; indeed an entire genre of pilgrimage grew up in Australia, and even more strikingly in Britain. In Australia, to mention the other (in)famous literary case, Jack Lindsay penned an apologetic titled *The Way Ahead.* Moreover, in our own time, although this distinct genre has evaporated, there is now a new wave of communist biography and autobiography, for the subjects of these are still viewed as interesting people, and rightly so.[9]

Not all the pilgrims were as effusive as Hardy or Lindsay. In 1958 Australia's premier historian went in search of flaws in the Russian clay, and of course found them. Manning Clark reported in his study *Meeting Soviet Man* that he had seen not the future but the past, and it was melancholy. By 1958, Clark recognized, communism was already in crisis; few but the dwindling ranks of the CP and a handful of fellow-travelers took "Soviet man" seriously.[10] Clark traveled to the Soviet Union as an archaeologist; he claimed to have found there a relic, for Soviet man was triumphalist, given to the values of the Enlightenment, believing in the triumph of the human spirit, while intellectuals in the West had already packed up and gone home in despair. Clark evidently felt unhappy about both modernism and postmodernism. For him, the irony was that the country of Dostoevsky had lapsed back to an age of faith. The Soviets were religious in the bad, narrow sense rather than the open, existential sense.[11] Unlike Hardy, Clark was troubled by Soviet puritanism and by the caricature of Western decadence. But his real attraction was less to "Soviet man" than to the "tragic grandeur" of Russia.[12]

Into the 1970s, the membership of the CPA was heading toward two thousand. The institution, as Clark observed, was already in decline before that. The CPA split in 1964 and 1971 and again in 1984, when the majority of its Victorian leadership liquidated into the Australian Labor Party (ALP).[13] Its collapse, significantly, preceded the collapse of communism in Eastern Europe. The CPA was always a vanguard among Western communist parties, at least since the Prague Spring; it led, even, in closing up shop. This was a courageous act: it takes great courage to acknowledge that a party is finished, and this signals a loss, as well as an advance of sorts. It signals the loss of a tradition in Australian culture. The CPA was a tradition, a literature, a public sphere. There is now one fewer stream in civil society, and this is a loss. For communism, at the least, has been a kind of halfway house for Australian radicals. As Rupert Lockwood used to joke, the biggest party in Australia is the party of former communists. Alongside the Stalinoid tracts of Hardy and Lindsay sit all their other brilliant works and those of Ian Turner, Russel Ward, Brian Fitzpatrick, Bernard Smith, Noel Counihan, Jean Devanny, Dorothy Hewett, Judah Waten, Katherine Susannah Prichard—and, more recently, Stuart Macintyre, Tim Rowse, and Alastair Davidson—and the efforts of the thousands of ordinary communists and fellow-travelers who argued for socialism in office, kitchen, and factory and were active throughout the unions and social movements.

This is one aspect of the loss. Viewed in larger, historical terms, the loss was entirely predictable. Communism in Australia was primarily a generational phenomenon. There are two dramatic symbols that capture the vitality of the Soviet experience for an earlier generation—the Wall Street crash and the siege of Stalingrad. The historic strength of communism in Australia was the power of Depression communism. The 1930s was an era when everyone became a planner, just as today they become marketeers (mouseketeers). The Soviet Union *became* the workers' paradise in the specific context of the Depression. This crucial experience also helps explain the rise of Keynesianism and the particular path of Australian communists such as Lloyd Ross into the planners' office of the ALP with H. C. Coombs. For Stalinism was planism applied.[14]

Viewed historically, then, and sociologically, we would have been fools to believe that communism was an eternal force; it became dominant through the revolution against *Capital* and the tentacles of the

Comintern, and it has now terminated. Communism became dominant, supplanting social democracy in parts of Western Europe and splitting the entire labor movement into the communist and social democratic fractions, which helped lead to social fascism and then to fascism. The image of communism was tarnished by Stalinism and by its self-extension throughout East and Central Europe on the point of the bayonet. The Soviet bloc had begun to implode already with the Sino-Soviet dispute and the suppression of the Hungarian Revolution of 1956. Old communists began to vote with their feet. Then the emergence of the new left and the generation of 1968 played its part to extend the malaise; the old Depression communists found themselves in a party now colonized by hippies and sexual radicals, refugees not from want but from the excesses of the "me generation." All these forces had combined to bring about the death knell of communism's historic organizational form. Communist parties in countries such as Australia had all but wound down well before the great revolutions of 1989.

It is worth sounding a note of caution here. Amid the collapse of the institutional forms of communism there it has frequently been implied that the *problems* involved have also completely expired. In the Australian case we have yet to identify the attributes of local Stalinism in order to establish what there was in it that was new. Anti-intellectualism and the deadly combination of administrative heaviness and redemptive euphoria are arguably features of Australian labor that preceded and have outlived communism itself. In this sense, it is true not only that the positive impulse of communism, the pursuit of the image of the other, is alive, but also that its baser features have outlived the organizational form as well.

But the dissolution of communism represents a loss, too, when we consider the physiognomy of Australian political culture today. This is no sea-change. It is a glacial slide. Into the 1980s, what we faced in Australia was the transformation of political life. This had a great deal to do with the effective retirement of two sets of actors whose influence had hitherto been pivotal: communists and Catholics.

This shift occurred largely because of the modernization of the labor movement. Communism has always, in a sense, been the left wing of the ALP, so again this decline should be no surprise. But the administrative transformation of the ALP and the Australian Council of Trade Unions (ACTU) has effectively meant the elimination of its principled, or puritanical, edges. The demise of communism, in this regard, again constitutes a loss, for communists disappeared either into the labor bureaucracy or into their own private spheres of disillusion and high consumption. Where have the communists gone? The answer, as far as I can tell, is this: they have lapsed into technocratic laborism or have disappeared somewhere in the lounge rooms of their own narcissism. The "ordinary" communists have nowhere left to go—the new left party is *too* new for them—and newer generations are likely to end up in "fun" parlors or hanging around on street corners rather than selling the *Tribune*.

If the question to be asked of any component of the national culture is "What kind of personality type does it encourage?" communism (and likely anticommunism) brought out three character types—the administrator, the zealot, and the good citizen. *Zealots* we are happily without. *Administrators* we of course need, provided that they are prepared to recognize that administration is not politics (but this may be a battle we have already lost). *Good citizens* we cannot do without, and ordinary communists were, in my experience, more often than not good citizens; they had a morality if not always an ethics; and they had lived up to Max Weber's challenge: they had chosen a warring god. Their norms and values were worlds away from the flatulent self-indulgence of the 1990s. They understood at least *something* about principle and about difference, which makes little sense in a new world where politics consists of the seamless unity of the two central parties posited over the left and right of the very center. They may not have been as good citizens as the citizens we would like—this much is probably true. The distinction between the zealot and the good citizen from case to case breaks down. The levels of tolerance that one could ascribe to the good citizen were not always evident. Communists were probably more pluralistic in practice than they were in principle. Their cultural universe was monotheistic, not given to pluralism. Yet they learned that they were individuals in a world where there were higher things. They chose their god, but they also joined their church. Like their Catholic counterparts, they managed to contribute to civil life even from within the constraints of their respective fundamentalist socializations.

What is striking in retrospect is that, outside of the staging, communism and Catholicism were probably not extremities in Australian politics at all. Both traditions were actually mainstream in many regards: both argued for social justice, equity, family, and authority and disagreed violently over the particular question of communism and the Soviet Union. Take away the fatal fascination with the Soviet Union, add to the picture the modernization of Labor and the flattening of civic life, and you have the demise of Australian communism and political Catholicism alike.

However, we have no perverse nostalgia for the loss of the 1950s.[15] The Cold War ruined the lives of too many people, in Australia as elsewhere. There is no way back, nor should there be. The problem we confront is a new commonsense view. The new commonsense view is that the great ideological divide, this archetypical nasty dualism—*left versus right*—has been replaced by a new sense of contingent possibility. Would that it were so. But it is not—for there are *new certainties*. Margaret Thatcher tells us that there are *no alternatives*. Or was it singular? *No alternative*. Instead of Hardy hectoring us about the Soviet paradise, we now have Jean Baudrillard to tell us the good news that he has found the real utopia—in Disneyland.[16]

Baudrillard, this fellow-traveler of the new brave new world, raises some central hackles and issues for radicals. For there are at least two things that my generation of Australian radicals were never able to face up to. One was the issue of labor anticommunism, which was always simply explained away as some kind of bad false consciousness. The other was the issue of America itself, for my generation had still not been able to reconcile itself to the diversity of the American experience or to the vitality of the American Revolution. Anti-Americanism has always involved a strong element of self-hatred, which is one basic undercurrent in fellow-traveling. Ironic as it may seem, radicals actually need to feel *at home* in their own culture, to some extent, in order to fruitfully participate in it.

There may thus be utopias in America, but they are not those claimed by Baudrillard. More likely they are in its foundational myths, for revolutions confer myths of foundation, and this is one source of identity that the Australian left has always lacked, and consequently imported. Here it is important to remember that in an earlier epoch, French, German, American, and British radicals made the pilgrimage to Australia in order to see how the "social laboratory" of the fin de siècle worked.[17] As subsequent welfare historians have shown, this image of Australia as a world leader was also utopian, but at least it was a local utopia, and at the least it emerged from some kind of civic culture.[18]

A century later, we still have a great deal to learn about our own traditions, for the memories have gone, and it is memory that sustains the political identities on which we draw. The end of communism in

Australia represents the end of an epoch, the closing of a period of self-incurred tutelage. Now we are obliged to think for ourselves, and to make choices. The prospect is awesome, and the temptation is to go postmodern, where everything goes because nothing any longer matters, or else to fall silent, because the economization of public life proceeds apace and we have no vocabulary adequate to proclaim the profound loss of human potential that ensues from this process.

Communists chose, from the 1920s on, to replace other images of utopia with those of the Soviet workers' paradise. They already knew that their own situation was less than idyllic. What they often posited, before October, as the image of the good society was imported more predictably from the English tradition: the utopia of independent bushmen or yeomen. As I understand it, this image was replaced, probably in the 1930s, by the utopia of social security or minimal provision; its residual impulse is still to be felt in the enthusiasm for suburbanism. In the 1980s labor had two competing utopias, that of Saint-Simonian modernization—the hope of the ACTU—and that of abundance via the market—the hope of federal Labor. The ACTU's utopia is in some ways a refiguration of the security utopia of the 1930s. The government's image of the good society is closer to Baudrillard's.

Having taken their stance against the Soviet utopia, Australian radicals should now turn their attention to the socially influential utopias that are actually on the agenda. The challenge to Australian radicals in this is enormous, because with the previously mentioned losses there are also gains, but these are incredibly difficult to register in a public sphere that seems to be shrinking. We live in a culture that generates more enthusiasm for and against the Ninja Turtles than it does over the gains and losses of the way we live.

Max Weber was right, finally, that the Russian Revolution was the worst thing that ever could have happened to the course of socialism. Now that we are free of this dead weight, we should celebrate; the incubus of the Soviet imaginary is lifted. Australian radicals now have a better chance of resisting the two vocational temptations of Jacobinism and fellow-traveling, those vices that have bedeviled most of the history of Australian socialism. Now we shift, sober, more worldly, into this setting where it is necessary to respond to our own situation, to transcend the self-hatred of earlier leftism—to embrace our journey not into the future but into the present. Internationalism gives way to cosmopolitanism as we realize finally that communism, this exemplary instance of the pursuit of the other, made the vital mistake of earlier utopias: it imagined that utopia is a *place,* whereas it is rather a *norm.* After Hardy and his generation, after the collapse of Stalinism and then Bolshevism, with the final reabsorption of marxism into a broader critical culture, we need to recognize that our journey is no longer to a place or to a future; rather, our responsibilities are located in a culture and in a present. We have finished with the romance of revolution. We must now begin to live in history. Destiny will not knock at the door; it is open.

(1990)

Eight

Between Totalitarianism and Postmodernity

I

What is between totalitarianism and postmodernity, and what comes after? The two terms refer to significant markers or symbols of our times, even if they are of different types. From most perspectives, the collapse of communism between 1989 and 1991 had a radical effect on Western culture. For better or worse, marxism and communism have been combined, or at least associated, both in the popular imagination and in scholarship. Yet, as Derrida has written, Marx also acts as a specter, the alter ego of a capitalist or industrial civilization ever ill at ease with itself.[1] Postmodernity, or postmodernism, however, is a cultural (or, for some, a societal) form rather than a political order in the way that communism was. The idea of juxtaposing totalitarianism and postmodernity, therefore, suggests that the two phenomena might most usefully be read culturally, as signs of our times. The end of communism as a political or social regime leaves traces, as does the postmodern; in fact, increasingly, they both in common fail to elicit controversy but rather become part of the furniture, parts of the traditions we inhabit and the vocabularies we call on to make sense of modernity.

Between totalitarianism and postmodernity is therefore, at least from one perspective, the same thing—after Marx. At the same time, we have already been after Marx for a century, though it is certainly true to say that marxism was a dominant ideological presence in the twentieth century rather than the nineteenth. Within sociology, perhaps more so in England and Australia than in America, marxism was a dominant scholarly influence and intellectual ideology into the 1960s. Indeed, the currents influenced by humanism, then by Antonio Gramsci, Louis Althusser, and Michel Foucault, saw an efflorescence of marxist thinking; we all became marxists. The journal *Thesis Eleven* was founded in Melbourne in 1980 as part of this moment, before the collapse of communism or the cultural arrival of talk about the postmodern. The influences on the journal were many and varied, from Western marxism to structuralism and across the range of issues associated with a journal characteristic of social democracy at its best, like Kautsky's *Neue Zeit* a century earlier. It was also antipodean, some would say postcolonial, and it has remained so, even since its transpacific collaboration with the MIT Press from 1990. So the project is European in the sense that marxism worked as a continental series of traditions; it is antipodean, connected by subordination to Britain and America in the world system; and it is transpacific as well as transatlantic, at the same time importing and exporting radical scholarship.

The transformation of *Thesis Eleven* across this period is itself an interesting indicator of the times. Using its subtitle as a measure, its self-understanding shifted from that of "A Journal Working at the Crossroads of Socialism and Scholarship" to "A Socialist Journal," then to "Interpreting Modernity," the latter a paradox, for it directly violates Marx's Eleventh Thesis on Ludwig Feuerbach. The sense, however, is apparent—that processes of change have themselves served to destabilize marxism as a set of traditions. In this there should be no surprise, for marxism after all represented a confluence of various already existing currents in Marx's world and its extension, revision, consolidation, and ossification in the hands of various followers. The idea that marxisms, or socialisms, were somehow immaculate conceptions, outside of and against all other ways of thinking, was not only dangerously arrogant but analytically impossible.[2] Marx's work was a brilliant synthesis created from pre-existing themes and categories. To anticipate, then, what has happened to marxism today is to notice that it has returned to the cultural sources from whence it came, or at least to its present cultural inheritance in the 1990s. Marxism has become part of the cultural common sense of the planet; everybody knows that economy rules. This also means, contrary to common sense, that marxism is dead only in the most arbitrary or legalistic of senses. In the liberal arts it has become part of the way we think, at least in its critical register. Of course, it was part of European culture in the first place; now it remains so, whatever we call it. Socialisms emerge, in retrospect, as the alter egos of modernism and enlightenment. To mistake their formal evacuation for the end of their influence is to look in the wrong place, to fall for a kind of nominalistic fallacy rather than to read the traces of a movement that emerged from European culture and returns to it.

Between Totalitarianism and Postmodernity was the first MIT *Thesis Eleven* Reader.[3] It brought together some of the best representative essays published in *Thesis Eleven* over the years, divided into two sections organized around these themes. The first section was titled "Two Faces of Modernity," referring here to Bolshevism and democracy; it included essays by Peter Murphy, Johann Arnason, Julian Triado, Edgar Morin, Ferenc Fehér, Gunnar Skirbekk, and me. The second section was called "In the Wake of Postmodernity," picking up on the other axis. It included essays by Zygmunt Bauman, Axel Honneth, Alain Touraine, Andrew Arato and Jean Cohen, Agnes Heller, and Cornelius Castoriadis—all *Thesis Eleven* people in one way or another (though none of them, of course, were party members in this age of multiple identities). As litmus tests of concerns, many of these writers and their views are pivotal. From the disciplinary perspective of sociology, perhaps two stand out. Bauman now is recognized as one of the most significant sociologists since Georg Simmel because, like Simmel, he is committed to the idea of *ambivalence* as a central orienting device and motif of modernity. In sociological theory in general, it is probably fair to say that we have run out of gurus, which itself is no bad thing. Anthony Giddens remains enormously influential, if somehow uninspiring, and Pierre Bourdieu's work remains exemplary because of its insistence on substantive engagement. The work of Bauman does not offer a template so much as advise a way of thinking; there is no Bauman School, nor, exactly, is there a Touraine School. As an old man from Konigsberg had it way back when, autonomy means thinking for yourself. This is a lesson moderns have been slow to learn.

Bauman's argument in this case concerns the idea that sociologists have two basic choices about their practice—they develop a new field, postmodern sociology, or else pursue a new project out of the old one, a sociology of postmodernity.[4] Taking Bauman seriously, we probably need inevitably to do both together and not lose too much sleep over it. Bauman's argument therefore suggests a very useful way to look back over sociology and its essential relation to modernism, and to puzzle over what comes next. His own project works both as a sociology, a view of the new, and as an anthropology, a concern with the transhistorical practices and rituals that we inherit.

For the purpose of the present reflection, however, it is the essay of Touraine that stands out. Its title jars—"Is Sociology Still the Study of Society?"—but its message is powerful.[5] For Touraine, the problem of sociology is not that it is modern or modernist but that it is neither. It is schematic and mechanistic and therefore risks missing its vocation. Touraine's question is provocative. If sociology is still the study of society, can it grasp its own subject or process? Touraine's point is quite different from that of those who, like Ernesto Laclau, tell us that society is too much a hypostatization, that there is no such thing as "society." Touraine's claim is rather that, in a particular sense, sociology missed its moment: the project of sociology froze at its inception, for its guiding curiosity is about change, yet it fixed its categories in ways that, most famously in functional structuralism and then in marxist functionalism, rendered it incapable of addressing that change. This means that for Touraine, as for Jürgen Habermas, the story of sociology has really barely started.

According to Touraine, there are three major developments that characterized modernity—the acceleration of economic change, the penetration of social change into everyday and private life, and the internationalization of social and economic facts—which together constituted the background to the most recent transformations of the social sciences. Yet in sociology it is the structural image of society rather than the fact of change that counts. In other words, the sociological tradition becomes dominated by the idea of order rather than by the process of movement; this is the reason that Touraine is no ordinary fan of social movements but is rather a sociologist of action that movements can from time to time exemplify. For Touraine, then, movement or change is what sets modernity apart; these, then, are the orienting concerns of sociology, which (to borrow from Habermas) is best briefly defined as the philosophical discourse of modernity. Moderns and mainstream sociologists, however, identify society with the nation-state and tend to use organic or mechanistic systemic metaphors to think of societies as things that will fit into four-box schemes, general typologies that somehow manifest themselves in concrete cases, those of America, Argentina, or Australia. Though Touraine does not pursue the point here, the limit has less to do with the hegemony of Talcott Parsons and/or the Pax Americana and is caught up with the terrorism of general theory. To put it in different terms, although Touraine's own sociology is abundantly flexible when it comes to cases other than France, his work is also deeply historical, whether French or Latin American.

The disciplinary message of Touraine's essay is clear: sociology has in fact become the study of society, but this risks a consistent tendency to reification; sociology, therefore, should return to its more radical impulse, where it is the study not of the template but of change. As I have indicated, this suggests that a great deal of argument remains to be had over matters of truth and method. Sociology's limits have arguably been caught up with its tendency toward or weakness for modeling, at the expense of the contingent, the ephemeral, the marginal, and the historical. Comparative sociology since Montesquieu has sought to overcome this dogma of the abstract but often at the cost of reproducing it; a comparative sociology, for example, of the nations of the Organisation for Economic Co-operation and Development is likely by its very logic to take us back to boxes and schemata and away from the insights that come from juggling similarity and difference. At the same time, there are plain risks of particularism when analysis privileges the ideographic over the nomothetic. Part of the irony of this for marxists, who have always already been divided internally over history and theory, is that they, too, have been so completely seduced by the image of the system and by its identification with the nation-state (peripheral critics of imperialism notwithstanding). Despite tokenistic genuflections toward the world system, marxists in sociology have tended to think nationally, even if they have also added in useful notions of class contract or historic compromise, viewing order as something more given to contestation and negotiation than merely rule-governed.

To summarize what I have said up to this point, then: with the unfolding of the twentieth century, and from the vantage point provided by our own moment—somewhere between totalitarianism and postmodernity—marxism has come unstuck, and sociology has missed its mission. Obviously the phenomena of marxism and sociology are not identical; it is the connection between them that I am interested in. I am not convinced that it is a bad thing that marxism returns to its cultural roots or now occupies the academy rather than the downtown party headquarters. The project of sociology, by comparison, is institutionally alive even if it is still, as always, fumbling for the map. These kinds of confusions and uncertainties are what have given rise, since the 1980s, to talk about the postmodern. Now we feel (radicals in particular) considerably less clear about what it means to talk of interpreting the world, let alone changing it. It is not obvious, however, that much more has changed since 1992 (or 1991). These questions have been in the making for some time, not least of all in Australia, where, for example, the Eurocommunist Party in my hometown read the signs on the wall in 1984, effectively shutting up shop and joining the now hegemonic Labor Party five years before the fall of the Berlin Wall.

II

Those who come from the periphery will be likely to argue that it has its advantages; the view from the edge may be clearer. With reference to the weaknesses of mainstream sociology or marxism sketched out by Touraine, for example, it is surely no accident that the finest marxist work in historical sociology came early on from Trotsky, in *1905*, and from Gramsci, in *The Southern Question*. Even though classical marxists like Karl Kautsky developed finely tuned sociologies, they tended to view societies in the modular sense, which Touraine criticizes. Those who grow up in the direct context of uneven development, by comparison, are unlikely to go for general models of order and subsystems; life is far more contingent, both more hostile and more elastic than that. To use a different language, sociologists on the periphery are likely to begin with the sense that modernity is also largely dominated by tradition, that the postwar identification of modernity and modernization is dubious. Wits among our ranks have been heard to observe that places like Australia were postmodern before they were modern, not only because our cultures are always hybrid and mixed but also because the antipodean experience of modernization has been highly uneven itself.

Australia, needless to say, is not the only antipode, but it is the case I know. Its story is highly peculiar by comparison with the modular modernity begotten of the formula posed by the French and Industrial Revolutions. Like the United States, it has a new world society, but its origins are penal rather than frontier, without the dominant experience of slavery or civil war. Strangest of all, Australia has managed to combine a culturally bourgeois superstructure with a premodern, part industrial base; in other words, it has been modernized culturally but not economically. The period of the last twenty years or so has been especially turbulent, by Australian standards, because the now dominant Labor Party has sought to bring the marxian theorem back into balance, so the superstructure is held up by a more developed industrial base. The sociological difference has been compounded by a political distinction; whereas America and Britain have been deregulated by Ronald Reagan and Margaret Thatcher, the process of restructuring in Australia has been steered by an ostensibly social democratic party. In brief, this has meant that successive labor governments, undefeated now at the federal level since 1983, have set about the deregulation of economic policy with a vengeance but have followed a more benign course with reference to social policy. The awkwardness for the labor movement in this setting has been that its involvement in processes of radical change, such as undoing economic protection, has also seen its capacity to hold onto traditional sources of identity diminished. The Labor Party has been working an axis that combines dynamics of innovation and exhaustion.

These processes have not been subject to a great deal of sociological scrutiny in Australia. This has partly to do with the unexpected nature of the process of change and partly reflects the relative weakness and modest profile of sociology and, more especially, of historical sociology. The argument I have put forward in *Transforming Labor* is that Australia has entered a period in which a major civilizational shift is occurring.[6] Rather than postmodernizing, in any obvious sense, white Australian civilization is modernizing. For want of a better word or a more expressive symbol, it is Americanizing. Political life and marketing have been Americanizing for some time, since at least the 1950s. Since the 1980s, economic and social policy have been following a similar path. Again, this is a striking case because, although party political life in the institutional sense has been predominantly conservative since federation in 1901, both social and economic policy have been bipartisan, given to economic and social protection, proto-Keynesian and then Keynesian. Although the conservative parties dominated the directly political process until 1983, with only a few clear ruptures along that path, the labor movement, ironically, has dominated Australian culture, and life in the universities and in criticism has been dominated by leftist intellectuals largely in sympathy with labor. An agrarian-inspired labor movement has therefore been a major social actor throughout the twentieth century.

How can we explain this process? Marx and the peripheral marxists offer some useful insights, as I have indicated; applying the viewpoints of Ferdinand Tönnies and Émile Durkheim can be employed as an interesting way to open up some of the romantic and modernizing tensions within the local labor movement. Touraine's work is also helpful, this time as a countercase. Touraine's French study *The Workers' Movement* makes it plain that, in the French case, the workers' movement provides a contestatory utopia of socialism as modernization, a parallel to that of the bourgeoisie—an image of capitalism, in a sense, without the bourgeoisie. But the proletarian and communist utopia in France has been symbolically modernizing.[7] What is striking about the Australian experience is the relative absence of exactly this impulse and this utopia. Hitherto, the dominant ethos and culture of the labor movement has been more in line with Tönnies than Durkheim (both, it is important to remember, socialists). Its motifs have been rural, then suburban, romantic, craft-oriented, nomadic; at this point, the situation reminds us of the earlier work of Bauman, *Memories of Class,* where Bauman, like Craig Calhoun, argued that in the case of Anglo labor movements, historically it is the past that orients their activity in the present and their imaginary conceptions of the future.[8] In Australia the period since 1983, then, represents something like the modernizing of the labor movement and labor itself. It is no accident, in this setting, that it has been the marxists and the former marxists emerging out of the Political Economy Movement and the metalworkers' unions who have provided so much of the intellectual brief for modernization; this was, after all, why the Victorian communists liquidated into the Labor Party, for they came to the conclusion that the central imperative, industrialization (and therefore industry development policy), could be effectively steered only though the major political party associated with the labor movement, the Australian Labor Party itself.

Surprisingly, then, paradoxically marxism has had an extensive sphere of influence in Australia, in part because of its privileged relationship to a dominant labor movement. As I see it, this is related in turn to the ways in which marxism is a modernizing current, in the East and the West alike. In Australia there are at least two vital mental connections to marxism—one to the fact that Marx's own work, after its romantic, Schillerian moment, became both accommodated to and enthusiastic for Promethean forms of development, the second evident in the sense that whatever else the Soviets did, they did modernize (observe the 1930s enthusiasm for megalomaniacal construction schemes, the Moscow Metro, and so on). Through these kinds of associations, then, the connections become more apparent. An agrarian, romantic, backward-looking labor movement has a substantial cultural hold over a nation with a weak and dependent bourgeoisie; when the moment of modernization arrived with a vengeance into the 1980s, it was former communist advisers and policy makers who advocated industry development policy in particular and societal modernization policies in general. From a local perspective, however, the problems are various, even if we agree that modernization—social change—is in some ways simply inescapable. One major problem from a leftist perspective is that to modernize labor tradition is also to empty it out, denying in the process that the peculiarly Australian version of the historic compromise achieved much at all; but it did, in fact, achieve a great deal, including high levels of public civility, social cooperation, and welfare support.[9] An attendant problem that follows directly on from this is that deregulation of a hitherto protected culture often disregards its modest scale. The Australian economy is a small fish; its deregulation now coincides with globalization, which, like free trade, favors the already strong.

In *Postmodern Socialism* I develop a kind of second-order argument around this theme.[10] The scale of reference is more global as well as local; in a way this book is an attempt to think through what some of these civilizational changes mean. The points of connection back to Touraine are significant. The subtitle of *Postmodern Socialism* refers to three terms: "Romanticism, City and State." Romanticism is drawn out as a complement to the Enlightenment, with which it is culturally and empirically coextensive. These categories, after all, are ex post facto constructions that consistently blur the way in which patterns of thinking from Rousseau to Marx crossed over these alleged boundaries. To make the obvious connection, romantics are often also modernizers, and moderns, as well as being traditionalists, are often also postmodern. In this way postmodern talk represents some sense of the urgency of change, actual or desirable, though it necessarily uses pre-existing vocabularies to address these processes. The references to city and state are suggestive of different concerns, though critique of cities tends also too easily to dichotomize talk of cities and suburbs, where again the actual distinctions are less clear. Cities are ancient as well, and not only modern; only the focus on state serves to signal its overshadowing by globalization, for while economy and culture increasingly become global as well as vernacular or indigenized, politics remains more governed by national referents, though (especially in Australia) politics is also teased into regionalism of a putatively transnational kind (in Australia "globalization" is a synonym for "Asianization").

Cities have been a major focus of sociology since Simmel, Berlin, and the Chicago School or, earlier, Engels and Manchester. My own sense is that, together with examining other themes such as money, looking at the city is one of the best ways to make sense of modernity. To connect back to Bauman, both money and the city are extraordinarily rich indicators and expressions of modernity as ambivalence. My argument in *Postmodern Socialism* is that to return to questions of space, as well as to questions of the acceleration of time as speed, it is also important to think of cities hierarchically, for cities rest on undergrounds, whether actual or metaphorical (and suburban or on the edge) or both (as is especially evident in places like New York City or Los Angeles). The disciplinary awkwardness in this, however, is that the city, like money, is not viewed as a core expression of modernity so much as a subdisciplinary genre, the realm of urban planning or of economic sociology. The connection of the theme of the city to that of the state is more tenuous. The modernist project, as exemplified, say, in Henry Ford, John Maynard Keynes, and Talcott Parsons, presumes the identity between society and nation that draws out Touraine's criticism in "Is Sociology Still the Study of Society?" Processes of internationalization or globalization, however, make it increasingly difficult to locate classes as national actors. State structures are the victims of globalization, even as globalization (like the world system of imperialism that preceded it) works directly through nation-states. Connecting up the images of underground and state, it now becomes increasingly significant to rethink the relationship between economy and state. The modernist gaze of mainstream sociology conventionally has behaved as though economy were public, as though informal or underground economy were merely a traditionalistic residue (much in the way that marxists mistakenly treated the petty bourgeois and petty commodity production as leftovers of obsolete modes of production). Modernist sociology has therefore, to some extent at least, been guilty of mislocating the economy, presuming as it has that economic activity increasingly becomes legal and public as modernization proceeds, assuming simultaneously that all subjects can be placed as (or raised to) modern citizens, that margins and the underground are, so to speak, dysfunctional rather than functional to modernity. This, finally, has transformative effects again on the state, which is as active invisibly and locally as it is at formal state and federal levels, and, at the same time, the reproduction of formal state activity depends on public revenue, which is inversely related to underground economic activity.

The argument of *Postmodern Socialism,* then, is that while major civilizational shifts are occurring in Australia, there is also a global shift beyond that usually associated with the idea of economic globalization. This is a cultural shift of political horizons. For the century that ran roughly from 1880 to 1980, a modernist or liberal or social democratic consensus emerged in the West that the Social Question could be solved by social reform, guided by notions of citizenship and economic integration through the public workings of the labor market and the nuclear family. All that is now going or gone, not least of all as a social model. Change has gotten the better of us, as scholars and as citizens; the processes that go on behind our backs have left us to face what looks like a new world.

III

Thesis Eleven was formed in the period before these various tendencies became manifest or even were posited. The choice of title itself was part accident, bequeathed to us as a legacy by a friend of ours who died, whose idea and whose title for the project this was. Nevertheless, we also chose it, and in choosing it we showed the period, maybe the youthful arrogance of the left. For the left presumed that "change" was its prerogative. What has happened in the interim suggests that we misunderstood or misvalued exactly how central the facts of change were. In the words of Marx, "The philosophers have interpreted the world; the point, however, is to change it." But since the 1980s the world has changed beyond imagination, marginalizing marxism as an independent tradition and helping to remind us, as Bauman and Calhoun argued, that radicals are also conservatives. The theses on Feuerbach remain, in retrospect, a fruitful text of the tradition; but it is no coincidence that the text for today is that line of Shakespeare's *The Tempest* that arced through Thomas Carlyle to arrive in the *Communist Manifesto* and then became the emblematic title of Marshall Berman's great book *All That Is Solid Melts into Air*.[11] The sentiment in Marx runs together with another, the image of the sorcerer's apprentice. Sociologically speaking, the point today is that the world is reaching a level of complexity and opacity in its relations such as to make leftist propositions for "change" irrelevant. Not because reforms are irrelevant, as the inhabitants of two-thirds of the world and the inhabitants of the underground in the first will tell you.

Nor is this to say that the processes of change that we gather under the category globalization are without author. Globalization represents a will to power, a political choice, especially in places like Australia, to license economic imperatives above and beyond the realms of social policy.

Where does this leave marxism as an ideology or as a theory? Inasmuch as globalization represents an extension of imperialism, marxism or its inheritors will likely remain a peripheral ideological presence among the outcasts of the world system. Marxism as a theory, I have suggested, may have lost its appearance of independence, but that was also illusory and proprietary, the result of too much pride and arrogance and imaginary independence. What we end up with, facing the millennium, is in one way what we started with, as Marx read Hegel's *Phenomenology* in 1844 and as we read Marx's *Manuscripts* in the 1960s: a sense that the struggle of master and slave never ends—never triumphs but never ends, either. The redemptive or modernist illusion to which marxists clung imagined that this struggle could be overcome. Now it looks as hard as fate. But yet, it moves.

(1995)

Nine

Socialism after Communism: Liberalism?

What is left of socialism after the collapse of communism? That seems obvious: liberalism. Certainly there are strong indications of this, as in the redefinition of socialism as "democracy" or "civil society." If we look at social democracy, its own politics were and are often indistinguishable from liberalism: notions of rights, social justice, and citizenship draw together social liberalism and social democracy whether we talk of Eduard Bernstein and Leonard Hobhouse or of the later Keynesian consensus. Although all this seems neat enough, what it raises, among other things, is the question of the status of liberalism. A more precise answer to the question might indicate that what we are left with is pluralism, that is, the identification of difference and struggle as both normal and desirable. At least one thread of marxism still speaks to this: the image of master and slave that Karl Marx took up from Georg Wilhelm Friedrich Hegel. These arguments are developed in my book *Postmodern Socialism*.[1]

That what is left of socialism after communism is liberalism is a sensibility that Francis Fukuyama only named. After 1989, most people probably view capitalism and democracy as triumphant on a global scale. The social question, which called out socialism, remains, or at least the problems grouped together under that term stubbornly persist. What is less apparent now is any sense that social engineering or social reform has a purpose or a feasibility. Indeed, the widespread sense is likely closer to that of a residual muddling through, as though we can talk about social problems but not do anything about them. This essay seeks to discuss and extend the common sense of the moment by contesting the obvious.

The twentieth century was arguably marxism's century if we view marxism as the "other" of capitalism. Bolshevism became a major actor, and communism became a world power. Social democracy, meanwhile, was initially marginalized by this path of events, only to revive in the West after fascism and alongside communism as an alternative form of administrative regime for the postwar West. Viewed theoretically, Bolshevism was primarily a theory of party that became a tyrannical practice of state. Classical marxism itself developed no sufficient theory of politics. Marx and Friedrich Engels defined the party as the class and imputed it a historic vocation; the proletariat would change the world. The penultimate chapter of Marx's *Capital* said so, Q.E.D. The immediate legatee of marxism, in the form of the German Social Democratic Party (SPD), took on this sense of spontaneism, maturation, or fatalism; August Bebel awaited socialism like the falling of ripe fruit. Karl Kautsky notoriously defined the SPD as a revolutionary party, not a revolution-making one. Bernstein wanted to pursue democracy, which meant in effect taking liberalism more seriously than earlier. Rosa Luxemburg shared Marx's sense that sooner or later the whole operation—via the working class-act—would collapse. The political project of the SPD became the pursuit of an independent community across these arguments and reformist practices, the proverbial state within a state.[2]

The Russian October Revolution changed all this, because the Bolsheviks dared to act more decisively. They had no internal empire to defend. They seized power and dismissed the Constituent Assembly. If Marx had no sufficient theory of politics, Vladimir Lenin was armed with the prosthetic device called the Party. There began a long and unhappy story that ended (more or less) in 1989. Within the history of communism, the most fascinating and potentially fruitful of interludes that followed was that associated with the work of Antonio Gramsci. Gramsci's more expansive political sensibilities introduced into subsequent discussion notions such as "hegemony" and "historic bloc"; yet the Modern Prince, the vanguard party, remains in the shadows, so that Gramsci's political theory embodies an unresolved tension between Bolshevism and democracy. It is this that explains the great debates over Gramsci's legacy into the 1980s. For a part of Gramsci's work in prison, thinking practically, still privileged the party form, whereas a warmer stream of his thought contributed to the more recent enthusiasm for social movements.[3]

Luxemburg; the Council Communists, such as Anton Pannekoek; and the early Gramsci all maintained some connection with the spirit of Marx's spontaneism. In the shadow of marxism there always stood the figure of Jean-Jacques Rousseau, thinking that good people would change the world, if they could, and opening the strategy in possibility that in their default the self-appointed representatives of public virtue could stand in for them.

Marxists, historically, preferred to evade the question of what form the good society might take. They were always, even if despite themselves, utopian, but their utopias too often consisted of negation. Marx's own great work indicated that commodity production had to go, but not what would replace it.[4] Lenin's great contribution was to indicate that socialism might look like the post office.[5]

More pressing, perhaps, for socialists in the twentieth century was the task of locating a revolutionary subject. They focused on the putative instrument more than the goal. Socialism, it was presumed, would lie somewhere between not-capitalism and better-than-capitalism. Marx privileged the proletariat, as did Luxemburg; it took Georg Lukács to formalize the claim that the proletariat was epistemologically privileged, as he did in *History and Class Consciousness*. Lenin was a better sociologist; he knew that classes could not be relied on to act politically, that particular concrete organizations or institutions were necessary to this task. Into the 1960s, however, councils seemed anachronistic and romantic, parties bureaucratic and paternalistic. Into the 1980s, social movements were increasingly constructed as potential actors.[6] More modestly, perhaps, others began to defend the idea of civil society or the slogan of citizenship. Leading radical thinkers, from Jürgen Habermas to Cornelius Castoriadis to Agnes Heller, replaced the idea of socialism with the values of democracy, "radical democracy," autonomy. The path of the century that brought marxist politics to a close thus apparently resulted in the confirmed politics of liberalism. Radicals could still combine marxist political economy with a liberal superstructure. On a scale of closer to two centuries than one, marxism and liberalism began perhaps to renegotiate their initial terms of separation, world denying and world affirming.

So what is left of socialism? Liberalism? To the extent that this is true, it may also be an expression of the crisis we are living. Liberalism can quite easily be defended as less dangerous than marxism; but it is not less problematic. Socialism, semantically, refers to the place of the social against individualism. Socialism semantically opposes individualism, not capitalism; these are moral and normative vocabularies, not originally arguments about productivity or economic efficiency. These are arguments about how we choose to live, not measures of economic output; they invoke attitudes about social forms, not juxtapositions of static imaginary modes of production. Liberalism's great weakness in this regard is its insufficiently socialized conception of action. Liberal thinking typically rests on one hypostatized couplet: individual and society, state and citizen. Even "liberal socialists" like Hobhouse have bent this way. In *Liberalism,* Hobhouse favored the individual even as he argued the centrality of society: "Liberalism is the belief that society can safely be founded on this self-directing power of personality, that it is only on this foundation that a true community can be built"; or, against the imaginary Hegel in the margin: "Society consists wholly of persons. It has no distinct personality separate from and superior to those of its members."[7] Perhaps the latter is so, but there are more than persons in societies; there are groups, families, networks, organizations, corporate actors such as firms and unions, social movements, religious or ethnic groups, political parties, and so on. Once these latter are added in, the whole idea of lonely individuals somehow miraculously contracting with the "state" begins to look vaguely comical. Part of the problem with Hobhouse's text is that although it was more social than many liberalisms, it was not yet strikingly modern; it was of its moment, monocultural, and insufficiently complex in its imaginary form. Later on in the text, Hobhouse began to discuss voluntary association, so community came to work largely as a synonym for society; Hobhouse could allow this but not the more corporative identification of state and society.[8]

Of course, the social is not an absolute absence. Hobhouse's argument is shadowed by the idea of voluntary association. Earlier, central liberals such as John Stuart Mill had also focused on the dyad state and citizen, even if Mill also took seriously economic classes, for example, in his *Principles of Political Economy.* The Fabians, if not quite liberals, nevertheless working within a tradition shaped by positivism and utilitarianism, wrote extensively about trade unions and conducted social research into the household.[9] Perhaps the Fabians did better here precisely to the extent that they were sociological thinkers, concerned with the web of associative and institutional forms within which social life actually occurs. Yet it nevertheless seems to be the case that within mainstream liberal thinking, the reductio ad absurdum implied by state and citizen is always present. If there is no state qua state, as Hobhouse warned, there are only citizens. It is not a bizarrely long jump from this graphic mess of individuals to the proposition that there is no such thing as society. But more severely, in our context, there is a foreshortening here of everyday life itself. For we act as individuals only within the fabric and dependency of all those institutions and are placed within them by the accident of birth. Our formation and the conduct of our lives is irredeemably social and sociologically thick.

To place the social thus, first—to begin from the premise that there are only social individuals—is not a defining feature of the liberal tradition. Not all liberals will be individualists, but they will tend to begin from claims regarding the individual and at most will add in society when it comes to complementing notions of obligation with those of right, although obligation can also be limited to obligation to individuals or to the state on their behalf. Socialism, in this regard, is a tradition related to but different from liberalism.

Socialism, in short, is not just liberalism with a social twist or result, even if social liberals and social democrats are often difficult to separate practically. As I have argued elsewhere, social democracy in its richest version is to be located in the German tradition associated with classical marxism.[10] Social liberalism starts from these different premises, of individuals thrown together, and makes specific allowances that might materially or spiritually support weaker individuals, i.e., those who cannot support themselves: infants, the infirm, those without hope. For better or worse, social democrats think in terms of community, even if they also allow community to be overdetermined by class. In Marx this sense was usually overstated, in the *Sixth Thesis on Feuerbach* or *the Paris Manuscripts*, where individuality makes sense only in terms of the ensemble of social relations, or, more obscurely, species being, or later, in *The Eighteenth Brumaire* or *Capital*, where individuals wear the character masks ascribed them by class relations. But there have always been other socialists alongside the marxists, and they too have argued this sensibility in different ways.

So Richard Tawney, for example, in the 1929 lectures that became the text *Equality*, argued as had others that socialism was the next phase that might fulfil the promise of the French Revolution. On this view, the good society could be conceived only as a community, a community bonded by solidarity through service.[11] Yet both communitarians like Tawney and early guild socialists like G. D. H. Cole, for whom the local was preeminent, were vulnerable with the passing of time and the rise of organized labor to the association of community, society, and state that had made Hobhouse twitch. But these are general problems to do with the increasing presence of the state into the twentieth century, for the various socialists, such as Cole and Harold Laski, who began from social premises, had also earlier insisted on pluralist arguments concerning the composition of social arrangements.[12] Although all these English arguments are shadowed by the desire for simplicity and by the relative fact of monoculturalism, they do in common nevertheless presume that it is social relations that come first rather than social contracts between imaginary individual actors in a society whose relations are constructed ex post facto and without proper respect for the household or the private sphere let alone for other forms of voluntary association.

The irony for marxists is that this sense of plurality is something their own tradition never caught up on. Between state and citizen orthodox marxism placed *classes,* and the third term became the first. Individuals largely disappeared from marxist theory, and the state fared little better. This raises the question of a significant tension between Marx and his followers, for Marx, too, remains more thoroughly individualist than is often thought. The anthropology of wholeness that Marx inherited from Friedrich Schiller and that explained the possibility of alienation posits as ideal an imaginary person who is whole and independent. This way of thinking is still evident in Marx's later work, for example, in the idea fundamental to *Capital* that exchange relations are vitally relations of loss.[13] The image of the collective laborer haunts the pages of *Capital* but does not deeply inform its logic. Similarly, the focus on so-called public economy replays the bourgeois occlusion of household economy; family form remains marginal, and classes remain conceived as though they are actors rather than the organizations, unions, and parties that actually work on their behalf.

Further, as Zygmunt Bauman has argued, the proletariat that Marx constructed as a modernizing actor often rather carries a communitarian memory and pathos. Classes, in marxist argument, often thus stand in for community or communities.[14] Even critical theory fared no better in this regard. For although it sought to theorize family, media, and culture, the legacy of the Frankfurt School for Social Research took on the Lukácsian premise of a privileged proletarian agent, then dropped class analysis altogether when the proletariat failed to rise to the occasion. Critical theory, then, turned to its own variant of state and citizen, this time presenting the standoff as that between man and mass. Thus the Frankfurt School turned from sociology to philosophy, ending like other projects in expelling the social, all that goes in between.[15] On one side Behemoth, on the other the atom; totalitarianism, real or incipient, everywhere.

Modernity, as we know, is the age of the subject, self-forming, self-regulating, narcissistic, mobile and fluid, contingent, sometimes even Promethean. And the twentieth century has been an age of disaster, whatever else it has been, corpses piling higher on corpses, Behemoth and corpses. Little surprise, then, that today we feel compelled to celebrate the individual and defend the individual against violation. Little wonder that we should feel backed into liberalism, like Richard Rorty, because we dislike cruelty.[16] However, there is even more at risk than this.

The twentieth century was arguably the century of socialist presence, whether we date it from the emergence of the social question to the events of 1989 or construct it more compactly, symbolically, as the short century 1914–89, in which wars and revolutions resulted in a postwar Western sense that social progress was nevertheless still possible. Socialism, the idea that humans together could renegotiate and reform social relations so that inequality could be minimized and citizenship encouraged, is now apparently over. Sociology viewed as a national politics of reform and civics seems also to be passing, not least of all because of globalization or the will to globalize. Socialism has thus ceased, today, to refer to a realizable project or an imaginary state of affairs that can abstractly be opposed, juxtaposed against that which we know as capitalism.

Socialism emerged as the name for a process, a process of conflict and struggle. The society of the future, it was imagined, would be harmonious, still, often simpler, more like the *Gemeinschaft* of Ferdinand Tönnies than his *Gesellschaft*. The idea that socialism might be a condition or a place rather than the name of a process of struggle also became dominant in Marx's work. In order to rethink this, it is necessary to return to Hegel's dialectic of master and slave, which Marx reconsidered in the *Paris Manuscripts*. Hegel's dialectic is one of the most often revived of symbols, not least of all in our own times, when talk is frequently influenced by notions of the need for recognition. Talk of recognition thus often coincides with problems of narcissism. As class politics has receded, initially to be replaced by the politics of social movements, so has antistatism revived the politics of civil liberties. What is called postmodern politics, as in the case of Jean François Lyotard, is often a minimal politics of self-defense against Power, based on the individualism of incommensurable difference. Modern politics, by comparison, at least until recently, rested on senses that individual identities are socially formed and marked and thereby drawn together by similarity of experience or interest as well as spaced out by difference. Modern politics still presumes that politics also occurs in public spheres.

The politics of recognition does not refer clinically to a process in which one individual forms an abstract relation with another. The significance of the dialectic of master and slave is rather that it contextualizes culture within power. Identity thus occurs within asymmetrical relations of power that are constantly subject to renegotiation. Workers and capitalists engage in different kinds of struggles that shift; so do men and women, within the relations of sexual politics, as do races, regions, and ethnic groups in the politics of multiculturalism. The point, however, is that history is struggle, and history, contrary to Fukuyama, never ends. The prospect of perfect harmony is illusory, a bad utopia. Utopias need to be defended as historically competing hopes for the good society, not as models of conditions actually to be achieved. For if they were to be achieved, the struggle would be over, and so would life, and politics with it.

As Leonard Woolf put it, recalling Michel de Montaigne, it is the journey, not the arrival that matters. Marx was willful to imagine that history, or prehistory, could ever come to an end. Socialism therefore continues to remain one point of orientation in radical politics when it reminds us that the point is to struggle, to reform the world, to follow our values regardless of whether we believe that they might ever be realized. Liberalism cannot help us here, for it lapses back at best into varying sensibilities suggestive of the struggle between individual and state but not between all the various groups of actors within which we actually find ourselves located as social individuals. What comes after communism might then include liberalism, but not only it, for this kind of defensive or minimal politics can only then protest further against cruelty against the state. Humans need to say no, but they also need to do more than this.

Let us leave the last word not to the marxists, then, but to the liberals who thought they knew better. John Stuart Mill, John Maynard Keynes, and William Beveridge all left space, an open codicil, within their writings, that perhaps their own traditions would not suffice, in which case it would be necessary to take more seriously the arguments associated with socialism.[17] This, as they understood, is a process without end, in which we cannot reasonably expect to anticipate outcomes yet fully to be shaped. Socialism remains, in this sense and as Marx understood, a practical question. After communism, we return not to liberalism but to history. This is the political legacy of socialism.[18]

(1996)

Ten

Socialism in Europe—after the Fall

One hundred years of socialism . . . these words, which make up the title of Donald Sassoon's recent book,[1] resonate, as if spoken by a lonely, Magrittelike voice in the solitude of an empty room. Not a hundred years of socialism, or a hundred years of struggle, but one hundred years of socialism, the one and yet the many expressing somehow in minimal eloquence the grandeur and twilight of this great movement and ideology, this extraordinary phenomenon that changed everything and then, seemingly, disappeared into the cultures from whence it emerged. How could all this be possible? What is and was the phenomenon of socialism, and what are its legacies and consequences for the grimmer times we now apparently inhabit? These are the kinds of issues opened up by Donald Sassoon. *One Hundred Years of Socialism* is a brilliant book; probably we have seen little like it since G. D. H. Cole's multivolume *History of Socialist Thought,* though Sassoon's book is also more, and less. More in that its scope is more sociological, taking in social developments across Western Europe; less in that its geographical vista is tighter and its claims to encyclopedia status are more modest, even if it is a phone book of a thing, physically massive, placing demands on the reader's physique as well as on his or her intellect and time schedule. All of which is to say that its publication is a major event, for this book should be compulsory and compulsive reading for all of us who care about these topics.

So who is Donald Sassoon, and what is his project? Sassoon's earlier work has been just as exceptional as what we see in this book, though hitherto its nature has been more particular, or monographic. His previous books include *The Strategy of the Italian Communist Party, from the Resistance to Historic Compromise* (1981), *The Italian Communists Speak for Themselves* (which he edited, 1978), and *Contemporary Italy* (1986). Read as signs, these are perhaps already symptomatic of some positions and curiosities; for Sassoon is plainly an Italianist by trade, and the story of Italian communism from Antonio Gramsci to Enrico Berlinguer is one of the most extraordinary of such stories in Italy or elsewhere. The Italian Communist Party (PCI) was a communist party without parallel. Into the 1970s the Italian party became conceptually syncretized with the Spanish and French Communist Parties, emerging as the great hybrid hope of that period, Eurocommunism. (Remember Eurocommunism?) Radical hopes on the left were rekindled from England to Melbourne in Australia and the San Francisco Bay Area in the United States around the new spark of life given to the old and elusive idea of a "third way," an alternative not only to capitalism and communism but also to the inertia of social democracy and the brutality of Soviet communism. Thus Sassoon's project might be located in these kinds of matrixes of hope and fear. For Eurocommunism, embodied in the Italian "historic compromise" and the French Common Program, looked like a way out of the impasse then. Now the view has altered, but the interpretative puzzles remain.

Charting the Terrain

One Hundred Years of Socialism is an expansion of this optic throughout Western Europe and the twentieth century. What went wrong, and what went right? Looking back now, after the hope of Eurocommunism and the anger or mourning of loss, Sassoon sets his markers around a neat century. The symbolic collapse of socialism per communism in 1989 is an obvious marker even if, as Sassoon knows, its precise interpretation is less obvious or apparent. Sassoon chose to begin his story a clear century earlier, with the foundation of the Second International in Pigalle in 1889. Socialists, these most revolutionary of political advocates, have of course always also been deeply traditionalistic. Like fascists and other political moderns, social democrats have always played a cool hand at inventing traditions. So they met, then, to anticipate the Second International a neat century after the obvious symbolic marker of their time, the great French Revolution. All the tensions that were to hold up modern socialisms in effect were already there. The hope for apocalypse, the dream of peaceful transition; the desire for ruptural change, the simpler slogan of a better life, revolution and reform nestle together like jealous siblings both loved yet spleenful. The location is useful. Sassoon was, I think, right to follow the tradition that aligns socialism with the French Revolution as much as the Russian. Not least of all because, as Max Weber is reputed to have said to Georg Lukács, the great Russian experiment was likely to set history back by a hundred years (but is it still too long for us to wait? perhaps, until that centenary, one hundred years after October). For the logic of Sassoon's book, in a way, is exactly that the great success of socialism was as the legacy of the French Revolution, this time read, however, as reform rather than as Jacobin tragedy. I take Sassoon to be arguing—and in this I think he is correct—that while the twentieth century is the great century for capitalism, it is also the century of socialism. The great irony in this for those, including socialists, who are used to simpler dichotomies, is that the two run together, inseparably, one as alter ego to the other even if now dismissed. As Sassoon puts it, we now know that the left offered up the first political casualties of capitalist crisis in the 1930s, and we now know that the left's achievement was greatest exactly during the golden age of capitalism between 1945 and 1975. Capitalism held up socialism; now it refuses.

These are, in a sense, what might be called Gramscian sensibilities. For Gramsci knew that instability fed reaction, not progress, and that socialists needed to develop arguments not for disorder but rather for a new order. Yet Gramsci remained a residual Leninist, notwithstanding various more recent attempts to turn him into a historically misplaced member of the Birmingham School of Cultural Studies who accidentally strayed into Turin. And Gramsci knew that although tradition was always behind us, modernity was perpetually before us, that the wretched of Europe needed more modernity rather than less. There has always been a degree of intellectual conceit in that middle-class critical rejection of modernity that has remained formal and rhetorical, launched from the comfort of well-padded armchairs in the centers at the expense of those without shirts or shoes. Thus the further apparent irony, which Sassoon notes, that the idea of socialism was generated not by those whom we today think of as the absolutely wretched of the earth but by the skilled and by their articulate middle-class allies. Communism, in turn, for better and for worse, became an ideology of modernization, a point widely acknowledged but insufficiently contemplated. For communism is still, I think, widely discredited on the bogus grounds that it was a throwback, an anachronism, a way out of modernity rather than through it. In other words, both fascism and communism are still often misunderstood as premodern or antimodern, whereas both these experiences actually need to be conceptualized as alternative modernities. This is an important issue, in Sassoon's view of the century, because he knows that socialism is caught up with modernity. It is not only the case that the Soviet path became a model for a kind of authoritarian or primitive modernization; the larger issue is that capitalism and socialism jostle and mingle together as modernity.[2]

But Sassoon's canvas is not quite global, nor is it comprehensive. His book is not, he insists, a history of socialist ideas, nor is it a history from below of the movements themselves. Rather, he indicates, it is a comparative history of West European socialist parties in the contexts they faced—capitalist development, the nation-state, the international system, dominant ideologies, the past. Sassoon behaves like an historian, yet the net effect of his book is something we encounter as more like sociology. The stress on comparison is one aspect of this; the overarching curiosity about modernity is another. And, as we shall see later, the curiosity about, for example, women, the labor market, and social movements also suggests that this project works as a sociology more than as a strict analysis of socialisms. Questions of inclusion and exclusion in a work of this strength and significance are likely to become trivial, if not silly; yet the issue as to why, for example, women figure so prominently in a history of socialism (not feminism) is one source of curiosity, while another, only partly resolved, is the question of why fascist parties that also constructed mass or labor movements are largely marginal to the analysis. As Sassoon indicates in introducing his narrative, the detail and intensity of analysis in his book escalates after 1945; so to be clear about the text as we enter it, its key concerns are with the Western European socialist parties in comparative perspective through the postwar boom.

Yet Sassoon is a historian, too, and even a sociologist would have properly to deal with beginnings. Sassoon acknowledges the inspiration of Gramsci again here, this time the Gramsci who put it profoundly that to write the history of a party is like writing the history of a country from a monographic point of view. This insight may be more pertinent to Italy than to other cases in which the experience of communism or social democracy was more marginal. What it means for *One Hundred Years of Socialism* is that Sassoon was writing the history of Western Europe from the perspective of the history of the Western European Left. But this, like every beginning, is difficult. It is difficult, in the first place, because there is no necessary causal link between socialism and the rise of the labor movement. The widespread tendency to identify socialism and the labor movement may be connected, in part, to marxism's propensity to privilege the image of the revolutionary proletariat as the universal subject of history. Thinking back on these matters, Sassoon argues that socialism virtually invented the proletariat as the political class necessary to its own desires. Marxism then became dominant as the smartest kind of socialist ideology, for it combined the best available theory of exploitation with the best available theory of history. In addition, marxism was capable both of incredible theoretical sophistication, enough to keep the intellectuals off the street, and of being translated powerfully into the context of life on the factory floor. Germany then ruled the new Second International, and Karl Kautsky ruled the International; short-term reformism coupled with long-term apocalypse blended neatly into maturational reformism. By 1914 the German Social Democratic Party (SPD) had a million members and a clever program that bridged reform and revolution by accommodating both of them. Karl Kautsky's *summa* of this wisdom out of the Erfurt Program in *The Class Struggle* was translated into sixteen languages before 1914. The other socialists lived in the shadows of the Germans, though perhaps not just in the way that Sassoon portrays it; in wondering why France, for example, produced no marxist theorists of the calibre of Kautsky and Eduard Bernstein, he sidesteps the figure of Georges Sorel, and the issue of Sorel's filiation into fascism. The Fabians, meantime, were too busy acting elsewhere to develop stronger theoretical claims; hiding behind the shared cultural mythos of pragmatism or practicalism, they nevertheless developed sophisticated social theories, as I have shown in *Labour's Utopias*.[3] If Fabianism became the de facto collective consciousness of British laborism, the minimalist demands of the SPD meantime anticipated the basic features of the postwar welfare states; thus do utopias become enacted, less as the grandiosity of Jacobin social engineering than as the incremental politics of reformism that go together with economic growth.

Through the entire period up to 1914, socialist parties remained firmly committed to the politics of opposition. Their transformation into parties of government was gradual, peaking through and especially after the Second World War. And what a transformation this was; for the shift from a politics of negation to one of affirmation was massive, fraught with danger as well as offering great promise. Sassoon does not make the connection, but for many it will be difficult not to think here of Roberto Michels and his masterly study of 1915, *Political Parties*. Michels is a useful symbolic connection here not only because he also took that extraordinary and fascinating personal shift from left to right but in addition because he anticipated the argument that in the SDP's great success its failure could already be discerned. If 1914 changed the world for socialist internationalism, however, everything changed after October 1917. Whatever else their contemporaries thought about the Bolsheviks, they were mesmerized by their capacity to act. From Sorel and Gramsci to Bernard Shaw, they clapped, wide-eyed, stunned and beguiled by the cheek of the Bolsheviks. Although the Soviet experiment then became the major imaginary of socialist thought as well as its modern historic crucible, the reformists meantime plodded on, serving rather than snatching. Thus, as Sassoon observes, between 1932 and 1938 the Swedish social democrats practically laid the foundation for what would become the West European conception of social democracy after the Second World War: the compromise between labor and capital, with a welfare state and full employment. Although it is beyond the scope of Sassoon's argument, it may also be worth adding that similar visions were not only constructed and informed ideologically by other experiences, including those of socialists like the Fabians; they were also lived out in the so-called social laboratory offered by the antipodes, Australia and New Zealand, into the new century. Nor was it any accident that these experiences were notionally connected through colonial traffic like that of Fabians such as Maud and William Pember Reeves from New Zealand to London. Settler capitalist labor movements, too, were at the forefront of innovation, as I have outlined with Mark Considine and Rob Watts in *Arguing about the Welfare State*.[4] The lives of the peripheries always also affect those of the centers, in matters of socialism too.

The real achievement of the SPD, meantime, was the Weimar Republic. As Sassoon observes, the SPD could and did claim that the Erfurt Program had been incorporated into the new constitution. Only this, again, was something like defeat in victory, for what Rudolf Hilferding called "organized capitalism" came too readily to accommodate not only the forces of socialism but also those of its mortal enemies. Still there were other voices, like those whom Sassoon groups together as the "neo-socialist" planners. Planning, of course, had become a new orthodoxy.

This may be as close as Sassoon gets to the important problem of left-right collusion or coalescence. He notes, for example, that the British fascist leader Oswald Mosley was also in an earlier life a labor minister and observes the Nazi leader Gregor Strasser's enthusiasm for public works. Probably it was Hendrik de Man who best exemplified these kinds of fatal contradictions. But various others also acted them out, as did Benito Mussolini himself, and even Nazis like Joseph Goebbels were affected by marxism in various different ways. The fascist emphasis on action and will resembled Bolshevism, and the idea of the organic or corporate state was no right-wing monopoly, manifesting itself also as far away as France and England in the work of Émile Durkheim and John Maynard Keynes. So where does the left start and the right end? Sassoon acknowledges the problems here, both moral and intellectual, but he does not much probe them. He claims in passing that no leading social democrat or communist joined the Nazis in Weimar Germany, but if that is true, the converse is not; Otto Schuddekopf, for example, published a book-length study in 1960 concerning exactly the idea of left actors who came from the right, *Linke Leute von rechts*,[5] while for his part Zeev Sternhell has upset the neatness of left-right cleavages in his major work *Birth of Fascist Ideology*.[6] Sassoon agrees that there is a problem here, a still "insufficiently lit danger spot" connecting the extremities of left and right, but he passes on the opportunity to push further. Let me offer to push a little more here instead, even at the expense of being perhaps provocative.

Sassoon dismisses too readily, as many today might say, modernization theory, the "anti-socialist" polemicists who allude to convergences in the totalitarian mind, the old idea that the left-right spectrum actually links together, so to speak, around the back. Just as many socialists today would look with less hostility than hitherto on some aspects of the work of, say, Friedrich Hayek or Karl Popper, so might it be possible to construct a socialist argument that connects Jacobinism in the manner of Bolshevism with something like fascism. Fascisms, after all, built mass movements and constructed economic and social programs that in many ways resembled those of Stalinism. To put it more bluntly, it could certainly be argued that left and right coalesced together into the 1930s around two points of political and economic affinity, the first evident in the hostility to parliamentary forms, the second manifest in the enthusiasm for planning. They were also bound together by larger cultural enthusiasms such as mass mobilization and eugenics. More generically or analytically speaking, it is not so obvious that fascism should be excluded from the labor movement story once Stalinism is included. Italian fascism was certainly a hybrid form, and Nazism contained clear components of anticapitalist romanticism as well as of the technological imperatives described by Jeff Herf in his study of the field, *Reactionary Modernism*.[7] The Belgian Workers Party, as Sassoon observes, encapsulated this awkwardness in their 1933 call for *le socialisme national*. Only Sassoon here exclaims, "in 1933!" as though this would have seemed odd in a world where communist street gangs beat up Nazis, and vice versa, and everybody argued for planning, all in the name of some sort of socialism or other. And these were, emphatically, yet in a different sense obviously or necessarily *national* movements. We should not be at all shocked by the idea of national socialism before 1933; arguably, before Auschwitz it simply meant other things. International socialism at the formal or diplomatic level collapsed in 1914. Thus it is no surprise, in this light, that the Fabian Society published the Belgian Henri de Man's *Plan van den Arbeid*, with an introduction by G. D. H. Cole, in 1935. Nor, in retrospect, should we be too surprised by the news, as Sassoon reports it, that de Man finally became a supporter of Nazism, announcing that it was "the German form of socialism." Oswald Spengler anticipated the argument way back, as a choice between the good German socialism and a nasty utilitarian, Manchester species of marxism, in *Preussentum und Sozialismus*.[8]

Not all claims to socialism have come from our side of the fence. But it was also the case that not all the news of the period was this cheerless. Austromarxism arguably got about as close as Gramsci did to arguments for the third way, beyond technocracy whether Bolshevik or social democratic. Even if, like Otto Bauer, Gramsci was perhaps too much a cultural product of the old game, his thinking in prison also began to open up out onto those demanding challenges of modernity that Sassoon insists frame our lives. For Gramsci understood the centrality of the American experience of modernity, of Americanism and Fordism. American culture was more open to modernity because it was less constrained by the kinds of traditionalism that Italy had yet even fully to recognize, not least of all as the "Southern Question." Perhaps it is unfair to observe that more than Gramsci could realize, the United States would also ever be hamstrung by the consequences of its own southern question. In any case, the result, for critical marxism, was the considerable embarrassment caused by the likes of Vladimir Lenin, Leon Trotsky, and Gramsci arguing that for socialists factory civilization was a good thing, especially if one came from Naples or Siberia. For marxists were also modernists, no matter how much some of their number were given to fantasies about images of the good life spent in hunting, herding, fishing, and especially criticism.

After Bolshevism

As far as Western Europe was concerned, the vital impetus of early Bolshevism was spent by World War II. Before long Joseph Stalin was to close up the Comintern, and Palmiro Togliatti was to celebrate polycentrism in the wake of Nikita Khruschev's denunciation of Stalin. As Sassoon says, then, from this point, after Stalingrad, the focus of this particular set of stories shifts more principally to cover the social democratic traditions that dominated the scene after 1945. Now we enter the period of success, consolidation, and unwinding, the playing out of socialism's great influence into the golden age. It could perhaps be said that both fascism and communism resulted in the mutual ruin of the contending forces; socialism, which had nowhere led the antifascist struggle, in a sense emerged into the hiatus that followed the war and this mutual grander exhaustion. For this was also the remarkable moment, now forgotten in the wake of 1989, when the credibility of capitalism slumped. In ideological terms, the Second World War was continuous with the Depression and its unexpected result, planomania. Paradoxically, capitalism's independent claim to generate the good society was retrospectively in discredit, this at the very moment when output was approaching cornucopia levels and Fordism truly arrived in the suburbs, delivered by the 1957 Chevrolet, sugar coated by Hollywood and symbolically represented on television serials. As somebody once said—was it Robert Hughes in *American Visions?*—when one saw those cars, one understood what freedom in America meant. In Europe it meant other things, equally miraculous, for this indeed was the epoch of "miracles," Japanese, Italian, then Brazilian, Mexican, and other. Whether propelled by Fiat or Detroit, the results were similar; consumerism had arrived. Khruschev had dreamed that the Soviets would outdo the Americans by outproducing them; America won the war of ideology in the supermarket. There was another nail in the coffin of communism; once "polycentrism," or the idea of national roads, had been adopted, there was no real need for a revolutionary international, but neither, in the strict sense, was there any longer a need for distinct communist parties. Communist parties, following Bolshevization and the Twenty-one Conditions of the Comintern, had been designed to do what socialist parties could not—to seize power, to act as combat parties rather than as passive if positive countercultures in the manner of the SPD.

If, now, social democracy was again sufficient to steer national politics, communist parties were moribund. This was exactly the story as it unfolded, for example, in Australia, where the Communist Party, founded in 1920, dissolved back into the Australian Labor Party in 1984. Plainly the story is different in Italy, where the PCI has been more like a labor party than anything else, a "broad church" capable of holding together Catholics and communists, intellectuals and workers, and even cultural apparatchiks and entrepreneurs. The postwar period made the PCI respectable, as it did the British Labor Party and its Australian equivalent. For this was a moment when national-patriotic identity went to the left. The most brilliant yet ordinary strategy of class alliance came to fruition; and this, of course, is what we have lost in the meantime, as both workers and a globalizing new middle class take their votes elsewhere. More, as Sassoon argues, this was a period when mainstream sensibilities moved left, and Christian democrats did as much as social democrats to web out the welfare net. If Sassoon's own chosen century began in 1889, other connected stories opened just after that, even in response to the politics of the labor movement, in the form of Pope Leo XIII's encyclical *Rerum Novarum* and its associated Catholic radical streams around distributism. The confluence of factors, again, should not surprise us too much; if the contemporary idea of the welfare state is something we associate with Britain or Sweden, its origins lie with Germany, but with its Bismarckian initiatives well before Lloyd George's national if partial insurance scheme of 1911. The welfarist consensus was contested, yet it was powerful for all that; it was not only the voice of William Beveridge but that of Winston Churchill that in 1943 advocated support "from the cradle to the grave." For even Churchill argued for full employment, compulsory national insurance and health insurance, and a massive housing program, and, as Sassoon reminds us, all this reflected precisely the amazing unpopularity of capitalism everywhere in Europe immediately after the war. Between 1945 and 1950, not a single pro-capitalist liberal party was elected to government anywhere in Europe. But the practical victory for socialists and labor was largely fuelled by social liberalism, per Keynes and Beveridge, both of them characteristically open to the intellectual possibility of socialism if politically skeptical about its independent feasibility.

That social democrats were unable to generate new and vital positions in this situation is hardly surprising to readers of Georg Wilhelm Friedrich Hegel; we understand too late. Thus it seems a little harsh for Sassoon to characterize postwar leftists' fears of further depression as "pessimistic" and "erroneous'; they too were living out of the shadows of war and the Great Depression, and the golden age, as most critical commentators now seem to agree, was the most exceptional of epochs, one we are unlikely to relive again after any obvious fashion. At the same time, these fears were to open up into more positive expectations, such that into the 1960s it momentarily seemed plausible that Bernstein had been right after all: there was some kind of process of socialization from within under way; we were all (again) socialists now, liberals at least. Yet many socialists simultaneously remained attached to the sense that, whether by the accumulation of reforms or by some other imagined route, socialism could be conceived as an end state, as though we could arrive there, finally, and know it, and as though we could remain there. Marxists, for their part, often behaved as though it were capitalism that was revolutionary and dynamic even if crisis prone, whereas socialism would be still and calm and, once achieved, would be so conspicuously superior a state of affairs as to remain unchallenged. Such longer-term species of paradox coexisted with more immediate kinds. Thus socialist parties, more specifically social democratic parties, had to come to grips with the fact that capitalism and reformism were symbiotic. In order to pay for social welfare, it was imperative that markets be made as efficient as possible. As Sassoon puts it more sharply, to follow "socialist" policies it was essential to be pro-capitalist. These were not the high dramatic kinds of ironies of history contemplated by Bolshevik scholars like Isaac Deutscher, but they were equally puzzling as his theorems concerning defeat in victory or victory in defeat.

Sassoon makes the conceptual connection more explicably on some occasions than others. If socialism really is to be understood as a phenomenon of modernity, its relation to capitalism remains as necessary as it may be enigmatic. Even the period's leftist enthusiasm for nationalization was based on the sense that, left on its own, capitalism would not sufficiently modernize. Karl Marx's own fundamental ambivalence in the critique of political economy echoed across the radical common sense of our century: capitalist dynamism was the great incipient hope, while capitalism as we knew it was sloppy, disorganized, hopeless. Though Marxists then willfully dismissed the older idea that socialism was best defined as capitalism without capitalists, they also smuggled this sensibility in the back door. Perhaps they could not do otherwise, within the practical and conceptual constraints that modernity carries. If socialism was no longer to be conceived as an end state, after history rather than historic in its inception, then this may be as much as we can reasonably hope for.

If socialists were thus capitalists by default, then, as Sassoon reminds us, they were also frequently colonialists. Indeed Bernstein was typical in sharing John Locke's theorem that those who mixed their labor with the soil laid more true claim to it than those who merely occupied it. Not that socialists were not also internationalists, yet the complicity of modernity in colonialism itself could not prevent socialists from the same kinds of racism and elitism. If socialists were capitalists of a kind by virtue of embracing modernity, they were also colonialists by virtue of the same civilizational fact. So it is that modernity remains the big issue, even if it is in the margin or frame of Sassoon's view rather than offering its substance. When Sassoon turns, for example, to the discussion of revisionism between 1950 and 1960, he revives the theme of modernity in the claim that in Europe the left-wing struggle against consumerism, only later to be formalized in famous contemporary texts like Herbert Marcuse's *One Dimensional Man*, often took the form of local opposition to the Americanization of society. Coca-Cola became a major issue, and not only symbolically, for continental leftists would often find themselves directly allied with local wine and beer producers against the importers of logos and consumer goods. Sassoon quotes Maurice Thorez on the matter: "In literature as elsewhere we must ensure that Coca-Cola does not triumph over wine."[9] McDonald's, of course, made Paris, even if Eurodisney is a flop; the processes of globalization will always be uneven, though the symbolic and economic connection between Americanism and globalism is lost on nobody. The argument could be taken further. Certainly sociologists such as Zygmunt Bauman, in *Memories of Class* (1983), and Craig Calhoun, in *The Question of Class Struggle* (1983),[10] have argued the point that socialism is deeply traditionalistic and even in a technical sense reactionary, claiming to represent the communitarianism of the lost past against the corrosive acids of modernity. Ferdinand Tönnies, we must not forget, was also a socialist. Or, if we were to put it differently, and in sympathy with the work of Arnold Toynbee or the antipodean theorist Bernard Smith, just as all modern societies combine archaism and futurism with the present as new, so do socialisms project backward and forward at the same time that they accommodate the present.[11] This can be seen to have been so even more so into the 1980s and 1990s, as conservatives have behaved radically and as social democrats and liberals have argued for civil legacies and traditions disappearing from national cultures under the expanding influence of globalization and its key value, individualism. Thus the apparent irony that trade unions look like dinosaurs today because they owe their national outlook partly to the fact that, however selectively, they *were* the nation. As Marx had put it, right again if diagonally, the working classes were fixed, stuck, whereas it was the members of the bourgeoisie that knew no ultimate fatherland or motherland; they could always leave, catch a plane, and carry on regardless in the next safe walled city or middle-class enclave. European liberals and social democrats faced the localized version of these problems for those who would stay at home—how to generate American consumption levels without an American regime of production. How to achieve the European version of American consumer society was, as Sassoon puts it, the real political issue of the 1950s, which is where all those miracles came into the picture. What remained less well situated in this picture was Pax Americana, the cold war, the international as well as consumerist imperatives of the United States. If socialists really lusted after something like capitalism without capitalists, perhaps they also found themselves in a modern field where nirvana looked like Americanism without America.

Socialism after Modernity

In Sassoon's interpretation, then, the modernization of socialist tradition became the form in which socialism eventually renounced the ambition of developing noncapitalist economic relations. A different twist could also be put on this view, for in a way it aligns the various socialisms too exclusively with the marxism that came to dominate them. The local socialisms that opened up into and after the 1820s were given not so much to the idea of the negation of private property as to gentler notions of its distribution; in the words of Francis Bacon, "money is like muck, it needs best to be spread around." Socialisms of these other kinds were more opposed to individualism, socialism-individualism, than to private property as such, as in capitalism-socialism. Anyway, as those representing the long trend from Marx himself to Joseph Schumpeter suspected, socialism was a variation on capitalism rather than its negation, as the Marx of the *Paris Manuscripts* hoped. Revisionism, then, whether in the hands of Bernstein in fin-de-siècle Germany or later in those of Douglas

Jay, Tony Crosland, and Evan Durbin in postwar Britain, was again the symptom of an imaginary adjustment to modernity. To open to the right, in this sense, was also to open up socialism to its old and rejected sibling, liberalism itself. Marxism was let go as the image of an end state; the idea of stasis as utopia was gradually rejected. The socialist movement's own imperatives lapsed into the minimalist demands of the *Communist Manifesto* and the Erfurt Program. The ghost of Kautsky was, as Sassoon says, finally exorcized, and with it the schizoid coupling of revolutionary rhetoric and reforming practice; as Kautsky had it, infamously, the SPD of his reign was a "revolutionary but not a revolution-making" party. Crisis theory finally went out the window, together with the two-class model and "the worse, the better" claims of emiseration theory. Proletarian mythology in any case had long been compromised by the necessity of constructing class alliances. The road from Crosland to Tony Blair, Bernstein to Willy Brandt was less convoluted than it may at first have seemed. But the interim was also a fascinating experience, for as Sassoon narrates, the left returned with a vengeance in the meantime.

The very arrival of abundance helped to trigger the 1960s with its politics of refusal, the most visible form of romantic anticapitalism yet encountered, as hippie culture spurned capitalism before discovering how to put the counterculture to profitable ends. As I tried to show in my 1994 book *Postmodern Socialism,* it seems actually to be the case that so far from generating its own forms of modern consciousness, modernity calls on romanticism perhaps even more than it relies practically on the Enlightenment.[12] If we are moderns, we are also ambivalent or hesitant moderns; think only of the sociological classics—Marx, Weber, Georg Simmel, Durkheim, and Tönnies—or think of the practical impact of suburban utopia across the twentieth century. If the left became the advocate of local modernization, it also often held this ambition together with the nostalgia of tradition, especially in places such as France or Britain, where modernity was less a capitalist than a nascent technocratic creed. In Britain in the 1960s, as in Australia into the 1970s and then the 1980s, it fell to labor parties to seek out modernization. Marx's premises concerning capitalist dynamism were somewhat selective; some capitalisms were more dynamic than others. Some capitalisms consistently denied Marx's prognostications regarding the relentless thirst for profits; some firms seemed to continue almost forever turning in minimal or negative profits. Capitalists, it seemed, also seemed to enjoy not making profits, at least where Anglo traditions encouraged ruthlessly adversarial industrial relations or, as Michal Kalecki had put it, where the pursuit of more strictly political desires for control dominated economic desires for productivity. Like some welfare states, some capitalisms work better, more effectively, and more humanly than others. As Sassoon insists, however, the idea of national models will not really work, for although all governments might learn from others, the modular sense of an exportable Swedish or Austrian package will not wash, for these experiments are all irredeemably local in their grounding or comparative advantage. When it comes to matters of class struggle, parochialism or local culture rules, except in those instances in which internationalism intervenes. The challenge for local labor movements, as I tried to show in *Transforming Labor* (1994),[13] is to work tradition and modernity together without succumbing absolutely to the imperatives of globalization or the fuzzy nostalgia for imagined pasts. But to say this is also only to return to Sassoon's analytical observation that socialists have far too blithely projected socialism, their own desire, onto labor movements that, while sometimes radical or at least solidaristic, have also been deeply committed to the politics of consumerism in the material world. So, as Sassoon suggests, even the halcyon images of the 1960s also contain a more sober note, of trade unions hitting hard to improve wages and conditions in the here and now. High levels of strike activity in the 1960s are open to various possible interpretations, just as it is difficult finally to isolate any single explanation of why some welfare states became more comprehensive or minimalist than others. Wildcat strikes or occupations remain far more symbolically loaded than annual strike day measures, which obviously indicate intrasystemic economic struggle more than they do breakouts of radical politics.

The main union game, however, was less wildcat than corporatist. So income policies or social contracts became a major motif or aspiration of postwar social development in the West. Planomania's slimmer legacy from the 1930s slipped into the postwar period with a modicum of formal participation added. Those on the left, meantime, gushed over the slogan of worker-student alliance, though as Sassoon recounts, even the roseate mystique around the May '68 "events" in Paris tended to keep each social group marching separately, if together. The social movements of the 1960s affected the socialist parties in other more tangible ways. If, as Sassoon nicely puts it in slogan form, modernity meant America plus Sweden, modernization also meant the liberation of women into labor markets. The events of 1968, too, fit the schema of modernization after the fact. The new left, in retrospect, seems less impressive than the women's movement. Maybe this is because we were in it, dressed up in clothes that now seem ridiculous, and substituted sex, drugs, and rock and roll for politics. As I suggested earlier, and as I argued more extensively in *Postmodern Socialism*, what this also revives is the issue of the attractions of romanticism and antimodernism for moderns. Sassoon takes up an agnostic stance when it comes to problems of explaining the hippy culture, not least of all the fascinating moment when the British pop invasion turned the tables on America. How could it be that the traditionalistic British could outrock the Americans who had pioneered the cultural transformation of blues into rock and formed a new modern and popular culture with it?

Part of the explanation can be anticipated in terms of the flows of cultural traffic and in more conventional claims about the historical significance of seaport cultures in the flows of cultural traffic. The British also had at their cultural disposal a neat romantic channel to orientalism in their postcolonial relationship with India. The Beatles and the Maharishi were a new symbolic representation of an old colonial relationship, one based not only on imperial arrogance but also on romantic desire for the other, not-Birmingham, not-Manchester or -Liverpool. Thus, as Sassoon reminds us, the British (and Australian) student radicals of the 1960s were fundamentally anti-American but in deeply ambivalent ways. Criticizing the rotten leaders of the United States, separating the corrupt establishment from respect for the decent people who were screwed by them, radicals still often remained aligned with the American model of modernity, even if they disliked Americans. Perhaps more than this, though, radicals the world over embraced romanticism because they wanted out of America in their heads; as Marcuse put it, they wanted out of the asphalt car parks and back into the fields of grass. Whatever the case, these people mixed styles and cultures; they were often given to authoritarian antiauthoritarianism, to the romantic cult of Che Guevara and Leon Trotsky taped together with putatively antiestablishment bands like The Who and the Rolling Stones.

So why did "alienation" become a symbol of the 1960s? Sassoon also pokes at this issue and finds it puzzling. Perhaps the question is too close or confining. The "1960s" occurred in various places across different times, especially, I think, actually into the 1970s, and the cultural attributes of that decade have since been recycled and are presently being recycled in various different places. One key connection that eludes Sassoon's commentary, even if it is a textual one, is the translation of Marx's *Paris*

Manuscripts into the 1960s. Here was a marketing opportunity made in heaven, if only it could have been anticipated at the time. Probably very few actually read Marx, though it seems likely that many read his momentary romantic reincarnation in Marcuse. For Marx named what was perceived to be a problem as alienation, and the term arrived at the peak of the romantic anticapitalist or hippie response to modernity in the 1960s. Translated into English twenty years later or twenty years earlier, Marx's *Manuscripts* would have simply disappeared, as the *Grundrisse* did into the 1970s. None of which is to say that the translation of Marx's work itself had any necessarily historical effect; the point, rather, is that these kinds of elective affinities can be drawn out of the period in order to make it less baffling than it might appear. Just as Sassoon observes elsewhere, it was also the case that the work of Louis Althusser (and later, Michel Foucault) had a striking effect on the new left culture, for it combined an apparently libertarian or maoist politics of refusal with a picture of modernity as the fixed state apparatus or the immovable prison house. The oddities of theory may not lead or even just reflect, but they do offer some keyhole optics into processes elsewhere, apart from the academics and the bookshops.

Social Democracy's Failure in Success

Feminism, meantime, was a theory that also ran together with movements and with the patterns of social transformation increasingly characteristic of this period. Does Sassoon overplay all this? Certainly Tony Judt has protested so in a review of Sassoon's book in the *Times Literary Supplement* (November 8, 1996). Although Judt praised the book, he also criticized the proportions of its coverage—not enough concern with Eastern Europe and too much with feminism for his taste. As Judt complained, there is something intuitively wrong with a history of socialism in the twentieth century that devotes more space "to the 'woman question' in the 1980's than to the Social Democratic Party of Germany between 1890 and 1933." This is no simple misogynist wheeze, however; Judt's complaint is that Sassoon's own optic is too presentist, too much caught up with the politics we now (some of us) inhabit, where feminism in some ways has displaced socialism, in the politics both of the street and of the academy—as though one cannot talk of socialism without talking about feminism. In one sense, this is entirely correct; for one cannot talk about socialism without talking about fascism, Catholicism, eugenics, theosophy, or ecological radicalism. Yet (to make a connection that would horrify

Judt) there is also something in this critical response that Althusser would have called the failure to properly constitute a theoretical object: we cannot by the nature of discourse speak of everything at once; woe betide us if we do. My own response to this issue is therefore slightly different; as I anticipated earlier, it does seem to me that Sassoon, the self-described historian, is more engaged in sociology than perhaps he would like, and as *One Hundred Years of Socialism* increasingly focuses on the postwar period of West European social democracy, so does the theory and practice of the women's movement become more central to his story. In other words, this may be a historicist slide in itself; if, as Gramsci recommends, we find ourselves puzzling over national paths of development and transformation, the strictly defined analytical object of "socialism" may actually give way to other patterns of movement.

If we accept this kind of methodological unfolding on Sassoon's part, the problems of interpretation become more interesting. In this instance, I think, Sassoon aligns feminism and socialism too singularly with the image of modernity or modernism. It is true, as Sassoon puts it, that both movements were children of the modern world. Only Sassoon proceeds to argue as though both socialism and feminism were modernist, not only of modernity. I do not think it will do to portray both movements as antitraditional; for both had, among other icons, their respective images of the New Jerusalem. Contrary to Sassoon's claim, feminists could and did hark back to millenarian claims, not least of all per arguments to matriarchy or mother right, just as the workers' movement could construct its own rhetoric back through lineages of peasant and popular struggle, back even to Spartacus, to Lilith or Hecate. What can it mean, then, when Sassoon insists that for socialists and feminists "the past had to become scorched earth"? Plainly both movements were modernizing, and both were formally dependent on the field we know as modernity; both also held, and still contain, a need and even a reverence for tradition that now, we should imagine, is itself also a defining attribute of modernity. Certainly the utopias of the labor movement act out and back as much as they anticipate and yet fear the shock of the new. What remains central here, in our lives if less in Sassoon's book, is the deep sense of modernity as ambivalence that was expressed in Marx's work and articulated later through Georg Simmel and, in our own time, in the critical sociology of Zygmunt Bauman.

The theoretical connection is important, too, because of the ambivalence that moderns of both sexes bring to the experience of wage labor.

We love it, need it, and hate it; we survive as actors in the public sphere, arguably, only because there remain private spheres to hold us up. Every other day we long for the past, even as we plunge wilfully into the future, and the present dissolves in between.

Returning to Sassoon's narrative, his argument is that the triumph of postwar capitalism was the triumph of regulated capitalism, to which I would add only one small qualification: it was the triumph of a particular kind of regulation, for the consensus since Karl Polanyi's *Great Transformation* seems rather to have been that all markets are licensed and regulated but in distinct kinds of ways. This is only to say, in more conventionally Durkheimian terms, that all capitalisms also need to deal with problems of social solidarity, however decisive or absent they may seem. The coincidence that worked for socialists, then, was that between high levels of growth and high employment levels. Unemployment, then, became the single most important factor in the decline of trade unions' strength. Social democracy's strength is inversely related to unemployment. Social democracy or welfarism retained stronger prospects in smaller countries such as Austria, Sweden, Holland, and Norway, where local cultures were more solidaristic and political habits more often consociational and consensual. Here the prospects for full employment, not only full male employment, also appeared stronger, though initiatives along the lines of increasing female labor participation now increasingly coincide with the restriction and privatization of welfare support in child care, health, and education. Industry development policy, in this context, arguably reflects the old masculine interests of the labor movement over those of the women who work part time and often in tertiary rather than secondary industry. The distinction serves to remind us that globalization processes can also be expected to have highly uneven effects for women, given the connection between globalization and service industries. Modernization, in any case, as Sassoon observes, is a strategy that points away from the traditional values of the socialist movement, away from state ownership and the working class. But where, then, does it point? In France, Sassoon argues, the arrow of postindustrial progress pointed to the value of self-management, *autogestion,* which has the combined virtue and vice of meaning all things to all people. Self-management saw the revived socialist forces ride to power while the French communists took out the garbage. Behind the good vibes of self-management, however, there stood no economic strategy except that of the old Keynesianism, reflation and public ownership. All those parties in the streets were premature, or else they became unwitting anticipations of the *danse macabre* of French socialism.

More than anywhere else in Europe, the French kept up their anti-American shutters, at least when it came to claims about culture and Coca-Cola. As Sassoon puts it, the strength of French socialism remained different, as a cultural phenomenon, because, unlike German or British socialism, French socialism can legitimately claim to be the inheritor of a national revolutionary tradition. The politics of nationalization could therefore still be defended, momentarily, as a national policy in France. Tradition still held on by its fingernails against modernization. In ideological terms, however, this process of socialist modernization had turned in on itself. At the end of the François Mitterand experience, the French left looked more bankrupt than it ever had before. The hopes kindled in the PCI, meantime, had come to little, while the collapse of the authoritarian regimes in Portugal, Spain, and Greece plainly represented progress, if not of the degree that socialists had hoped for. By 1980, while Althusser and others were still discussing the older theme of the "crisis of marxism," Alain Touraine announced, "Socialism is dead."[14] Yet, as Sassoon recalls, this kind of edict could not help, even then, but sound odd; ten years earlier it would have elicited laughter or scorn. Socialists may have responded to the economic crises with far too much narcissistic confidence, yet the sense that the problems remained itself echoed powerfully across the 1980s, became muffled for a few years after 1989, and then resurfaced as problems of German reunification and the Russian mafia expanded. Socialism, meantime, did not disappear; it coexisted with Margaret Thatcher and Ronald Reagan both domestically and elsewhere in Western Europe, with complications. The welfare state was subject to various lines of attack, but it did not disappear. Some socialists began to argue that markets could deliver socialist services, that the ends could be retained while the means of delivery were modernized. The industrial proletariat continued to shrink, but then socialism had never depended singularly on its support in any case. Sassoon expresses the problem more strikingly, however, in relaying the news that by now the typical member of the British Labor Party—one of the most class-bound parties in Europe in terms of image and rhetoric—was, by 1989, middle-class, middle-aged, and—here only, no surprise—still male. All of which suggests a Christmas bonus for Tony Blair, who mirrors this phenomenon as much as he seeks to harness it. Maybe modernization will get the better of him, as it did Mikhail Gorbachev and all those before him who unleashed change in order to ride it. As Marx had pondered in 1847, the path of modern history looked too much like the story of the sorcerer's apprentice, an image itself later appropriated for market purposes by Disney, now as a comic rather than a tragic motif.

Before the fall of the Berlin Wall, socialism had turned back to liberalism, already, to claims concerning citizenship and social rights, justice, dignity, and equality. This was also, paradoxically, a return to practice in a sense against theory, to the practical message of a century of struggle now embodied in institutions and traditions. This is exactly what Eduard Bernstein had meant by revisionism: not an antitheoretical theory so much as a theory driven by practice as well as by ethics. What has been lost in this is not only the scholastic side of socialism, in which marxists, in particular, specialized. Sassoon quotes Olof Palme, speaking in 1975: "We socialists live to some extent in symbiosis with capitalism. The labour movement was a reaction to capitalism."[15] But it was more. The labor movement or the working class also made capitalism. The image of authorship or agency so central to socialism a century ago has lapsed. None of us feels in control anywhere, except instantaneously perhaps in the shopping malls. The only apparent consolation that Sassoon can find in this is the possibility that movement is life. To stand still is to let go, even if moving forward is no guarantee of success.

In his epilogue to this story, Donald Sassoon returns, finally, to the status of communism and marxism at the end of our century. His verdict on communism is ambivalent: "Communism as an instrument of modernization was not a failure. Communism as an instrument for the emancipation of human beings from the servitude of necessity was a catastrophe."[16] Without making too much of the disagreement, let me suggest that Sassoon's assessment of the twentieth century fails completely to convince, in part because it is aligned too sympathetically with Eric Hobsbawm's in *The Age of Extremes*. Like Sassoon's book, Hobsbawm's is a great one that has rightly been widely applauded. My own reading of Hobsbawm, for what it is worth, is that it is too heavily biographical in its assessment of the respective status of communism and fascism. To make an obvious association, Hobsbawm seems to me to work within a Deutscherist view, incredibly influential especially in Britain and popularized on the new left through the work of *New Left Review,* for which at the end of the day the Soviet experience must be defended because socialist. I shall not labor the criticism here, because it is elaborated in a book I published ten years ago titled *Trotsky, Trotskyism, and the Transition to Socialism.*[17] To put it more plainly, Bolshevism is viewed in this optic as morally superior to fascism because it committed abominable acts in the name of noble ends. Now, this narrative may be defensible in the case of Hobsbawm's book because it represents the main radical explanation available to his generation, and Hobsbawm's case is distinct because his own life and his object of analysis, the twentieth century, directly coincide. As critics like Michael Mann have argued, however, Hobsbawm, too, bifurcates left and right, as is evident even in his choice of a title for his book, where the extremities never meet.[18] As I have suggested, though, left and right should be conceptually and historically aligned where the sympathies can be discerned, as well as separated because one stream (to truncate) is humanist and the other antihumanist. If, however, there are murderers in both sets of families, there is no point in denying this or in avoiding its implications. From a perspective or experience different to Hobsbawm's, the extremes are not communism and fascism but both against social democracy.

As Sassoon returns in closing to communism, so he necessarily returns to Marx. Certainly Sassoon foregrounds social democracy, where Hobsbawm focuses on communism. Was Marx responsible for all this mess, these roads to hell paved with the skulls of the well-intentioned as well as the bystanders? Here it seems to me that the cleavages are clearer. Marx may have helped generate some mischief, but he was no Bolshevik; probably he would have taken tea with Kautsky rather than the soapbox with Lenin. But Sassoon lets Marx off the theoretical hook too readily in asserting that Marx "never developed a theory of socialism."[19] My argument in *Labour's Utopias* is that Marx developed at least five varying utopias stretching from romantic in *The Paris Manuscripts* to modernist in *Capital* but failed to systematize these clues. To say, with Sassoon, that Marx was "contemptuous of those who wrote utopian blueprints"[20] is to repeat a cliché at the expense of arguing about utopia as a field of tension between modernity and tradition. Utopia remains vital not least of all because although it is one thing to recognize that all political arguments embody utopic elements, it is another to accept the sense that all that is left is what is in history today, that the only choices we have even in principle are between, say, Japan, Europe, and America. Even Bernstein hoped for more than that. Yet we need to acknowledge that Sassoon's is a tough brief—it is a brief with a moral problem attendant on all who believe in socialism and write about it. How does one tell the truth without encouraging radical depression? Sassoon knows, as did Gramsci, that this story is not over and that socialism remains a cultural current even if it is now formally unrecognizable, because it is so fully implicated in capitalism and in our fin-de-siècle turmoil. The irony, as he concludes, may be that the idea of socialism does not remain like a lone survivor from the lost Atlantis; rather, the idea may die at the very moment that socialist parties survive. As Sassoon laments, in his final words in this book, "these parties are the only Left that is left."

Conclusions

Let me conclude for my own part by drawing together some of these threads. Sassoon, in my view, is fundamentally correct in reading his period, 1889–1989, as a kind of watershed or historic moment that saw the consolidation both of capitalism and socialism. The two experiences are historically and conceptually inseparable, but not only because, say, marxism emerged as the critique of political economy that is also its mirror (Jean Baudrillard) or shares its imaginary universe (Cornelius Castoriadis). Sassoon's frame for thinking socialism is valuable because, although he retains many of the critical insights of marxism, he also steps beyond and outside it in order to locate marxism within modernity rather than the other way around. Analytically speaking, this is to step away from Marx via the traditions of critical theory, which combined Marx and Weber, via Lukács, to Weber's own project, where power is pluralized and capitalism is a key problem but not the only one. To become open to modernity is simultaneously to place or limit marxism and also to register the profundity of its critical claims. Marxism can no longer claim to be the sole philosophical discourse of modernity, but it is equally difficult to imagine modernity without marxism. The collapse of marxism, in this way of thinking, is less a loss than a transformation. We now inhabit the incredible moment in which at the same time nobody believes in marxism and yet everybody accepts its basic premise—economy rules, not least of all because globalization rules.

Although we can easily agree with those notional claims that, say, the twentieth century was the American century, it seems to me that Sassoon is onto something more profound with the idea that for socialists our century started and finished early. Although many would also draw inspiration from the older idea recycled by Hobsbawm, that our century started in 1914 and ended in 1989, that insight also has its limits. To speak of the American century is to raise more questions than answers, which is exactly the vocation intellectuals ought to pursue. Hobsbawm's short twentieth century also condenses, in different ways; 1914 leads directly to 1917, the beginning of the communist experiment as state power, so Hobsbawm is telling us very clearly (and profoundly) that the twentieth century was less the American than the Soviet century, or the century in which hope opened for the left because of the October Revolution. This, it seems to me, is a reflection of the kind of Deutscherism that views the Russian Revolution as the great fact, just as others constructed the French Revolution as the unifying and condensing symbol for modernity. But this is to truncate too much, especially when it comes to the Russian Revolution. If Weber's advice to Lukács was correct, as now seems clear, this is not only to truncate the story of modernity but also to reduce it thus, under the wrong sign. Trotsky was sharper than this even to begin to think modernity as the epoch of wars and revolutions. For it is arguably that experience of wars and revolutions that held up the twentieth century, and from which we are only now departing.

The rough dates I have chosen to mark these sea-changes in *Transforming Labor* and in *Postmodern Socialism* are only moderately different from Sassoon's. My own sense is that the period 1880–1980 marked a phase of coalescence in new liberal, labor, and socialist thought and practice that made capitalism strong and socialism its social partner. Blue Books, Birmingham radicalism, Friedrich Engels and Sidney Webb on housing, and guaranteed minimum—all this made a piece. To speak plainly, that century was marked by a disputed consensus that social problems could be both registered or recognized and resolved. Socialism was the answer to a question called the social question. The world we have lost on this account was one to do with the will to reform. The slide back to the individualism of the older economic liberalism is a slide back to the other side of the will to reform. Postmodern chaos and postmodern markets seem simply beyond control; we have chosen to construct them as beyond control, to accept that the game called civilizing capitalism is over, although it cannot be over for once and for all when a capitalist such as George Soros becomes a communitarian; nothing can remain the same, neither socialism (or what replaces it) nor capitalism. So there is no certainty at all that economic liberalism or so-called deregulation will last indefinitely; the more serious question is what the scope for renewal might be after the present wave of globalization. For social democracy is the most alive form of socialism, whether we compare Bolshevism with Fabianism and social democracy as national projects, as I have in *Labour's Utopias,* or whether we track, with Sassoon, the expansion and involution of communism and the reconvergence of social democracy in the wake of World War II. And social democracy is, as we have seen, a national project; that is precisely why socialism is so much endangered by globalization. Citizenship, in other words, is also national; the idea of global citizenship is a chimera, for social justice and social rights are delivered and protected (or not) by nation-states. Whatever the virtues of cultural globalization or multiculturalism, the kind of internationalization offered by economic globalization is both bourgeois and revolutionary; it carries the kind of creative destruction that Marx anticipated and Schumpeter then named—more creation for some, more destruction for others—too slow to capitalize on change or to take up cudgels for the sorcerer.

Finally, then, we come to face frontally a contradiction built into modernity and into Sassoon's attempt to capture it analytically through narrating the socialist tradition since the 1890s. None of us can escape change, nor can we control it, seek though we may to do so. There is no end state, neither a capitalist nor a socialist one. As I have argued in *Postmodern Socialism,* what this means for the left is not only that we have lost the comfortable illusion that socialism will ever actually arrive or arrive to stay. To extend Sassoon's argument just a little, the issue for socialists today is that we have lost the tension. The point is not that socialism has failed to conquer capitalism so much as it is that socialism has failed to keep its role as the alter ego of capitalism. Not victory, but the struggle, is what matters. Socialism is to capitalism as slave is to master in Hegel's image, adopted by Marx and spread by Alexandre Kojève; or so it was and ought to be. Not because we should believe in its certainty of arrival as an end state so much as because it is (so to say) the struggle between them that held together the fibers of our lives. What we have lost, today, is the painful yet creative tension between the forces and ideologies that we used to call "capitalism" and "socialism." As Sassoon puts it, as Michels and Weber anticipated, we are left with the ideologically empty or exhausted machines of institutionalized party politics. Or, to put it differently, the causes we imagined and hoped for and associated with socialism no longer have any institutional bearers; they have been reduced for better or worse to the norms and ethics that inform both socialism and social liberalism. Historically it has been the experience of unfreedom, as Orlando Patterson has shown in *Freedom,* that itself generates not only suffering but also the cry for freedom.[21] The risk today is that we encounter the unfreedom but less the call for its transcendence.

The challenge for socialists today remains not to achieve transcendence but to act as though freedom and dignity remain possible. In the context of the moment we inhabit, this is nowhere near as minimal an assertion as it may seem viewed from the lofty heights and the lower depths of the revolutionary tradition.

Donald Sassoon's book is a book for our time. We can only hope that its publisher will put it out in paperback and distribute it widely. What we are left with, at the end of the Hegelian day, may nevertheless be more than the parties; it may be something more like a culture. Sassoon does not refer to Gabriel Garcia Márquez in this connection, yet *One Hundred Years of Socialism* evokes *One Hundred Years of Solitude*. The conclusion of Márquez's book, if I remember correctly, is poignant; races that are condemned to one hundred years of solitude do not have a second opportunity on earth. Socialism may, however, as William Morris already hoped a century ago, yet recycle in other forms, for the struggle continues. It continues to hold up modernity as an attitude and a project; it continues to animate our everyday lives and our hopes beyond them. One hundred years of socialism is a story to be proud of, to draw strength from as well as wisdom. The ghosts of the radical traditions will shadow us in this, as is their wont. We shall see what the next century brings . . . promises as well as threats, new beginnings as well as closure.

(1997)

Eleven

Intellectuals and Utopians

Sociology, the textbooks tell us, depends on self-reflexivity; for we sociologists seem to have a characteristic knack of knowing what is wrong in what other people do, but never in what we do. Zygmunt Bauman's sociology is persistently self-reflexive; his view is that we, too, are part of the problem, indeed that we as intellectuals or legislators aspirant have been a big part of the problem of modernity. Our attraction to the modern possibility of change sometimes leads us to value change over everything else; yet we cannot deny, either, that the world needs changing, even if it is less immediately clear than ever exactly whose responsibility this task is. Thinking, acting, interpreting, dreaming — these are nevertheless some of our major activities. Seeking out the balance seems to be the most impossible of challenges, yet it is also the most interminable.

Socialism — the Active Utopia

Utopia is a ubiquitous presence in the lives of moderns. We love it, we hate it; we know that the world needs change, yet we resist or detest the changes sponsored by others, which often seem to make the world less inhabitable than it was before. Into the twentieth century the story intensified, for then we encountered utopia in power, in the Soviet experiment, and then under fascism. Utopia, dystopia, George Orwell's *1984*, Aldous Huxley's *Brave New World*, alternative models of living from the

Shakers to the hippies, dreams to go forward or back— utopia seems almost to enclose the modern experience, encompassing both the desire for self-creation and the horrors of rational mastery.

Attitudes toward utopia are also likely to shift historically and conjuncturally; these are not simply matters of personal taste. The practical and theoretical Western enthusiasm for utopia of the 1960s indicated the relative abundance of that moment; then we had the luxury of realizing that social arrangements did not mirror economic potentials. Utopianism, however, can also be romantic or modernizing, as the themes of Bauman's *Memories of Class* (1982) suggest. Some utopias are born in the blackest of moments, though we should also contemplate the fact that there have been, in a sense, no utopias after Auschwitz; at least utopia then became contemplative again rather than active.

Bauman's vision of utopia was positive when, in 1976, he published *Socialism: The Active Utopia*. This was a good moment in his life; settled in Leeds after years of disappointment and harassment, he dedicated the book to his twin daughters: "To Irena and Lydia—my twin utopias." Actually existing socialism, or its concrete representatives, may have expelled the Baumans from Poland, but in the spirit of that period of Marx renaissance, Bauman opened his book with a characteristic claim: "Socialism descended upon nineteenth-century Europe as utopia."[1] Reality was to be measured against the ideal, against utopia; it was the latter, the project of socialism, that remained both defensible and desirable. But more, utopia is real; it is part of us, the part that remains uneasy at the sense of the achievement or arrival of our great civilizations. If normality generates conformity, utopianism is vital even in its most fantastic or ridiculous guises. Societies like ours, based on the hegemony of instrumental reason, need mental space to discuss ends and hopes. Utopias were significant, for Bauman, in four generic ways. First, utopias relativize the present. They offer us criteria other than immanent measures in order to take stock of where we are and where we are heading. They open horizons of comparison, but unlike history, they evoke not only past achievements but also future possibilities, more or less imaginary (13). Yet second, utopias are also significant because they are aspects of culture in which possible extrapolations of the present may be explored. Utopias are driven by hope, but they can also be concrete; they express the possible hopes of an age, and they say something about its capacities (15). Third, utopias are useful because they pluralize; they generate dissensus rather than false harmony, even though individual utopian projects might themselves enthuse about false harmony or stasis. Utopias split the shared reality we inhabit into a series of competing projects for the future and assessments of the present. This is why one person's utopia is another's dystopia. Utopias are political, in the best sense of the word, in that they express distinct and competing images of the good society, images whose expression often coincides with the activity of distinct social groups (15). Fourth, utopias do in fact exert enormous influence on the actual course of historical events. Utopias have an "activating presence"; yesterday's utopia—like the idea of guaranteed income—may be on today's social policy agenda.

As Bauman summarized, utopia is an image of a future and better world, which is not at all inevitable so much as it is desirable; which is critical of that which exists, and in this sense is beyond practical realization; and which relies politically on the possibility of collective action (17). Not all utopias, then, are socialist, but socialism has been the most prominent member in the family. Of course, the figure of utopia is also classical, arcing back at least to Plato; but modern utopias are different, and this is where socialism comes into its prominence. For socialism has always been caught up with the sense of change that we identify as modern, and this whether positively, as futuristic, or negatively, as romantic in tenor (18–19). Francis Bacon, not Plato, was the face of its earlier vision; the distinction in Bauman's mind is similar to that in Émile Durkheim's lectures on socialism, where communism looks back, to simplicity, and socialism is a modern, future-oriented, modernizing force.[2] The commune seeks stasis; socialism, by comparison, is complicit in the very restlessness of modernity itself. Socialism mirrors capitalism, and this is one of its weaknesses as well as its strengths—it seeks out perfectibility rather than perfection (19). Thus the complicity of socialism in social engineering, and ultimately in Jacobinism. Jacobinism is based conceptually on the image of the weak individual who needs only to be led by Those Who Know (21). Jacobinism is a kind of utopianism based on contempt for the impassive, the ordinary, the present, the impure, the unwashed (22). Marx short-circuited this logic of contempt and leadership only by introducing the impossible, the idea that capitalism automatically generates its own fatal economic contradictions or else its own proletarian gravediggers. This false marxian solution to the problem of political organization, in turn, opens the door for the Bolsheviks or the New Prince as the missing link to fuse the gap between the proletariat and history (24).

Next Bauman confronted a theme that was to anticipate the path of his life's work into the 1990s: the problem of order. As he announced, with stark clarity, "It is only recently that we have begun to realise the extent to which modern thought is prompted by the cravings of order" (28). Although it is less than controversial to observe that the utopian impulse often historically takes architectural form, Bauman's concern here was rather to probe into the motivation involved. For architecture is coterminous with the thoroughly modern, scientific, social engineering attitude. Utopianism is based on the quest for order (29). With the advent of modernity, order shifted from the realm of "nature" to that of *techne;* this is a fact both "real" and "utopian" in its dimensions, for modernity is the field of social self-constitution. The anthropological and ethical issue here is whether we, as moderns, are prepared to live with the mess or whether we are to become obsessed with the idea of cleaning it up, once and for all (30). As Bauman noted, the central utopian socialists, including Henri de Saint-Simon, Karl Marx, and Edward Bellamy, all remained deeply ambivalent on this score. Their work combined in different ways the lust for change and progress with the very different, residual sense of loss of the past. Perhaps this is why Marx and Bellamy remained caught between Durkheim's imagined options, trapped between communism and socialism, stretched across the desire for simplicity and the thrust toward dynamism.

The emphasis in Bauman's argument, however, is on the distinction between the industrializing socialist intellectuals like Marx and the alternative currents that valued nostalgic dreams about the precapitalist world we had lost (31). As Bauman acknowledged, "Even the most ardent preachers of the new industrial world must have drawn their definition of order, as a safe and predictable situation founded on the regularity and recurrence of human conduct, from the living memory of the past, since it was never demonstrated by the system currently in existence" (31). Utopias, then, will not neatly be classified as exclusively oriented to the past or to the future; progress and nostalgia, hope and memory, will always be caught up together. The real dividing line runs between the preachers of greater complexity and admirers of simplicity, where simplicity conjures up the image of return.

If the presence of Durkheim is often apparent behind arguments in sociology, so does the ghost of Ferdinand Tönnies shadow many of its concerns. Bauman acknowledged this directly when he aligned the value of simplicity with the image of *Gemeinschaft* (31). *Gemeinshaft,* or traditional community, works as the usually unstated image by which much of contemporary sociology still will measure the present; modern sociology, that is to say, has at its heart a deeply traditionalistic core. Marx, too, was a follower of Tönnies without ever knowing it; for what else could the critique of alienation imply than a return to simplicity? For Marx was not only the son of the steam train; and Tönnies, who historically followed him, was also a socialist and a utopian.

Socialism has been, and to some extent still was for Bauman in 1976, the modern utopia. Or else, and here he drew from Tom Bottomore, socialism is the counterculture of capitalism, both within and without it. Yet if socialism has been historically important, its significance as utopia is more powerfully as the not yet. If it is realized, as state power, it will die; at the other extreme, utopia that rests always somewhere beyond would seem merely illusory (36–37). Yet it is modernity that ultimately frames socialism, not capitalism alone; it is modernity, not just capitalism, that is the problem, and in a certain perverse sense it will therefore be modernity (or later, the postmodern), that will be the solution, not socialism. For socialism is also caught up with, and continuous with, liberalism, not only capitalism (42). More precisely, in Bauman's words, "The socialist utopia could present itself as a genuine substitute for the bourgeois way of dealing with the issues of modernity, or as a further stage into which the previous stages smoothly and imperceptibly merge" (48). But the family resemblances across the different socialisms are weak, and dispersed, as in Wittgenstein's sense; they resemble each other, but only in mirroring a different feature. Bauman next addressed Durkheim's use of the specific category socialism to denote the idea of a state-directed economy. But this, too, is a specific rather than a generic image of socialism, and it privileges images of the desirable over the actually achieved (50). Socialism is made a program more than a critical spirit, which is to presume that utopia can be realized concretely, like a builder's plan. This is to substitute an accountant's conception of socialism for its ideal of freedom or equality. For socialism has these two goals, freedom and equality, both of which have been trampled by its enthusiasts (53). But it is also marxism, as an ideology, that opens this slide into economism and gray industrialism. For it is in the hands of its marxist spokesmen that socialism is centered on and thus reduced to economy, or "necessity," whereas early marxism and alternative streams of socialism actually sought to problematize economy itself, not to harness but to transform it. The workers' utopia thus in a certain sense became a bourgeois utopia (58).

Earlier in Bauman's text, as we have noted, he had cleared his throat regarding Antonio Gramsci's idea of the New Prince, the party to end all parties. Certainly the historical trajectory of Gramsci's own thought was away from council communism and toward the new party; likely under fascism and in Mussolini's prison, he could not think otherwise. At this point of his discussion, however, Bauman returned to Gramsci, for whatever the contradictions of the Sardinian's thought, his legacy to the Marx renaissance was among the richest, and Bauman had been contemplating this since the early 1960s, well before the English-speaking new left discovered Gramsci. Further, just as Gramsci was less ideologically available to the thinkers of the Budapest School, who recoiled at the mere mention of the New Prince, so was Georg Lukács more part of the problem for Bauman than part of its solution.

Why Gramsci? Ideology, culture, and civil society were keywords in the reception of his marxism, offering an alternative link to the Bolshevik Party between the socialist idea and its subjects, an argument at once more sophisticated and more democratic in its timbre. Where economy ruled for the orthodox marxists, for Gramsci humans did, even in manners mediated variously through habit, custom, and belief or common sense. Gramsci stood almost alone in viewing socialism as a popular challenge, neither as a historic inevitability, as did Karl Kautsky, nor as something to be seized, as per Vladimir Lenin. State and economy mattered for Gramsci, but citizens inhabited civil society, which was thenceforth where socialists might direct their attentions. The struggle for socialism, for Bauman as for Gramsci, was the struggle for a new culture (65–68). But Gramsci, of course, appeals also to intellectuals, not only because he was one, but also because he took intellectuals seriously; we know one of us when we see one. Popular culture counts, then, but so do the intellectuals who are its cultivators. Although Kautsky viewed social democracy as the confluence of socialism and the working class—an idea and an agent—Gramsci more accurately conceived it as the project of a potential class alliance or a new historic bloc including intellectuals and workers. To acknowledge the importance of the intellectuals, as Gramsci did, was also potentially to foreground them as a problem, as the aspiring social ventriloquists ready to educate and to speak for the uncultured proletariat. At least, in Gramsci's view, we would be spared the pathetic comedy of intellectuals masquerading as pantomime proletarians, at the beginning of the long drama that ends with "We rule you; we fool you; we eat for you; we shoot you; we serve all." The Bolshevik experiment acted on the possibility that economy, not culture, still ruled, that to solve one problem would still imaginably solve the other. Yet the spirit of marxism, as Bauman concluded, was not about the management of the economy, and not even about forms of ownership, but about the activity of the masses. Lenin took the baton, but was unable to run with it (76); perhaps he was actually running somewhere else.

The history of marxism, in any case, was transformed by the Bolshevik initiative. The Soviets were compelled to make a modernity of a particular kind rather than a socialism of a marxian kind. This meant that the Soviets were faced with an impossible challenge: to generate not only a modern economy but also a modern culture and forms of legitimation with it (81). This was exactly the feature that Gramsci had discerned, later and at a distance; seizing state power, as in the Soviet experience, was deceptively easy; the problems came later and were grounded rather in civil society, or perhaps in its weakness in this case. Nevertheless, in Bauman's eyes, one major problem in prerevolutionary Russia was to be located in the fact that the marxists belonged to the emerging civil society rather than to the state; state power was not thrust on them, but the change in mentality across the two spheres was nevertheless dramatic (83).

Lenin identified his party with the people, against the actually existing population. Both the people and the individual were occluded in that process, conceptually and politically. Seeking to sidestep the stage of individuation, as the Bolsheviks did, could only lead to the complete subjugation of the individual by a totally alienated social power (89). No individuals, no possibilities for democracy. Yet the Soviet experience was a path through modernity, of a particular kind. It was a modernizing revolution, bringing together industrialization, urbanization, and nation and state building, that compressed and outachieved earlier capitalist processes of primitive accumulation.

The dominant image of a socialist utopia was thus transformed, industrialized, flattened out; utopia was realized, in a sense, and therefore lost. As Bauman wrote: "It was no longer a utopia on the other side of the industrialisation process. . . . On the contrary, it is now a utopia of industrialisation as such; a capitalist utopia with no room for capitalists, a bourgeois utopia in which the private tycoons of entrepreneurship have been replaced by the grey, smart conformity of the bureaucratic octopus" (91). Socialism, after the Soviet experience, said Bauman in 1976, is a "populist" version of the old bourgeois utopia. Yet the Soviet claim is not simply capitalist, even if the opposition between those who control and those they control is a kind of bipolarization similar to that evident in capitalist class relations (93). One key difference, in the 1970s, remained in the way that politics was directly militarized (96).[3] Politics, in the classical sense, is notable in its absence; but unlike capitalism, it is not economics that sucks up politics but rather the militarized political realm that controls the economy. Bureaucracy rules here, not capital. A good ten years before the Western radical rediscovery of civil society, Bauman suggested that it was only the emergence of civil society alongside the end of scarcity that would potentially open this Soviet scenario up in a socialist direction.

Viewed from the perspective of utopia, however, the problem is even less shiftable; for the Soviet experience has aligned socialism with capitalism, whereas its critical role is caught up with the idea of socialism as the counterculture of capitalism. The hegemony of the Russian Revolution within socialism has meant the closing of radical horizons, the relative disappearance of alternative points of view or judgments of value. Socialism's "success" was now also to be measured by the number of factory chimneys, by the dominance of work discipline, by puritan morality, by all the indicators of industrial progress. The Soviet system came to measure its own perfection and its own progress in the "building of socialism" with the help of a bourgeois measuring rod (100). Socialism, like capitalism, became a dystopia, neither a noplace nor a good place. Socialism, therefore, had to start over (108). The narrowing of modern common sense into its capitalist confines meant that the mere possibility of social alternatives needed to be established again. What began as an idea in search of a constituency had become a constituency in search of an idea (109). Socialism in a sense had become real, practically embodied in both East and West, and therefore had lost its defining, visionary capacity (112).

The role of marxism in all this also became problematical. Although the young Marx imagined a radical solution in a utopia back beyond capitalism and alienation, the Marx of *Capital* had already opened this route in explaining the self-reproduction of capitalism. No guarantees about the negation of the negation could solve this (137). Marx's own vision thus shrank across the path of his thought. Hope, then, needs more than vision or insight. Marx's vision ultimately fell too low, too close to the reality of capitalism. Marx and marxism began to emerge, finally, as part of the problem, not only part of the solution.

Bauman's *Socialism: The Active Utopia* is an inconclusive study. It is a report on the desirability and difficulty of socialist hope. Three themes emerged in it that had special significance for Bauman's later work: labor, order, and intellectuals. The arguments about labor and socialism in this text plainly connect back, to *Between Class and Elite,* and stretch forward, to *Memories of Class* and beyond. Written in the middle 1970s, *Socialism: The Active Utopia* persisted in connecting labor and utopia, even if its referents were often more to the 1960s—Herbert Marcuse, André Gorz, and more generally Gramsci. Yet the impetus of the laboring utopia seemed already exhausted; labor was increasingly part of the problem of modernity. Socialism, then, is a utopia or a culture more than a movement; the labor movement is not a utopia in itself, except in the most immanent sense. Yet the problems of the labor movement, and the value of labor, nevertheless remain central, and the coming eclipse of the moment of production by that of consumption changes none of this; problems of working life remain central to our spiritual and material existence. For socialists, today the idea of utopia still cannot be reduced to the problems of labor, but the utopia that has nothing to say to work or labor is useless. The larger problem is that already in this book of Bauman's the closure of socialism itself could be anticipated. If utopia remains possible, at the end of the book, the future of socialism seems considerably less certain.[4]

The problem of order is also foregrounded in Bauman's *Socialism: The Active Utopia,* though its centrality emerges fully only in hindsight. Order shifts further into central focus in Bauman's *Legislators and Interpreters,* where it is intellectuals who seek to legislate order on behalf of the masses, and finally in *Modernity and the Holocaust* and *Modernity and Ambivalence,* where the quest for order becomes the central problem of modernity as such. In *Socialism: The Active Utopia,* the idea of order remains both less developed and more ambivalent. The impulse toward order is one fundamental motive in the utopian project; utopian intellectuals seek to redesign and rebuild the world, and as radicals we cannot but help being both attracted and repelled by these ambitions. Perhaps we are more attracted by the possibility of the thought experiment than by its prospects for realization; for the point, ultimately, may be less to seek actually to change the world than to know that the possibility exists, that we can live differently, that alternative ways persist. For Bauman, in any case, the negative credentials of the utopians as budding social engineers are posted here; the intellectuals are warned but not yet damned for their open-ended legislative ambitions.

A famous propaganda image of Lenin did have him wielding a broom, sweeping away the parasites, the vermin, the scum of the earth; and the

Bolsheviks were, of course, part of this problem, seeking to clean up the world once and for all. The Bolsheviks were less gardeners than surgeons; ultimately this part of their project, as Bauman would argue later, was in direct sympathy with that of the Nazis, only where the Nazis sought to exterminate Jews, for the Bolsheviks the vermin were a class enemy, the Kulaks. But both social forces waged civil war against one particular part of the project in order to cleanse the world. Neither was driven by intellectuals; rather, both sought to destroy them.

The debate about intellectuals is an old one, and it shows no signs of abating. Intellectuals, those who take themselves really seriously, have a residual problem with democracy. For if they—that is, we—know better, why should we not rule the world? As Bauman indicated, this kind of mentality rests on a spurious scientific and godly fantasy about mastery, as though the human world were amenable to "fixing." The Bolsheviks remained unable to transcend these barriers; Lenin agreed with Kautsky that workers would always need to be led, and Trotsky never escaped from the fantasy that the real crisis of marxism was only ever a crisis of leadership. The Western discovery of Gramsci in this context was a phenomenon in its own right. For Gramsci's marxism began from the recognition that everyday life was an extraordinary mixture of intelligence, habit, and prejudice, and Gramsci therefore insisted that in principle all citizens were intellectuals. Of course it remained the fact that some were more intellectual than others; yet it remained part of the socialist utopia, for Gramsci, that the marxist image of the future presumed that there was no genetic distinction between leaders and led. Gramsci, however, never escaped entirely from Bolshevism or from the Jacobin way of thinking. When push comes to shove, marxist intellectuals who have become professional revolutionaries cannot jump off the locomotive of history: democrats become demagogues; thinkers and interpreters become the legislators and hooded magistrates of history.

Legislators and Interpreters

Bauman's Polish brief as sociological interpreter had led to an impasse; the state in its mercy had decided not to shoot this messenger, but it compelled him and his family rather to leave their homeland. They became exiles, like so many other modern intellectuals who insisted on their vocations. Bauman's working life took him through Tel Aviv to Canberra to settle, finally, in Leeds, where he was professor and head of the Sociology Department for almost twenty years. By necessity, then, an academic manager of sorts, he obviously continued to write across that period. But it was on the cusp of retirement via a stay in Newfoundland that he produced *Legislators and Interpreters: On Modernity, Post-Modernity and Intellectuals.*[5] This was the next book, after *Memories of Class*, of his own transition. Bauman's opening ambit was apparent. The idea of intellectuals coincides with that of the Enlightenment. By this stage of the twentieth century, we had some justifiable right to be skeptical about the claims of both, whether separately or together. Part of this sensibility was openly Foucauldian. For it was in this era, when intellectuals and the Enlightenment began to generate some mischief, that for Bauman the power/knowledge syndrome, that most conspicuous attribute of modernity, had been formed (2). A new kind of state power coincided with a new form of intellectual discourse. So far, however, it remains clear that the field we inhabit is modernity. And so Bauman made it clear that for him modernity and postmodernity were not phases or crystal-clear conceptual markers. The two terms, he insisted, are not like "industrial" and "postindustrial" or "capitalist" and "postcapitalist." Nor, more emphatically, is modernity the same as modernism. For both modernism and its shadow, postmodernism, refer largely to self-conscious cultural and artistic styles (3). For Bauman, rather, the point of distinction at risk in the difference between "modernity" and "postmodernity" was primarily a matter of intellectual style, or the difference in context in which intellectual roles are performed. Modern and postmodern, in this way of thinking, might then be periodized as successive historical sequences; but the real point of distinction is the dominant image or model of intellectual activity in each. As Bauman wrote: "In referring to intellectual practices, the opposition between the terms modern and post-modern stands for differences in understanding the nature of the world, and the social world in particular, and in understanding the related nature, and purpose, of intellectual work" (3). To use the conventional distinctions, however limiting they are, the postmodern is then a phenomenon aligned with spirit, culture, or ideas and intellectual practices. The postmodern might then usefully be viewed as ontological or epistemological, philosophical rather than firmly historical or sociological.

Wherein, then, resides the difference between modernity and postmodernity? The two frames offer, according to Bauman, quite clearly distinct worldviews. Modernity presumes an image of the world as an ordered totality, open to the prospects of explanation, prediction, and control. Control itself is bound into the idea and practice of social engineering, planning, and mastery over nature. Effectivity of control and correctness of knowledge are tightly related. The typically postmodern worldview, in contrast, generates a plurality of models of order. Truth claims are connected to communities of meaning rather than higher or necessarily external goals. Localism and relativism rule, as they implicitly did before the modern. This, then, is the background against which types of intellectual activity are to be defined. For the typically modern strategy of intellectual work is best characterized by the metaphor of the "legislator" role. The legislator possesses final authority and ultimate knowledge; his power rests on the social distinction between those who know and those who do not. Legislation calls upon general and schematic knowledge that, as Max Weber said of bureaucracy, can be generalized in order to anticipate all future developments (as if!). Such is the extraordinary traditionalism of modernity. In contrast, again, and though Bauman did not summon up this precise word here, the typically postmodern strategy of intellectual work is hermeneutic. The postmodern intellectual is a translator, not an arbiter. He or she translates statements made within one communally based tradition so that they can be understood within the system of knowledge based on another tradition. Interpreters do not decide on behalf of others; they seek, rather, to facilitate communication between different autonomous participants. The postmodern strategy, in this way, might in one sense be imagined as closer to the practice of a certain kind of anthropology than to mainstream sociology. Yet these kinds of distinctions are bound to blur, for as Bauman insisted, "the post-modern strategy does not imply the elimination of the modern one; on the contrary, it cannot be conceived without the continuation of the latter" (5). As Bauman explained, there are levels of meaning at work here that make all this persuasive. For although, say, the postmodern strategy entails the abandonment of the universalistic ambitions of the intellectuals' own tradition in the world, it does not abandon the universalistic ambitions of the intellectuals toward their own traditions (5). Interpreters maintain a great deal of power or influence. Fundamentally, Bauman's was a Weberian or Kantian case seeking to reclaim the distinction between proper spheres of analysis or activity. For the real issue is the public claim of the intellectuals to power, as legislators, as phoney representatives of Reason or the People, when in actuality they have their own agenda to bear.

Legislators and Interpreters was, then, Bauman's attempt to reconstruct a hermeneutical circle of his own, where hermeneutics could be brought to bear on the problem of hermeneutics and its eclipse by managerial or legislative forms of knowledge and power (6). Yet the position of critique is not yet entirely clear, for Bauman insisted that he did not want to view the shift from modern to postmodern as necessary or progressive. He did not, at this point, further entertain the possibility that the hermeneutic might be a return rather than a progressive or regressive shift. Instead, Bauman returned to and departed from an earlier topic, the aetiology of the intellectuals. Via an extended discussion of the analysis of primitivism in the work of the anthropologist Paul Radin, Bauman arrived in effect at two provisional definitions. Intellectuals are ideologists, and they are defined relationally, by the role they perform in the reproduction and development of the social figuration (19). Again, the frame of reference is reminiscent of Marx's discussion of the emergence of the division of labor in *The German Ideology*, though Bauman did not invoke it here. Rather than referring here to Marx's priests, Bauman introduced Michel Foucault's critique of the "pastoral," for it was the power/knowledge nexus to which he drew attention here. Marx's argument was still, ultimately, one concerning economy more than culture, leading to the focus on exploitation rather than domination. Here, for Bauman, it was domination that counted.

Not that the road from interpretation to legislation was simple, however. For as Bauman emphasized, one model for the intellectuals in formation was the "active utopia" of *les philosophes* (24). The *philosophes* were not intellectual entrepreneurs seeking to sell a paradigm. Thus the ambivalence of the entire problem at hand: intellectuals are never only just power-hungry experts in the making. The root of the contradiction can nevertheless be located within the field of education. For the long change associated with the Enlightenment privileges reason over experience, coming to the conclusion that humans most need instruction in what lies outside or beyond them. "To acquire excellence," according to Bauman, "men must be taught. They need teachers. They need those who know" (33). He thus opened one possible path to his later discussion of the Holocaust and then ethics, for whatever we can learn outside of us, whatever procedures and rules we can learn or are taught, they cannot teach us how to act or when to say no.

In this, modern society nevertheless resembles images of traditional society, where proximity and the relative transparency of social relations ostensibly go together with higher degrees of stability and control. The process we have made familiar to ourselves under the name of the

Industrial Revolution has changed this by generating a category of vagabonds or "masterless men" and their attendant institutions of disciplinary control, from the school to the poorhouse, the hospital, and the asylum. What Bauman added to Foucault's adoption of Jeremy Bentham, here, was a heightened sense of actors within these formative institutions. For the far-reaching consequence of the asymmetry of surveillance is the demand for a specialist in a position of supervision, that is, super vision. The practice of surveillance itself depends on the existence of a category of surveillors (47).

But at this point Bauman changed metaphors, from the Panopticon to gardening, or cultivation, and replaced Foucault as his marginal authority with Ernest Gellner. Whence came modernity and its penchant for regulation? It was as though the gamekeepers of an earlier moment had become gardeners; and it is the specific image of cultivation here that drew out Bauman's critical ire. For the emergence of modernity rested on the process of transforming wild cultures into garden cultures. The sensibilities underlying this critique seemed to be recognizably romantic, valuing nature over culture; but this was also the beginning of a case in Bauman that led to *Modernity and the Holocaust,* to the exposure of Nazi theory and practice in antisemitism of constructing the Jew as the weed. Nazism, too, was based on an attack on nature, not only on rhapsody or rhetoric sung in praise of a weedless Black Forest.

The gardening state opened the way for eugenics. The power presiding over modernity (the pastoral power of the state) was modeled on the role of the gardener (52). The gardener became the image of that pattern of social engineering that in turn defined modernity. All of nature needed to be civilized, including the vagabonds and the motley members of the dangerous classes. The great unwashed would have to be reeducated, in their own interests. The specialists had arrived just in time to save us all, with experts, teachers, and social scientists in their vanguard (67). Education would free us all of our prejudices. The good citizen could be grown, like a grafted tomato or the blue rose. Before our eyes, historically speaking, we saw the philosophers turning into legislators. Whether this is a fair representation of the Enlightenment, however, is another issue, for the Kantian idea of regulation as self-regulation seems to disappear from these pages. Its central figure, in Bauman's argument here, is rather that of Jean-Jacques Rousseau forcing people to be free (74). The men of the Enlightenment doubtless had the contempt for the rabble that Bauman described; the critical question, however, is whether this exhausts their contribution to modern culture. If the project of the Enlightenment is reduced to its tutelary outcome in education or instruction, we are all in consequence far poorer indeed. Yet it is indubitably the case that, if the West has given us, for example, the modern project of democracy, it has also simultaneously given us the civilizing project in its dirtiest sense. The singular ideal of "civilization" has always pitted itself against the actual contents of other, actually existing, civilizations (93). And in this regard, as Bauman intimated, to civilize is not a qualitatively different act than to enact culture, or to cultivate. The pox of humanism here meant not only that nothing could be left alone but that everything was open to change. As Bauman wrote:

> The forms human life and conduct assumed did not seem any more part of the "nature of things" or part of a divine order which would neither need nor stand human intervention. Instead, human life and conduct appeared now as something which needed to be formed, lest it should take shapes unacceptable and damaging to social order, much like an unattended field is swamped with weeds and has little to offer its owner. (94)

At this point of the argument, Bauman turned more directly to discuss ideology, including the humanist ideology of marxism.

Marx's own obsession with changing the world rather than merely interpreting it places his legacy squarely within the tradition of thinking that Bauman was rejecting here. For Marx, too, knowledge could lead to a certain kind of collective mastery. *Savants* wanted not only to explain the world but also to save it. Yet this was also part of the worldview that had sustained Bauman from the 1940s to the 1960s. What, then, had changed? Marx now appeared to Bauman, as per Marshall Berman's portrayal in *All That Is Solid Melts into Air,* as an unqualified modernist (112). For Bauman, in other words, the later Marx lost the balance that had earlier seen him weigh up the respective gains and losses of modernity. For Bauman, as for Cornelius Castoriadis and Jean Baudrillard, marxism became the mirror of production. Entrapped within modern significations, marxism then became a theory of state-planned modernization. Bauman, in turn, discussed the image of Faustian man but connected him here with Nietzsche rather than Marx; as I shall suggest later, it seems to me that it is Faustianism rather than humanism that best deserved Bauman's critical contempt. It was the Marx that stretched out through Trotsky who turned most fully from the spirit of Prometheus to that of Faust the developer (113).[6] Marx, in any case, remained, I think, both a romantic and a classicist, as well as an ideologue and a revolutionary modernist. At this point in Bauman's own project, however, Marx began to appear at least as much the problem as the resource for its interpretative solution.

Yet it was Marx whose visage remained on Bauman's study wall in Leeds, and it is Marx's critical spirit that animates much of his work. For our new world, brave or not, remains continuous with these older worlds and their problems. What becomes open to question is whether the classical sociological interpretations, from Marx to Georg Simmel, managed to determine either the uniqueness of modernity or the continuity of its concerns with all hitherto existing social forms. Bauman's level of sympathy with classical sociology of this critical kind was high, yet his sense was also that from our vantage point, a manic century later, the world also looked rather different. Or, more precisely, the ways available to us to look at the world seemed more diverse and contingent in nature. How so? Three factors are involved. First, the critical classics tended to assume the irreversible character of the changes that modernity signified or else brought in its wake. Second, the critical consensus conceived of modernity in critical terms, as an essentially unfinished project. Third, the critiques of modernity were all "inside" views. The philosophical discourse of modernity became both self-referential and self-validating (115–16). The idea of the postmodern is significant if only because it offers a margin for critical maneuver or detachment from these positions. At the same time, as Bauman consistently was given to emphasize, there is, in another sense, nothing "outside" the modern or the global. So the postmodern is necessarily continuous with the modern, both in historical and in conceptual terms. Thus the irony, often, of various postmodern critiques of modernity that insist on their novelty and nevertheless reproduce, for example, the first attitude of classical sociology, its principle of the irreversibility of change. The postmodern often presumes an end to the conception or epoch of modernity, a view that is itself quintessentially modernist in substance (117).

For Bauman the postmodern referred usefully not to an alleged change of epoch or to the arrival of "postmodern times" but to this change in attitude or self-consciousness. The postmodern is a manifestation of the crisis in modern, and modernizing mentalities:

> The post-modernist discourse . . . is about the credibility of "modernity" itself as a self-designation of Western civilization, whether industrial or post-industrial, capitalist or post-capitalist. It implies that the

self-ascribed attitudes contained in the idea of modernity do not hold today, perhaps did not hold yesterday either. The post-modernist debate is about the self-consciousness of Western society, and the grounds (or the absence of grounds) for such consciousness. (118)

The emphases are characteristic of Bauman's thinking and are worth dwelling on. First, the postmodern is a debate about, or a critique of, culture rather than, say, economy or history in the first instance. Second, the argument looks backward as well as forward: we may never have been modern in any thoroughgoing sense; indeed, the modernist or boosterist model of modernity may be impossible, less unachieved than simply unachievable. But this also would mean that the "premodern" is probably "modern" in various different ways, for if high modernity is not modern, neither is early modernity; in this case, what does it mean to speak of modernity at all? Perhaps it is rather the case that we have always been modern, or open to change. And third, even though the argument here refers primarily to culture and has a historical inflection, its ultimate message is ethical, for it is not practically the case that culture thinks through subjects or actors but rather that they, we, think through culture. The postmodern is also, then, a question of how we see ourselves, and, as Bauman showed so painfully in *Modernity and the Holocaust,* there is at least one way in which the most modern of totalitarian actors and subjects are also the most excessively traditionalistic, or morally dutiful.

To put it in plainer terms, the postmodern attitude reflects a basic unease with high modernity and its humanistic claims of individual perfectibility to be achieved via social engineering. At century's end, we—many of us, or Western middle-class radicals in particular?—are no longer convinced that these ends are either possible or desirable. The ethical problems raised in a global register by these kinds of claims have long been identified as Eurocentric. It is as though we, the privileged, further down the path to the abyss of futile consumer hedonism, cannot resist calling back to those behind us that it only gets worse the further we progress. Yet it is also this unease with our worlds and ourselves that drives the critical enterprise that in turn sustains sociology. As Marx observed somewhere, one cannot but help from time to time contemplating whether we have generated too much civilization; this is the case for all concerned, north and south. What Bauman thought we cannot do is to translate this interpretation directly into legislation. We do not have the ethical right to decide for others if this means trying to help others avoid their own mistakes. It is as though, for Bauman, it should be the primary universal right of all peoples to make their own mistakes. To behave otherwise is to behave as though it is only the other who is capable of mistakes, or of evil. It is this sense of difference that has been lost in the rush of modern intellectuals to become legislators of taste, or of the world. Even so, the final claim of intellectuals remains Martin Luther's, to speak the truth as we see it; we can do no other.

The implication is clear: intellectuals should embrace, again, the logic of interpretation so that what we or others routinely call the postmodern also includes the practice of hermeneutics. This would mean recognizing that if we all inhabit the one world, we also at the same time occupy different life worlds. If this is the case, avants-gardes, whether artistic or political, are bound to collapse, for the absence of all clearly defined rules of the game renders innovation impossible, which explains the predominance of the images of pastiche or collage; even surrealism is no longer iconoclastic (130). Yet in this situation the ethical problem remains. For if the intellectual obsession with classification always carries with it the act of valuation, the question remains, how should we live? and with it remains the traditionalistic and modernist insistence that the moral responsibility of intellectuals is to tell others (our readers) how to live. But the unpalatable truth in the story told by Bauman is different: all we can tell others is the hardest thing, that they have to decide for themselves. The ultimate register of decision, then, is ethical rather than aesthetic, and this regardless of whether we view ourselves as modern or postmodern. The point is not that we should each of us cease to judge, but, to the contrary, that the fragility or provisionality of judgment must be recognized. So this is a call for more debate and argument, not less; it is a call only for a different style of dispute, whether in politics or aesthetics.

Bauman's own debating partners were various, but they included Richard Rorty with his relativism and Hans-Georg Gadamer with his hermeneutics, both of them traditionalists of different sorts (144). The issue then becomes one of community and of whether we inherit or make the communities we inhabit or hope for. Philosophers, henceforth, can behave more authoritatively in their own communities of scholars than they can in the community at large. Intellectuals, in other words, should no longer dream of themselves as heroes. Bauman proceeded to connect this theme to Weber's Protestant ethic, which he presented as a sociological myth, or at least as a myth made for and by sociologists. To view the arrival of capitalism as something other than intentional was one thing, for Bauman. What was more striking, to this critic of Weber, was the sense that the intellectuals, more than anyone else, liked Weber's tale immensely. As Bauman wrote: "In the myth of the puritan, they immortalized a mirror reflection of themselves" (149). If the noble captains of industry were the obvious tragic heroes of this story, the projection involved revealed that the interpretative heroes were we sociologists, hardworking, righteous, and stoical. Bauman's interpretation of Weber here is stunning and reveals perhaps more clearly than elsewhere his relative indifference to the formal corpus of Weber's work, at least in its philosophical dimensions. His interpretation is as shocking as it is idiosyncratic. Yet a moment's reflection also reveals its immense power of suggestion. For Weber plainly was nostalgic for a lost world inhabited by great men, and he himself aspired to greatness. The Protestant ethic, in that sense, involves a projection, just as by extension we could say that Marx's critique of alienation includes a projection, for the new world of capitalists was one that denied him a place in history, and not only the proletariat. The critique of alienation also indicated Marx's own sense of having been misplaced by a history out of joint.

Against the sociological projection of puritanism, Bauman called on the support of Richard Sennett and John Carroll. Whether the puritan was the figure of the capitalist or the sociologist or whether he was entirely fictive, the dominant cultural model today is rather remissive or hedonistic. The contrast implied is nevertheless difficult to avoid: if the modern or postmodern personality is hedonistic, it is the figure of the sociologist that acts as the censor or puritan (152–53). The sociologist has become the Man of Reason, which is exactly the thesis of Bauman's book; in other words, interpreters become legislators. Culture is tragic rather than humanizing; the surplus of its achievements, as Simmel argued, serves rather to numb than to enable us (156–57). We drown amid our cultural achievements because their abundance blinds us to each other. Ours is the story, still after all these years, of the sorcerer's apprentice. As intellectuals, we cede our autonomy to the institutions that control us at the very same moment that we style ourselves independent, mavericks, puritans, or outsiders. We end up looking like the Marlboro Man, with an aura of strength and independence yet held up by the highway posters of the culture industry, supported by the very agent that poisons us. And even postmodern culture, this new critique of critical criticism, is delivered up to us daily by the market, like toothpaste or cornflakes (163).

But if Bauman sought to avoid the narcissistic self-projection of the sociologist as hero, he was clearly not in all this giving up the right to judge, and to judge harshly. For the undercurrent in Bauman's worldview remained, and it involved both a sense of loss and some sense of continuity in the form of anthropological street wisdom. Bauman criticized sociology persistently but never deserted it; at work here is an insider-outsider dialectic of the most extraordinary quality, and for us—as creatures of ambivalence—it is exactly this that appeals. It is as though the sense of loss encountered in modernity is precisely civilizational or, in that sense, cultural; as though it constrains us powerfully and yet brings out the best in us, as creatures of habit, persistence, routine, and innovation. Modernity becomes second nature, as it were, but it does not impinge directly on our souls, for human beings are smarter and more resilient than that. We may be fools, in this way of thinking, or creatures of habit, but we are not idiots. We retain our need for dignity and freedom, and this is what generates the critique of modernity and its illusions. For consumer culture can satisfy only our second natures. We do see ourselves in the mirror of consumption, but we do not recognize the whole of our being there. Thus Bauman damned the world of consumption but also decried the exclusion of the poor from its apparent rewards and riches. There are now, he concluded, still two nations in Britain, as there were when Benjamin Disraeli first discerned the dichotomy in *Sybil*. If the market economy is now the kingdom of freedom, the striking social division is that between those who can participate in this world and those who are excluded from it. The two nations are no longer those of Disraeli or Marx, those of exploiters and exploited, bourgeoisie and proletariat (169). Our two nations are those of the seduced and the repressed. "Without the second of these two nations," Bauman wrote, "the picture of the post-modern world is totally incomplete" (169). Thus our most ambivalent of sociologists returned to the path of sociology; for the postmodern must also be viewed sociologically, precisely because, in the old language, it is a culture that is delivered (or denied) through an economy.

The irony of the way in which intellectuals identify with History or Progress, however, is that they also insist on insinuating others into the picture. So it is, for example, that peasants or proletarians come to be portrayed as stereotypical heroes. The flaws of the socialist imagination and those of sociology are often connected. Indeed, although the history of sociology should never be reduced to that of marxism, there is nevertheless a particular sense in which their fortunes across recent times have been intertwined, for better or for worse. So here Bauman's thinking connected back to *Memories of Class*, where the "Progress of Reason" involved a process in which the fact of factory confinement was substituted for what memory held alive as the image of the freedom of the petty producer (174). But this dream of reason could not hold, even if this fact, in turn, was until recently too painful for us to recognize. The middle classes, socialists included, were so entranced by their own civilizing mission as to occlude their vision when it came to popular desire. Lenin agreed with Kautsky that, left to themselves, the proletariat would fail to come up with much; probably they would rather kick a football than get really serious. Marx's views were more complicated but remained ambiguous; he presumed that the members of the working class were capable of self-organization but analyzed the problem away in what Lukács later constructed as the epistemologically privileged proletariat, positing alongside this the simultaneous sense that only those who had really understood Georg Wilhelm Friedrich Hegel could respectably call themselves marxists (175).

Bauman did not use these words here, but his arguments were caught up with representation and social ventriloquism. Marxists have long claimed to know and to represent the interests of the workers better than the workers could themselves; there is therefore a kind of weird sense in which marxists magically become the proletariat made articulate in a kind of substitutionism that even the young Trotsky might have marveled at. But at the same time this is an issue more easily identified than resolved, for representation nevertheless remains a fact of modern life. If social ventriloquism is a moral problem, institutional representation also remains a political fact. Bauman's purpose here, however, was less to resolve the issue itself than to argue forcefully for its recognition, for intellectuals are both narcissistic and self-denying. They both project their own problems and insecurities onto others and deny that their interest is in between that of those who rule and those who are dominated; they identify with superiors or inferiors as they choose, in the process making invisible the specificity of their own project or ambition. In other words, the ambiguity of legislation and interpretation is built into the position of the modern intellectual itself, which results in the combination of all rights with no responsibilities. The radical intellectual is the pantomime proletarian, the son or daughter of the people until the people get out of hand. If the proletarian therefore lets the intellectual down, this is only because the intellectual has constructed the proletarian in his or her own heroic image. The workers, in the meantime, stubbornly persist in identifying themselves as they will; they have better things to do than listen to the hectoring speeches of others.

And this is part of the problem, in turn, for the institutionalization of the working class by capitalism was never fully realized and is now again unraveling, as labor is being expelled from Fordist capitalism. Whereas marxists hitherto pondered the prospects of labor after capitalism, today we are faced with the puzzle of capitalism after labor, at least in the Fordist sense. That capitalism which, vampirelike, sucked the lifeblood from labor, in Marx's image, has been replaced historically by the international mobile phone, the don't-call-us of footloose finance (179). Today we are locked into economic life less by the imperative to sell our labor power than by the proliferation of things to consume. So class remains an actuality, for there is an apparent connection between personal income and expenditure, even as some categories of the population are being redefined as economically redundant, surplus to the system's need. The old marxian theorem that the unemployed belonged to a reserve army no longer holds, then; and at this point Bauman began to develop what became a standard claim in his work, that the dysfunctional can now be held up as examples, as human scarecrows, as the rest of us scramble to keep up paid work. The new poor fail, on this account, to make good the transition from the old, productive way of life to that of consumptive bliss. They are not good consumers, or rather, their consumption does not matter much for the successful reproduction of capital (181). Even worse, they are known to consume outside of market circulation, an antisocial act if ever there was one.

For Bauman, then, this new postmodern population can either be seduced by consumerism, glitz, and neon or risk repression and harassment, being moved on endlessly at other people's insistence. So it is in this text, *Legislators and Interpreters,* that Bauman's work meets up with Jeremy Seabrook's, most notably *Landscapes of Poverty* (1985) (186). The virtual realities of endless orgasmic consumption, sex, lies, and video have generated a world that makes Weber's Protestant ethic seem a universe, rather than merely a lifetime, away. The outsiders, those without goods or hope, are the cultural other of those elegant yuppies who spend money as if there was no tomorrow. Yet this pair of others is not like that bourgeois and proletarian, set, as it were, against each other implacably, bearers of two different cultures. The "achiever" is rather a trend setter, an example to be followed, in Bauman's words "a pioneer on the road everyone must aspire to follow, and a confirmation that aspiring is realistic" (187). Within these parameters it is impossible to criticize this endless noonward race; we can only be enjoined to catch up, to run faster.

But at this point Bauman closed this book. He did so by returning to the two possible optics before us, offering two conclusions, one each in modern and postmodern style. For although his purpose was plainly to criticize the modern, his stated intention was also to avoid viewing the postmodern merely as its victorious or superior historical replacement. And as the foregoing shows, there will be ways in which the postmodern involves more senses of gain than of loss, at least for some of us.

Bauman's modern conclusion to *Legislators and Interpreters* invokes the spirit of classical sociology with its core concern, that capitalism unregulated would erode society as we knew it. Markets rule; consumption replaces needs and transforms identity. Modernity in this sense has failed (191); or perhaps it has merely lived up to the blackest sociological scenarios anticipated by Weber or Simmel. To argue in this way, however, as Bauman recognized, is nevertheless to hold open the principle of redemption. On this account, he thought, the "potential of modernity is still untapped, and the promise of modernity needs to be redeemed" (191). Bauman's terms of reference in this modernist scenario are evidently Habermasian, which in a way surprises us given the effective absence of Jürgen Habermas's work from Bauman's analysis in this text. In any case, the coincidence is enough to make one wonder how much plausibility Bauman gave to this "modern" conclusion. Yet he did insist that the modern prospect remains open: we still strive toward the possibility, in principle, that we can combine the dual values of personal autonomy and societal rationality (192).

Bauman's postmodern conclusion seems more resonant with the sympathies of his book. Here the general scenario is that the puritan gives way to the consumer, bracketing the poor and oppressed out of the social picture, socially or sociologically invisible, beyond redemption. The oppressed are no longer imagined as the antithesis of the system; rather, they are the failed attempts of the mediocre to fly (193). If, then, Bauman's analytical sympathies stretched toward the idea of the postmodern as the critique of the modern, his personal sympathies were more old-fashioned. This is a world of hedonism where cynicism reigns. Bauman, the old utopian, had to protest; even for moderns, utopianism ruled (194). It is as though Bauman recast Durkheim's insistence, in *The Elementary Forms of the Religious Life* (1915), that the society that has no image of itself—no tradition or vision—will surely die. Bauman, in contrast, thought that the society that cannot sustain a plurality of imagined futures is already dead, closed, at least, to its own possibilities. So how can we do better without endlessly retreading these old paths? The essential clue to the postmodern alternative in Bauman's work remains with the idea of interpretation, or legislation. The refusal of strategy is still, as he put it in discussion of Rorty, a strategy in itself (198). Bauman's final conclusion is, in effect, to step out of his text altogether: "Rorty's anti-strategy seems to fit very well the autonomy and the institutionally encouraged concern of academic philosophy with its own self-reproduction. Until further cuts, that is" (198). Philosophers are permitted to abuse philosophy, for internal consumption, as it were; but then the postmodern huns arrive at the academy door, offering to confirm the diagnosis of the philosophers by closing the university. Thus do we speak authentically in one voice to our colleagues and in another to our enemies, without undue fear of inconsistency; and in sociology it is just the same.

Conclusions: Out, Toward Understanding

The path of the twentieth century may well lead from utopia to dystopia. Modernity opens the skies on our sense of possibility, even if it leaves us entering the new millennium clutching only showbags or glossy brochures. The limit of utopia, in Bauman's argument, emerges as connected to its operationalizability. Utopia should remain in the realm of hope rather than program, ending up in the brochure or in Disney World. The attempt to make utopia raises the question of the status of Jacobinism. Bauman's temptation was to identify Jacobinism and the Enlightenment, or at least Reason and State, with the project of *les philosophes*. We might choose to criticize this identification on analytical or historical grounds, but then the task of explaining modernity would remain. For we may well be prepared to grant that modernity is by nature ambivalent, but how does that help us explain the damage done in its name? Bauman's achievement in this context is that he contributed more, I think, to the sociology of intellectuals than any other such writer in the twentieth century. Was this a confession on his part, as a lapsed marxist? No more so than on the part of the rest of us. It remains morally necessary for someone to call the injustices of the world we have made.

It was not Bauman's claim that we can do without intellectuals; in one residual respect, his is only the Weberian reminder that forms of authority should not be inflated or illegitimately transferred from one sphere into another. Yet the messenger, the hermeneut, will never only bring the mail. Some interpreters will also bear utopias, which we can accept or reject or pass on for the consideration of others. The point is that, at the end of the day, the political opinion of the intellectual is worth no more than that of any other citizen; and this is why we are bound to muddle through, occasionally shooting the messenger, metaphorically speaking.

In Bauman's work, in any case, it becomes apparent that language matters as communication, and not the other way around. Utopian horizons count along with traditional horizons, cultures, activities, and habits, whether real or imagined or both. The oddity about modernity, in this regard, is what centrality of place and value it has given to ideas and to their bearers, we intellectuals. Modernity truly is, or was, the age of ideology, but this holds true only as it reveals to us the worst and the best of its potentiality. We believed in the possibility of reform; we hoped for human perfectibility. As Bauman indicated, various interpretations or conclusions can be drawn from this assessment. The more damning is this: what a disaster modernity has been; the more modest, in turn is this: perhaps we still need to persist, to do better. The latter, more powerful, implication, I think remains more resonant in Bauman's work. For contrary, say, to the legacy of aristocratic radicalism worked out through critical theory, Bauman's project seems to retain the sense that humans do not fully internalize the disasters of the cultures or civilizations that they inhabit. Second nature remains misleading. We still retain our own ways of going on.

(2000)

Twelve

Modernity and Communism: Zygmunt Bauman and the Other Totalitarianism

Zygmunt Bauman's most influential work is without doubt *Modernity and the Holocaust*.[1] There is no companion in his work to *Modernity and the Holocaust*, no *Modernity and Communism*, or perhaps it should be *Communism and Modernity*. For his life's commitment, in political terms, was to the left, to socialism, to utopia, or, differently, to Polish reconstruction after the devastation of the war. Communism survives, as a ghost, for it ghosts us all, those on the left or those who came from it. In my book *Zygmunt Bauman: Dialectic of Modernity*,[2] I have suggested that there is a samizdat text on communism in Bauman's project. It is *Legislators and Interpreters*.[3] If it is the case that *Legislators and Interpreters* does not fully hit its own target, the enlighteners, this may well be because it has another, more explicitly political, target in Bolshevism, or communist humanism. The intellectuals who sought directly to legislate—and did so—were not the *philosophes* but the Bolsheviks.

Where is communism, then, in Bauman's work? In one way, as in *Legislators and Interpreters*, communism appears as the core narrative of modernity. Americanism is its boosterist capitalist version; Nazism is the racial imperialist or human engineering modernity par excellence.[4] This echoes further in the way in which for Bauman the postmodern also meant the postmarxist. Part of the marxist story is inextricably bound up with the Soviet experience, so that to be after modernity (or at least, after modernism) also means to be after actually institutionalized marxism in its Soviet and satellite form.

Modernity and the Holocaust, then, also signals or anticipates the idea of alternative or multiple modernities. To think across Bauman's work, there must have been at least three primary forms of modern Western regime—liberal capitalist, communist, and fascist—across the twentieth century. Developmental regimes, as in Latin America or East Asia, have something in common with all three of these, for they are all models of modernization. As we read Bauman's work, it might be tempting to add a fourth, social democratic modernity. As Bauman put it in *Modernity and Ambivalence*, Bolshevism genetically was social democracy's hot-headed younger brother.[5] Yet social democracy from Weimar to Bad Godesberg was also liberal capitalist, even as it connected to communism and fascism in different ways. This is not to say that social democracy was politically indefensible, no matter how compromised it may have become, but rather that it cannot lay claim to the category of a separate modernity rather than a particular type of political regime within it (though the persistence of a Scandic model remains significant here).

Two other, larger themes cut across this field: totalitarianism and utopia. *Totalitarianism* is used here as a term of convenience. From my perspective, the Bolshevik and Nazi experiences need to be aligned rather than identified or radically separated. The shadow texts here might be those of the Frankfurt School, though neither of the classics, Herbert Marcuse's *One Dimensional Man* or Max Horkheimer and Theodor Adorno's *Dialectic of Enlightenment*, directly fits our needs. *One Dimensional Man* came close enough to arguing that all modernity was totalitarian, a charge that misreaders of Bauman have been known to direct at *Modernity and the Holocaust*. *Dialectic of Enlightenment*, paradoxically, might itself be read as an anticipatory critique of communism, for unlike fascist rationality, communism was a direct and self-conscious extension of one stream of enlightenment rationality. Against the Frankfurt School, or complementary to it, this difference in Bauman's work serves to remind us that if his is a critical theory, its orienting point alongside the Holocaust is its East European context. Where members of the Frankfurt School were relatively silent on communism, Bauman's work grows out of it, alongside it, against it.

Yet Bauman remained, at the same time, a socialist, and the theme of utopia persisted in his thought, even as utopia itself persisted as a necessary noplace, rather than (as per Bolshevism) as an image of a world to be achieved, now, whatever the cost. This ambivalence toward utopia connects back to the problem of enlightenment. For the Bolsheviks did violence to their people in their own name. The murders were committed in the name of noble ends. Where the Final Solution was rational in its own terms, a murderous solution to a Nazi-defined "Jewish problem," the ethics of communism were worse than those of fascism, for the Bolsheviks were prepared to commit murder for noble rather than ignoble ends. Thus the irony of the fellow-traveling insistence that Stalinism was superior to Nazism because it sought to improve Humanity. Unlike the Nazis, the Bolsheviks meant well; this was supposed to be some kind of compensation for their victims.

Alongside the samizdat critique of Bolshevism in *Legislators and Interpreters*, there are two other fields of analysis of communism in Bauman's work. One addresses the Soviet experience, the other Poland in particular. These notes are offered as hints for those who follow.

The Soviet Experience

Various commentators have identified the centrality of Antonio Gramsci to Bauman's project, and Bauman would be the first to agree. There is, however, another marxist soulmate, a fellow Pole, whose presence can be felt in his work. This is Rosa Luxemburg. Their compatriot Leszek Kolakowski noted the affinity in his 1971 critique of Bauman's "Pleading for Revolution."[6] All the sympathies are there—the view from below, the keen opposition to "barracks socialism," the maturational sense that history will not be forced. Less than spontaneism, there is in Bauman's work a sense that the world keeps moving; unlike Luxemburg, perhaps, he was ambivalent about both types of social actors, workers and intellectuals alike. As in the work of Bauman's teacher, Julian Hochfeld, here it is both Bolshevism and reformism that are the problem.[7] If Bauman shared this old sense that Bolshevism forced history where reformism merely rolls with it, however, his sociological sensibility was more open to the role of the peasants. This is especially apparent in his 1985 Leeds sociology paper "Stalin and the Peasant Revolution: A Case Study in the Dialectics of Master and Slave,"[8] where it is Barrington Moore rather than Rosa Luxemburg who sets the scene, for here the problematic is framed by Marx, peasantry, and modernization, with Georg Wilhelm Friedrich Hegel of course to come. Vladimir Lenin, like Petr Tkachev, viewed the peasants as the battering ram destined to smash the existing order out of pure rage, leaving power to the revolutionary minority who would start the real revolution. For Bauman, it was this unholy alliance between Bolsheviks and peasants that became a new dialectic of masters and slaves, the two locked together in asymmetric dependence just as Hegel had described. The problem, of course, was that the peasants were not really interested in communism. The master found himself at the mercy of his slave. In Bauman's words, *"The horror of the peasant beast on the loose was never to leave them—until the master would murder the slave, turning into the slave of his own crime."*[9] The revolution devoured its children, but they were, in the first instance, not the noble Jacobins but the peasants. Having painted themselves into a political corner, deprived of any possible options, the Bolsheviks then destroyed themselves. As Bauman wrote: *"The possibility that this would happen was created by the original sin of deciding to force the socialist utopia upon an overwhelmingly peasant, pre-industrial country."*[10]

Bauman revisited these issues in the 1986 *Telos* symposium on Soviet peasants. Here, again, it is the peasantry that plays the central role of the Bolshevik tragedy, even though it is now a minority class. Here its legacy is, among other things, ethical. Peasants steal to live, not to get rich. But stealing becomes universalized, in consequence, which means that the ethics of everyday life are jaundiced and larger hopes of autonomy dashed. The same impulse informed Bauman's response in the *Telos* symposium on the classic *Dictatorship over Needs,* by Ferenc Fehér, Agnes Heller, and George Markus. For there is a sense in which, as Robert Michels wrote *Political Parties* so that Max Weber did not have to (and Friedrich Engels did Karl Marx a favor in *Anti-Dühring,* all these remaining of course the views of the writers rather than the others), it is *Dictatorship over Needs* that fills the gap in Bauman's work. Bauman accepted this psychological take, that dictatorship is about control, over bodies, souls, and needs (this was the same moment, of course, when Bauman brought this kind of Foucauldian critique to bear on the primitive accumulation of capitalist relations in *Memories of Class, 1982*). Bauman accepted categorically the sense of the Hungarians that Soviet-type societies are modern—not lapsarian socialist, not capitalist, absolutely not historical throwbacks. Socialism was born as the counterculture of capitalism, a legitimate offspring of the bourgeois revolution eager to continue the work that the latter had started but failed to complete. Here Bauman connected rationalism and the social engineering of the Enlightenment project with capitalism and socialism. The argument parallels that in *Modernity and the Holocaust* in its implications:

To sum up: the Soviet system, without being a sequence to capitalism or an alternative form of industrial society, is nonetheless no freak or refractory event in European history. Its claims to the legacy of the Enlightenment or to the unfulfilled promises of the bourgeois revolution are neither pretentious nor grotesque. And thus it contains important lessons for the rest of the world.[11]

The Soviet system is an acid test for the Enlightenment utopia, for it sets the idea of a *social* rationality against that of *individual* rationalities by substituting state order for individual autonomy. Its failure indicates the hiatus of all socialist utopias and at the same time puts the global drive to rationality and order on notice. Moreover, its failure indicates the renewed possibility of grassroots movements, as in the Polish Solidarity (and here there is again an echo of Rosa Luxemburg).

By the time of *Postmodern Ethics*, Bauman was suggesting that we should no longer live in the shadow of the Age of Reason, for the twentieth century was the Age of the Camps.[12] Here the critiques of the Final Solution and of *Dictatorship over Needs* meet to indicate the necessity of a sociology of modern violence. Auschwitz meets the gulag in the modernist will to order, the liberal face of which is apparent in incarceration. Yet if the genocidal urge of these regimes was ineluctable, the regimes were not identical, only similar. And if they were exemplary of the dark side of modernity, those experiences did not in themselves capture what followed in the experience of Eastern Europe.

East European Modernity

How can one best explain these similarities and differences? Plainly Bauman rejected one analytical temptation, which was to subsume Soviet and German totalitarianism. The next problem then emerged: how to explain the foundational Soviet experience in its connection to the satellites in Eastern Europe. If it is meaningful to describe the Soviet Union as Stalinist, what does this mean for its echoes in Budapest, Prague, and Warsaw? Is it meaningful to talk about Soviet-type societies as sui generis, or is each case, Poland in this instance, sui generis in itself? Bauman maintained an appropriate degree of ambivalence about this classificatory bind, for it is, of course, *explanans* rather than *explanandum* that matters. What did Bauman tell us about Poland? His analyses of Poland are acute, and they are local and specific but powerfully sociological.

Bauman's essays available in English on Polish experience all combine the language of class and elite in the Weberian sense: class as appropriate to economic life, elites as political leaders, in this regard, preeminently the Communist Party. Bauman's analyses of Polish communism are also consistently historical or generational, drawing specific attention to leadership styles and rationalities, for example, with reference to the distinction between the revolutionary political skills of the pioneers and the routine administrative skills of those who followed.[13] Here party connections work as the transmission belt or line of the available "fixers." Into the 1960s, party connections in the work sphere were increasingly technocratic rather than ideological. This generational curiosity was connected to the Weberian interest in personality types. It also registered an acute sensitivity to the Weberian sensibility regarding shortage and endless struggles over goods material and symbolic. Bauman's critique of Soviet-type societies rests on the Michelslike sense that socialism, too, was an alternative career ladder, like the military or clergy in other circumstances. Socialism might have been about good or evil intentions, but in its institutional forms it represented ladders to be climbed, or what Michels called career escalators in the case of the Social Democratic Party (SPD).

Into the 1970s, Bauman's essays extended this Weberian interest in the duality of power structures, or what he separated as "officialdom" and "class," as the bases of inequality in socialist society. Power is not bourgeois; rather it represents a web of dependencies.[14] In Bauman's self-understanding, this also followed Marx, as interpreted by Julian Hochfeld, and the distinction between the two-class model of the *Manifesto* and the multiclass model implicit in *The Eighteenth Brumaire*.[15] Nevertheless, it was Weber who offered the animating spirit here, not least as Bauman offered a marxisant twist on the idea of patrimonialism as referring to the issue of the "futuristic" rather than the traditional legitimation of the *partynomial* ruling authority in Poland. His contention was that the socialist societies that emerged in the last half century in Eastern Europe do not fit Weber's proverbial categories—traditional, charismatic, rational legal—but may fit a fourth category, parallel to patrimonialism, where it is rule of the party rather than strictly rule of the fathers that is predominant. Bauman did not make the point here—it was central to Heller's contribution to *Dictatorship over Needs* ten years later—that Stalin's reinvention of tradition, the Great Patriotic War, and Mother Russia shifted Soviet legitimation from future to past, for his curiosity was not about Stalin or Soviet foundationalism but about the East European results of Yalta.

Bauman enumerated the features of partynomial rule as follows. First, their claims to legitimacy were futuristic, not traditionalistic; these claims were to the society of the future, not to Mother Russia, *Blut,* or *Boden.* Second, party rather than person was the object of loyalty. Loyalty to the party took the place of obedience to the person of the ruler, and faith in the desirability of the social order replaced respect for tradition. Third, the vanguard legitimation of partynomial authority required teleological, not genetic, determination of macro social processes. The plan was the major instrument of teleological determination. We speak of the *emergence* of capitalism but of the *construction* of socialism. Fourth, planning and the will to order nevertheless relied on markets. Plan and market were mutually dependent, as in master and slave.[16] Fifth, the struggle of plurality and market principles meant that there was a permanent and dual structure of inequality and a duality of power elite that reflected this, itself manifest as *officialdom* and *class.* As a result, in the socialist societies of Eastern Europe each individual's situation was shaped by two relatively autonomous and to an extent antagonistic power structures, neither of which was entirely reducible to the other.[17] As Bauman noted, however, this was not a case of the common weberian-marxist addition, where (as George Lichtheim put it) Marx explained base and Weber superstructure. Bauman's case was that the two essential planes of inequality in Eastern Europe did not overlap. There was no direct correspondence between officialdom-generated and class-generated inequalities.[18] Each individual in these societies was a member of two largely independent power structures: officialdom and class.

The dialectic of master and slave appeared again, then, in this tension between state and market, for here the demand for freedom often meant freedom of market forces. The peculiarity of this structure was apparent in political terms, where there emerged a kind of populist alliance between party and workers—against managers and professionals. Yet the problem of equality seems to have been in the realm of class structure, while the problem of freedom was related to officialdom, so there was little obvious room for maneuver where large groups whose interests were definable in terms of freedom and equality could act in concert. The oldest socialist demand, for bread and freedom, could not here be voiced as one. The Polish rulers authorized by Stalin were not about to destroy themselves in the way that the Soviets did, nor did they show any capacity to generate structures open to political change or social reconstruction from within. As Bauman concluded, in anticipation of *Solidarity* a decade later, a new alliance might result not from a new common goal so much as from a common dissatisfaction with a social reality mutually perceived as unbearable.[19]

Bauman returned to the historical or generational aspects of the satellites in "The Second Generation of Socialism" (1972). Here the question was about the class effects of the reproduction of the new social systems over time. More literally, Bauman's question was this: What are the forms of the transmission of inherited advantage? Here we can see Bauman puzzling over the Polish version of what were to become British problems later, in his period of exile. Not only was there a dialectic of freedom and security, whether in Poland or later in Blair's Britain; moreover, the value of discretional goods can be registered as signs and not only as use values. Beyond the subsistence level, goods also work as signs: there is a semiotic role of consumption.[20] The infamous institution that emerged to indicate the distinction took the form of closed shops. At the same time that market forms of delivery indicated a shift from "welfare state" to "welfare individualism" after 1956 in Poland, the political apparatus had to come to grips with the crisis of the "second generation." Joseph Stalin in 1937 and Mao Zedong in 1968 had dealt with the succession problem by purging. By the time of Nikita Khruschev, it had become apparent to the aging rulers that a more peaceful approach would allow them to die in their beds.[21] In 1968, in Poland and Czechoslovakia diametrically different processes ensued. In Czechoslovakia workers and intellectuals united against the regime. In Poland, no such alliance could be achieved. Polish industrialization came later; new Polish workers were still culturally peasant, susceptible to the attractions of urban consumerism and drawn to political quiescence.[22] The socialist revolution of 1945 was mounted in the name of an almost nonexistent working class. Paradoxically, this revolution produced a social class that could challenge the claims made in its own name. They could pretend to work, while the rulers could pretend to rule. But no one could pretend to be outside the system, or outside the state. These patterns were common to East European societies, but the way they were played out was shaped in large part by indigenous factors.[23] Features common to Soviet-type societies nevertheless included a "new middle class," where access to education was the key, though there were also deep conflicts between "rulers" and "experts." In sympathy with Luxemburg, again, Bauman worried over the loss of proletarian collective memory through the Second World War and the rise of institutional actors or *apparatciks* who were happy to pretend to represent the peasants cum proletarians from the comfort and safety of their dachas. Into the 1980s a new industrial working class was formed, but it was laborist or corporatist in program. Until 1980.

Solidarity and After

The emergence of the Solidarity movement in 1980 took everyone by surprise, even if in retrospect this process looks like a belated trade unionization of a belated industrial proletarian arrival. Bauman's 1981 essay, at the cusp of the movement, was more optimistic, speaking indeed of "the maturation of socialism."[24] This was because—and here Bauman talked like Cornelius Castoriadis—Poland in 1980 came close to the model of historical creativity. Though it is Castoriadis whom we associate both with the *Socialisme ou Barbarie* impulse to workers' autonomy and the later claim to an ontology of creation, the other absent presence in Bauman's margins is Jürgen Habermas, for Bauman also interpreted Solidarity as part of an enlightenment process. The Polish venture sought to alter the language of social discourse, to redefine social action outside both the logic of the regime and its powers.[25] The point of Solidarity, and its achievement, in this view, is that it did not talk to power, for to talk to the ruling party in its own language would have been to lose the battle before it started. Bauman wrote: "The hope to loosen the dead grip of dictatorship lies elsewhere, in winning legitimacy for a nonpolitical language."[26] The Polish events opened a new possibility, one of a civil society grounded in the autonomy of the public sphere, won by the workers. It was this conjunction, of the opening public sphere and the agency of the workers, that was the great historical novelty of Solidarity. Enough, indeed, to make Bauman ponder this as a premonition, if not the maturation of socialism.

Bauman returned to the Polish story in 1989 in "Poland: On Its Own." Here the view, again, was of Polish socialism sui generis. The Polish regime emulated Soviet Stalinism only into the 1950s, losing its impetus by 1953 and ending with the death of Lavrenti Beria in 1956. The "Polish Road to Socialism" emphasized differences rather than similarities with the Soviet Union. As a result, there was little synchronization of the political histories of the two countries.[27] The Polish regime prided itself as Polish, Western, over the Russian, Eastern ways. The problem with Solidarity, now, in retrospect, was the logjam it confronted. Although various social actors and interests agreed in principle to all kinds of change, the practical steps to implement reform seemed to conflict with everyone's immediate interests. Conflicts were channeled into the distributive sphere, yet longer-term struggles over life chances were frustrated, as in all such communist countries mobility was *nationalized*. The Polish elite had circulatory problems. The purge, the original Stalinist solution, fell out of favor with the generation of rulers who in their youth had captured power through such means. The only obvious alternative was to make more room at the top by multiplying positions of high status, prestige, and material rewards.

Thus Bauman revisited the Michels problem in its post-SPD, totalitarian version, where the party was not the opposition but the power, and all ladders were internal. Solidarity, in this context, offered not only an alternative, public sphere, but also the prospect of other ladders, other life chances. The emergence of "free trade unions" offered a space for the flourishing of talents, skills, and ambitions of all kinds. Even if some of the Solidarity actors were less elevated in their motives, they were obliged to promote pluralism.[28] It was in the logic of their action to support pluralism. Politics, here, might be a life chance or a vocation, but its impulse was bound to be positive, even if its impact would be short-circuited. The result, in the Polish case, would be all glasnost and no perestroika, at least until larger world-historic forces came into play.

Finally, then, there came Bauman's "Communism: A Postmortem."[29] The anticommunist uprisings were systemic rather than merely political revolutions. The Polish problem was that none of the established classes demonstrated, or could have attributed to them, "transformative" interests. In the first instance, none of the major actors wanted a new society; they wanted only some relief from the tragicomic aspects of the existing one. To move forward would mean dismantling the "patronage state" (the phenomenon earlier described as partynomialism). This would mean opening up a new trade-off between state and market or security and freedom, where more freedom, like the earlier excess of security, would cut both ways. Alongside this scenario, Bauman reintroduced the frame of modernity and after. Communism was socialism in overdrive, socialism in a hurry, the younger, hot-headed and impatient brother. Lenin's political impatience had led to a sociological rupture. Lenin had redefined socialism (or communism) as a substitute for, rather than a continuation of, the bourgeois revolution. Communism would be modernity without the bourgeois revolution, without bourgeois democracy or a public sphere of any kind. Communism was an image of modernity one-sidedly adapted to the task of mobilizing social and natural resources in the name of modernization.[30]

Those who would urge capitalism onto Soviet-type societies after 1989 often failed to acknowledge that these economies lacked not only capital and capitalists but even workers, in the puritan sense. Bauman's conclusion here was that this was one sense in which the events from 1989 on indicated a postmodern revolution: postmodern because post-puritan, and culturally overwhelmed by a sense that capitalism ruled victorious less in a productivist than in a consumptive sense. Bauman wrote: "It was the postmodern, narcissistic culture of self-enhancement, self-enjoyment, instant gratification and life defined in terms of consumer styles that finally exposed the obsoleteness of the 'steel-per-head' philosophy stubbornly preached and practiced under communism."[31] One could say that Americanism had won, or perhaps the prospect of the culture of the postmodern, even as the masses toiled for subminimum wages the world over.

Conclusions—Full Circle

I began these notes with the observation that there is no text in Bauman's project called *Modernity and Communism* to match his most prominent book, *Modernity and the Holocaust*. There are other traces and indications: the samizdat critique of communist humanism in *Legislators and Interpreters*, the de facto authorization of *Dictatorship over Needs* as a theory of Soviet-type societies for sociology, and the essays on Poland, some of which have been scanned here. The implication is clear: while the Polish story cannot be told outside of the Soviet story, its internal dynamics are peculiar. Although the idea of stalinism needs to be connected to the Polish experience, it cannot sufficiently explain it. The Polish communists were not utopians, the hot-headed younger brothers of Lenin. Their initial brief, after World War II, was less revolution than reconstruction.

The Polish context is crucial. The commonly encountered criticism of *Modernity and the Holocaust* is that in foregrounding problems of modernity, the book fails to say enough about Germans and Jews. One of Bauman's intellectual or writerly habits has been to continue a discussion in the next book, so his discussion of Jews in particular continues in his next installment, *Modernity and Ambivalence*. There, as in the Holocaust book, the shadow of Polish experience falls heavily; after all,

Auschwitz was in Poland. In *Modernity and Ambivalence* Bauman discussed, among other things, the internal struggles between German Jews and Ostjuden. Not all Ostjuden were Polish Jews, but all Polish Jews were Ostjuden. Bauman turned full circle on this point in his 1996 essay "Assimilation into Exile: The Jew As a Polish Writer."[32] Many good Polish Jews, like the German Jews into the 1920s, imagined themselves to be Poles or Germans. Yet the Polish assimilation of Jews—which Bauman elsewhere connected with Claude Lévi-Strauss's idea of the anthropophagic culture, which swallows the outsider up rather than vomiting him or her out, as the Holocaust did—was as successful as it was contingent, indeed was successful because contingent: the Jews would always still be exposed, found out.[33] Then came the war, German invaders and Soviet. To the Poles, there was little difference between the invaders. For the Jews, the difference was between life and death. Horrified, the Poles watched the enthusiasm with which most Jews greeted the Red Army.[34] The Jews of Poland made excellent material for the new power: here were ladders, opportunities to change the world, or so it seemed. This treachery was neither forgotten nor forgiven by the Poles, who periodically returned to antisemitic purges, including the turn that expelled Bauman from his chair in Warsaw in 1968 and opened a longer road to Leeds. It was time for Zygmunt Bauman to move on, to leave this life behind, though it would follow him.

(2002)

Thirteen

Looking Back: Marx and Bellamy

No two images of socialism or utopia were more influential a century ago than those of Karl Marx and Edward Bellamy. Marx and Friedrich Engels famously denied the utopian dimension of their own project; Bellamy celebrated it, at least in the formal sense. Bellamy's utopia was as public as Marx's was practically invisible. Marx behaved as though utopianism were the preparatory phase of modern socialism; Bellamy embraced the form, both literally and as literature. The extent of the influence of Bellamy's *Looking Backward* is legendary: it was the second-biggest-selling work of fiction in the United States in the nineteenth century. With regard to Marx's work, in comparison, the primary texts now available to us were then often still unpublished. Marx was widely imagined to be a state socialist in the secondary literature of the period. Bellamy was also widely viewed as a state socialist, though there was a more sufficient textual basis for this reading in the utopia of *Looking Backward,* where nationalism, indeed, stood for socialism and society was organized as one great trust. In Marx's case, English-language readers of the nineteenth century had more work to do. They had odd glimpses of a socialist utopia in *Critique of the Gotha Program* and *The Civil War in France,* and they could counterintuit an image of socialism as the negation of capitalism in *Capital.* They had an image of the regime of direct producers there, in the third volume of *Capital* assembled by

Engels, but little else to go on. They could not access *The German Ideology* until much later.

The reception of socialist ideas is always compromised; understanding is always framed by misunderstanding. In this essay I sketch out some clues for revisiting images of utopia in Marx and in Bellamy. My claim is that Marx, as is often the case, failed to develop a systematic utopia or image of socialism. We are left with a series of hints toward five different images of utopia across the path of his life and work. Bellamy's image of utopia is more consistent across the path of his work, but, contrary to common understanding, it reflects the unresolved tensions of nineteenth-century American modernity expressed through the prism of New England small-town radicalism. Bellamy's utopia is connected to the later image of the machine in the garden; contrary to William Morris's assertion, he was not an unmixed modern, and this is one quality at least that he shared with Marx, where the impress of romanticism remains profound.

Marx's Utopias

Marx played with at least five images of utopia in his work. They are to be found in the *Paris Manuscripts*, *The German Ideology*, the *Grundrisse*, and *Capital*, volume 3, and scattered through the comments on the "Russian Road."[1] From the first to the fourth image, the change in Marx's thinking was consistent with changes across his moment and his project, as it shifted the image of redemption from a romantic frame to a modernist, industrialist way of thinking about possible future social organization. The hints in the later comments on a possible "Russian Road" violate the logic of this trend and the power of Marx's own conviction that socialism could emerge only from industrial capitalism. Three other sources of hints on utopia are *The Communist Manifesto*, *The Civil War in France*, and the *Critique of the Gotha Program*. These last three sources are more politically suggestive than indicative of how production or political economy might be reconstructed in the socialist society of the future.

Marx's project was culturally formed by the stream we call romanticism as much as it was by the Enlightenment. The path of its development might indeed be viewed as the transition from the romantic critique of capitalism to the enlightened conclusion that its dynamics must be embraced in order to transform them.

The *Paris Manuscripts* rest on the labor ontology so central to Marx. Even after forty years of argument about Marx's humanism in English, the premise is unavoidable. Marx's early work is based on the critique of alienation. It remains a central problem, whether viewed in its marxian inflexion or in later encounters via Georg Simmel and Sigmund Freud. Marx's critique of alienated labor necessarily indicates a counterimage, of the unalienated society. If capitalism's redundance has to do with its merciless and structural denial of the autonomy of labor in the act of production, in the alienation of its result, its collective agent, and humanity as such, the utopia implied here is one of individual autonomy and small-scale, localized production and collective management. The early Marx, following Friedrich Schiller, was a vehement critic of the fact of the division of labor, and the motif persisted right through to *Capital*. There it was less the primitivism of Jean-Jacques Rousseau than the romantic critique of fragmentation of the whole in Schiller that was in the background.[2] Marx's desire was for the freedom of creation and expression of the romantics.[3] Here utopia is not a political society but a society of autonomous creation as and through labor.

The second image appears in *The German Ideology*. It is the now famous scenario of huntsman, herdsman, fisherman, critic. This suggests a plainly rural, and in fact horticultural, utopia. It indicates a green and pleasant land, like that imagined by William Morris in *News from Nowhere*. But is this playful image not then an instance of Marx's playing with us? Marx's interlocutor here is not Schiller but Charles Fourier. Marx's utopia in *The German Ideology* is a paraphrase of or a pun on Fourier's schedule for "Mondor's Day," in which a diversity of harmonious activities reflects the differences of the individual personality and its multiple reflections in different forms of small-group association, attraction, and activity.[4] Marx's more earnest sensibility appeared later in *The German Ideology*, where he agreed rather with the Renaissance position that socialism should not be a society in which each individual was Raphael but that all with potential should be able to grow into actuality.

Marx spent more than twenty years, from the time of writing *Paris Manuscripts* of 1844 to that of writing *Capital* in 1867, working on his critique of political economy. Its midpoint, and his laboratory, is available to us in the *Grundrisse*. If the *Paris Manuscripts* are the most evocative and *Capital* the most brilliant architectonic text in Marx's project, the *Grundrisse* fascinates because it is the most transitional and experimental of Marx's works. Here Marx played with the creative image of musical composition as labor but later toyed with the fascinating possibilities made available by the prospect of automation: "Labour time no longer appears so much to be included within the production process; rather, the human being comes to relate more as a watchman and regulator to the production process itself." The worker now "steps to the side of the production process instead of being its chief actor."[5] Plainly Marx was speculating, anticipating a process well beyond that of Henry Ford and Fordism; yet the implications are not only futuristic. Here the very labor ontology on which his early work had been based was placed in question. Labor's magic was transferred conceptually into technology itself; technology, rather than labor, became the transcendent force implicit within capital. The prospect of freedom, or at least of free time, shifted beyond the sphere of labor or production to the realm beyond it. Production, here, rather seems to be the prerequisite of free time and capacity elsewhere, though never for Marx in leisure. He left that fantasy to Paul Lafargue, in *The Right to Be Lazy*. The ontology of creation persisted across his work, but here it escaped from the realm of production. The presence of Raphael remained. This drift seems to be confirmed in one passage in *Capital,* volume 3, where the famous discussion of freedom and necessity shifts freedom more clearly beyond labor. Here imagination seems to be separated from work; the craft utopia implicit in the *Paris Manuscripts* is nowhere in sight. Freedom is defined as the work of the associated producers, who rationally regulate their interchange with nature, bringing it under their common control rather than being ruled by it. The realm of work is now conceived as the realm of necessity. Beyond that, there begins the development of human energy that is an end in itself. This is the true realm of freedom. Its very possibility depends on the shortening of the working day.[6]

Marx's fifth glimpse of utopia is a lateral one, available to us in his correspondence with Vera Zasulich. Here Marx's Russian followers asked the obvious question, later answered positively by the Russian social democrats, including Vladimir Lenin. Did the Russian marxists have to await the full maturation of capitalism before they could seriously argue for the introduction of socialism? Marx's answer should logically have been yes, and this was also history's answer in 1991. But Marx's actual answer was politically creative and tentative rather than necessitarian. Perhaps, he said, the Russians could follow earlier historic precedents, such as the communal form of the *mir*. Was this a lapse in Marx's past, back to the reveries of *The German Ideology*? I do not think so, though the implication that socialism could or should be rural rather than urban has its echoes. The Russian Road is more like a special dispensation than a strong utopia.

The larger contours of Marx's utopianism are evident. Marx, after all, was born in a time and place where socialism might still be imagined as before industrialism, in a craft utopia, or else as a return to that lost past on the Rhine in the years of his boyhood. The significance of his birthplace, Trier, looms large otherwise, too. Its Roman and French connections form shadows that remained influential over Marx's political thinking, and in turn shaped the hiatus of political utopia in his writing. The first source is the least striking, in *The Communist Manifesto*. At the end of the *Manifesto* we find a list of minimal demands, such as anticipated not Lenin but Eduard Bernstein. Following Henri de Saint-Simon, Marx and Engels here envisaged socialism in terms of the postpolitical, administrative utopia. Marx did, of course, make the fatal mistake of identifying politics (and often the state) with class, and therefore mistakenly imagined that socialism would be after politics. The second, more political, source, *The Civil War in France,* shows the same hesitance to develop a theory of politics. The Paris Commune became a momentary model for self-managed, local socialism, but the status of this hint is more like that in the Russian Road, indicating a strategic accommodation rather than revealing the presence of a robust utopia. The third hint comes in *Critique of the Gotha Program*. This was the source of the later notorious communist apologia for the hard distinction between a first transitional phase and a second fuller phase of socialist development, the first of which could be used to justify anything in terms of proletarian dictatorship.[7] Under the Bolsheviks, dictatorship would become permanent rather than transitional. Even the subtle intellect of Leon Trotsky could not escape this logic but rather transferred it into the economic base in *The Revolution Betrayed*. Trotsky's own utopia, itself best glimpsed in *Literature and Revolution,* was Faustian rather than romantic or merely enlightened.[8]

Bellamy's Utopia

Edward Bellamy, meantime, has often been thought of as an American Bolshevik. Trotsky claimed at the height of his own revolutionary career that this was his own aim: Bolshevism shod with American nails.[9] Bellamy, for his part, has been received, whether enthusiastically or critically, as another state socialist. This Marx never was, and arguably Bellamy's utopia does not fit this grid either, at least not in its authoritarian guise.

The preeminent source for Bellamy's vision of the future is of course *Looking Backward*. Occasionally critical argument extends further, to take in its sequel, *Equality*, though the suggestive supplementary texts actually came earlier, not least Bellamy's earlier fiction, such as *Dr. Heidenhoff's Process*. Bellamy's utopia is usually thought to be, like Melbourne or Manchester, flat and gray. Its actual location, in Boston, belies Bellamy's own small-town roots in Chicopee Falls, a small town near Springfield, Massachusetts, and it differs from Bellamy's original purpose, which was to locate the story and its future in the rural retreat of Asheville, North Carolina.[10] Bellamy's personal experience had this much in common with Marx, that he could remember his hometown before industrialization.

The utopia that influenced the world, however, was finally located by Bellamy in Boston, a European American city with a garden edge, designed like Central Park by Frederick Olmsted. Ironically, the influence of *Looking Backward* spread most profoundly westward, across the Midwest and to California. By the 1880s, Bellamy's desire was for social peace, abundance, and harmony. The standard features of Bellamy's utopias are widely recognized—an industrial army that releases its conscripts after age 45 into an age of leisure, a political regime elected by specialists rather than citizens, a technological fascination with gadgets and communal labor-saving devices; they are distributive utopias where production somehow seems absent in the face of this egalitarian consumer cornucopia, which nevertheless seems rather prim and puritan to late modern eyes.

The absence of democratic procedures was corrected in *Equality*. But Bellamy's utopia in *Looking Backward* remains a kind of state capitalism in which the military image of labor seems to reflect an ethic of service and the legacy of civil war rather than a desire for a militarized society. Whatever it is, it is neither barracks socialism nor war communism. Its private atmosphere is genteel, middle class, and closely familial; its public life again is reminiscent of the preference indicated by Saint-Simon, that the trouble of politics should be replaced by the smooth whir of administration. Bellamy's ethic might be one of civil militarism, but it is antimilitaristic. The economy works as one large trust, reflecting the early enthusiasm for trustification. Strife and waste are but thin memories of the past. Unlike Marx's early dreams, then, this is a consumptive, middle-class utopia of youthful work followed by mature rest. This is what gave William Morris a rash and prompted the rural counteridyll of

News from Nowhere, a text that resonates rather with the horticultural creativity of *The German Ideology,* if not its frenzy. For Bellamy, as for the later Marx, labor was the precondition of freedom, but freedom here means rest, whereas in Marx it remained connected to the energy of creativity.

What is less apparent in the general reception of *Looking Backward* is its basis in a kind of solidarism that might at first sight be associated with Émile Durkheim. For Durkheim, first in his *Socialism and Saint Simon* and then in *The Division of Labour in Society,* labor was the source of social altruism, the solution to problems of anomie generated by modernization. Durkheim's was a kind of guild socialism, itself modernized because industrialized.[11]

Just as Fourier stands in the shadows of Marx's utopia in *The German Ideology,* so is there a French utopian presence in the background of Bellamy's text. It is François de Fenélon, in *Telemachus.*[12] Bellamy's is a modernizing utopia, but it is also both rural and romantic in its inflection, gesturing toward New England transcendentalism, Ralph Waldo Emerson, and elsewhere Thomas Carlyle, and it has these Spartan connections with *Telemachus.* In Fenélon's retelling, Telemachus, the young son of Ulysses, travels the Mediterranean world in order to learn patience, courage, modesty, and simplicity. His is a Spartan utopia less of self-renunciation than of projection into the social other. Fenélon argued for a republican monarchy in which simplicity, labor, the virtues of agriculture, and the absence of luxury prevailed. The utopia of *Looking Backward* is not identical with this utopia, but the two images are connected.[13]

The strongest manifestation of this minimal egoism and maximal solidarism can be found in Bellamy's earlier fragment, "The Religion of Solidarity." Its guiding impulse is not the dull utilitarianism detected by Morris and others but rather a cosmological sense of the sublime. Bellamy's was a passionate, magical pantheism of sublime emotions. Bellamy believed that we are at the same time merely individual and universal. As he put it, the human soul seeks a more perfect realization of its solidarity with the universe.[14] Solidarity involves self-sacrifice; this is the motivating force for the invention of the industrial army in *Looking Backward,* not compulsion but service. However, even with the military ethic of sacrifice added in, this will not save Bellamy from Rousseau's predicament, that we must be forced to be free.

For Bellamy, then, the root problem was neither alienation, as in Marx, nor exactly anomie, as in Durkheim. The similarity with Durkheim remained, in that Bellamy viewed individualism as the result of industrialization rather than as its primordial condition. Solidarity, for Bellamy as for Durkheim, was a project, a challenge, whereas for Marx it was both an ontology, as the natural collectivism of species-being in the early work, and the result of industrial cooperation in the later work.

Alongside "The Religion of Solidarity," *Dr. Heidenhoff's Process* may be the most interesting supplementary text with which to locate Bellamy. Its plot concerns the use of period galvanic therapy to cure the guilt-ridden individual subject of the story. The plot thus resembles the narrative of *Looking Backward,* written eight years earlier, for it rests on a story of private and personal recovery and redemption. Here remembered sin is the most utterly diabolical influence in the universe. Dr. Heidenhoff's purpose is to extirpate it.[15] The presence of this text has prompted some, such as Franklin Rosemont, the historian of surrealism, to recast Bellamy as libertarian rather than authoritarian.[16] A more measured approach, exemplified by J. C. Thomas in *Alternative America,* portrays Bellamy rather in the company of other Americanist radicals such as Henry George and Henry Demarest Lloyd, contrary spirits rather than liberarians.[17]

In Rosemont's libertarian reading, Bellamy moves closer to the libertarianism of Herbert Marcuse. Perhaps a link between those utopian dimensions is in the work of Fourier, where utopia is activity rather than leisure, but it is also sexualized and playful. My own sense, rather, is that Bellamy can usefully be aligned with the thinkers proper to a field such as that surveyed by Leo Marx in *The Machine and the Garden.*[18]

Looking Back

Marx would remember the Rhine before industrialization, just as Bellamy could imagine Chicopee Falls before its water power turned it from an image of the natural sublime toward an image of industrial power, cotton, and guns. Did Marx and Bellamy alike dream of the future as an industrial sublime? I do not think so. Marx's enthusiasm for the revolutionary dynamic of capitalist expansion was never quite transferred into the giganticism of Fordism or the Bolsheviks. The conceptual basis of *Capital,* in fact, remains the image of the single factory; perhaps this was overdetermined by the nature of Engels's singular experience with textiles in Manchester. Marx does not sketch out the fuller details of political economy at either a national or a global level. The logical result of this is less the hope of socialism in one factory than a conceptual reliance on the singular unit of the factory and its socialist counterimage, which ends in *Capital*, volume 3, with the industrial rather than the craft regime of the associated producers therein. Sociologically, it is the middle, or the mediating institutions, that are left out. To put this more bluntly, Marx's brilliant elucidation of the centrality of the concepts labor and capital preceded the later, modernist indication that it was rather scale and complexity that should be established as defining characteristics of modernity. In this, Marx remained romantic more than modernist.

The gaps in Bellamy's conceptualization are structurally similar. The absences of democratic procedures in *Looking Backward*, to be remedied in *Equality*, indicate Bellamy's failure to connect the universal and individual via the particular. There are no intermediary associations or groups in Bellamy's writings, as there are in those of Durkheim, no civil society or particularity as in Georg Wilhelm Friedrich Hegel's *Philosophy of Right*. Both Marx and Bellamy were evidently antipolitical in their utopianism; it is this absence of conceptual mediation that explains the absence of organizational forms that could accommodate difference and help to articulate the political.

The stronger distinction between Marx and Bellamy concerns not the political but the literary. The Bellamy reception often screens out the fact that Bellamy was indeed a writer, primarily a journalist and novelist, whose greatest success in *Looking Backward* was an accident. Bellamy backed into politics, then discovered that he was obliged to stay there; such was the nature of the times. He was thrust into politics and was morally unable to refuse the sense of obligation. Marx's distance from utopia and its politics was distinct in formation, and there is no literary outlet for his dreamings. Marx's fatal mistake, self-explained in the 1859 preface to *A Contribution to the Critique of Political Economy*, was willfully to turn away from the sphere of civil society, now arguing rather that truth could be best located in the critique of political economy. The revival of the category civil society, not least with the decline and collapse of the Soviet empire, was in this sense a return to the other side of Marx. It does not make sense to blame Marx for Bolshevism unless we embrace both idealism and anachronism in thinking. But Marx's occlusion of politics, however widely shared in its predemocratic phase in world history, nevertheless shadowed the subsequent history of marxism.

Bellamy, in comparison, lost his followers into progressivism or into the movements that generated distinct practical aspects of utopia, such as the Tennessee Valley Authority. Bellamy began with what Leo Marx calls a pastoral middle landscape in which art and nature blurred until technology and immigrant labor displaced the Virgilian or, in a different sense, Jeffersonian dream of rural peace.[19] The attendant images might be those of Marx or at least Engels viewing Manchester, or they might be those of Charles Dickens. Thus Bellamy might be viewed as another transitional writer of American modernity, where the pastoral ideal remains of service long after the machine's appearance in the landscape. By such means could the United States continue to define its purpose as the pursuit of rural happiness while devoting its life energies to productivity, wealth, and power.[20]

In all this, it emerges that there are two moot issues and points of comparison for Marx and Bellamy: not only the nature but also the location of their utopias. Theirs were both imaginary futures made of images of the past, however different the two places and life experiences may have been.

Both Marx and Bellamy might be said, in this sense, to have longed for the small town, even as they also praised and set to work in their own thinking those forces that would accelerate scale and complexity. If we have failed, as scholars of utopia, sufficiently to identify this deep tension, this may be because we continue to extend it, as we, too, toss and turn between those streams that we call romanticism and enlightenment.

(2004)

Fourteen

Socialism and America

Why is there no socialism in the United States? Werner Sombart's question is famous; less well known is the answer. First published in the *Archiv für Sozialwissenschaft und Sozialpolitik* in 1905, the famous if clichéd answer had to do with the American working class's selling out socialism for reefs of roast beef and mountains of apple pie. Sombart's elongated answer was both more sophisticated and more interesting than this. C. T. Husbands, who edited the English version of the book that followed the essay, made a list, for the longer answer of course was multivariate. There were many reasons. First, American workers had a favorable attitude toward capitalism. Second, this favorable attitude extended to the American system of government, indicated by the high degree of civic integration. Third, the dominant two-party system sidelined socialist alternatives. Fourth, the working class had indeed been bought off by material rewards. Fifth, there were greater opportunities for upward social mobility in America. Sixth, and finally, the frontier reduced proletarian militancy.[1] In short, in the period language of the left, working-class culture was petty bourgeois.

Sombart's own argument resembles that of classical social democracy, as exemplified by its leading German theorist, Karl Kautsky: what was good for capitalism would be good for socialism. "The United States of America is capitalism's land of promise," wrote Sombart. "All conditions needed for its complete and pure development were first fulfilled here."[2] Here Sombart showed the kind of enthusiasm for American development that Marx had anticipated in *The Communist Manifesto*. Capitalism and America were a match made in heaven, the ideal type made real. Moreover, America already looked like the exceptional country, that which would know no bounds, locally or globally (4). Sombart shared that period enthusiasm for the New World, all finished with Europe. The marxian echoes here combine with Weberian sympathies. After all, Max Weber's essay on the Protestant ethic had first appeared in the same journal in which Sombart was publishing his essay and for which they shared editorial responsibility. So Sombart, too, insisted that the process of capitalist hyperdevelopment in America was culturally driven: "In fact, nowhere on earth have the economic system and the essence of capitalism reached as full a development as in North America" (4).

Yet the underlying sympathy in Sombart's essays is marxian, at least in political or prophetic terms. Inasmuch as American capitalism best approximated the concentration of capital described in *Das Kapital*, this also meant that America was ripe for revolution (6). On the one hand, America proves *Das Kapital*, including its unscheduled revolutionary outcome in chapter 32 of that book; on the other hand, it looks like a case sui genesis. America is obsessed with quantity and bigness, restlessness, and the ideal of constant self-advancement. Sombart's judgment was acute: "This competitive psychology produces a deep-seated need for freedom of movement" (13).

What surprises the reader of Sombart's book is the insistence, nevertheless, that this restless capitalism remains the prelude to socialism. America is counterintuitive for classical socialists. If it is the most developed, representing the highest stage of capitalism, it should logically also contain the most actively revolutionary proletariat.

Where, then, are the American socialists? Are there more than a few broken-down Germans in America, without any following? (15). And if there are no socialists in America, is this fact not sufficient to refute marxism? But no, Sombart insisted, it was absolutely not true that there were no socialists in the United States; there were two social democratic parties in 1905, neither exclusively German. What cannot be denied, however, is that the American working class does not embrace socialism (16). There may be socialists, but there is no socialism in America. There is no significant support for marxism in the United States. The American worker is too optimistic and patriotic; he may have some commitment to unionism or laborism, but he also has a fundamentally capitalist disposition. What explains the difference? Americanism, a specifically "American spirit," and the material conditions of its possibility (23). Now arrives the list of variables assembled by Husbands—a dominant two-party system, marginalization of third parties, positive citizenship rather than exclusion and resistance, American populism, and superior income levels. The latter, regarding the way American workers consume, brings us to the heart of Sombart's analysis. American workers do indeed eat better than their German counterparts, though Germans drink more (102). As Sombart concluded, tongue in cheek, "Abstinence fanatics who are favourable to capitalism will be ready to discover close connections between the [German] poison of alcohol and the poison of socialism" (105).

Perhaps, then, this is the stomach rather than the heart of the matter. The heart of the matter, more likely, is to be found in the social position of the American worker. In the United States, class knows less distance than in Europe; workers and bosses can more readily be viewed as partners in the great enterprise. And if not, there is freedom of movement: the working class can go west (116). Geographical and social mobility always appear to be possible. Sombart closed with Henry George, though the spirit of his argument is that associated with F. J. Turner; the west, after all, is finite. Then he exited in the spirit of Marx's apocalyptic scenario in *Das Kapital*, completely by surprise: "My present opinion is as follows: *all the factors that till now have prevented the development of Socialism in the United States are about to disappear or to be converted into their opposite, with the result that in the next generation Socialism in America will very probably experience the greatest expansion of its appeal*" (119; emphasis in the original). Unless this was a premonition of the Great Depression, its issue was awry, as was Marx's in *Das Kapital*. The logic of Sombart's work, so to speak, represents an unreconciled tension between what we might now identify as its marxian and weberian currents. The more powerful implication is that the purchase of socialism will continue to be marginalized by the power of Americanism.

The legacy of Sombart's question, or answer, is clearly more complicated than "reefs of roast beef" suggests. Others, like Daniel Bell, were also to focus on culture and on the politics of culture in seeking to explain the situation. Bell's essay, written in 1949–50 and published in 1952 as *Marxian Socialism in the United States*, remains one of the most important works in the field. Bell, like Sombart, begins from the question Why is there no socialism in America? But his response is in terms of the political culture of the left, not only American exceptionalism. Bell's question, rather, is Why did the organized socialist movement fail to adapt to American conditions?[3] Bell's answer is clear: the Socialist Party of America (SPA) was too marxist, in the American world but not of it. The Communist Party, even more emphatically, was neither in nor of the world but encapsulated in a world of its own. The American labor movement, in contrast, learned to live in and of the world but became American at the expense of socialism.

Bolshevism, in this account, is neither in the world nor of it but stands outside (13). In the American case, Daniel De Leon and then the Industrial Workers of the World stood outside, Samuel Gompers and the American Federation of Labor (AFL) inside, accommodating the world. The most influential American socialists, like Edward Bellamy, were nationalists or populists. The Socialist Party peaked in 1912, but at the high point its vote stood at about 6 percent, with one congressman (90). By opposing World War I, the SPA cut itself off from the labor movement and the people (116). The path of American economic and social development simply belied the marxian theorems, class bipolarization and all. As Bell concluded in his afterword, Sombart had the right answer but had asked the wrong question (195). There was and always had been elements of socialism in America, from New York and Chicago to Milwaukee and beyond. Yet the fault in the question remained, and it was obvious from outside the marxian tradition. As Bell put it, the real question was rather "Why Should There Be Socialism in the United States?" (197). European socialism had resulted from proletarian exclusion. In the United States, in contrast, classes were permeable and cultures regional. Socialism in America failed to put down strong roots, or, when it did, those roots overdetermined the outcome. The socialist impulse was rechanneled via progressivism and the New Deal until its romantic lineage was revived in the 1960s, though this again was too far away from the mainstream politically to effect it. Socialism was simply too romantic to connect sufficiently to a culture more worldly. As Weber had it, socialists were too much obsessed with absolute ends, insufficiently anchored in an ethic of responsibility. In Bell's view, the weberian motif plainly overcame the marxian desire for the new world in the new world. Socialists, in this view, spent too much time talking to each other, lived too long with dreams of redemption to make sense to their own imaginary audience.

Like Daniel Bell, Seymour Martin Lipset gave a good part of his work to the analysis of socialism in North America. The most systematic explanation came in the book he coauthored with Gary Marks, *It Didn't Happen Here: Why Socialism Failed in the United States* (2000).[4] Lipset and Marks, too, depart from the Sombart question Why is there no socialism in the United States? Their response is apparent: socialism was not absent but a failure. It failed because of American exceptionalism. The most central argument here is simply that America was different from Europe. Lipset and Marks follow Richard Hofstadter's line of thought that America's fate was not to have an ideology but to be one (29). The American ideology is sustained by five images: antistatism, laissez-faire, individualism, populism, and equalitarianism (30). Antonio Gramsci understood this, preferring Americanism viewed as a whole way of life to, say, Taylorism, understood analytically as its technology. The analysis in *It Didn't Happen Here* fans out other causal factors and explanations—the dominant two-party system, the presidential system, federalism, the split between unions and the Socialist Party, the distinctive business character of American unionism, the significance of Franklin Roosevelt and the New Deal. Also working against the prospect of an American socialism were the relative weakness of socialist subculture, with the exception of experiences like that in Milwaukee, itself exceptional; ethnic diversity and racism, relative material affluence compared to Europe; the "foreign nature of the party," first too German and then too Russian; the political sectarianism followed by socialists; the rejection of a labor party; political repression; and so on and so forth (chap. 1).

In retrospect it seems clear that, with all these factors and more militating against socialism and socialists, the cause was bound to fail in America. What Lipset and Marks make clear, however, is that this was not for want of trying. Hundreds of thousands of socialists dedicated their lives to these struggles, and failed. In summary, they failed for three reasons: they were unable to sustain a strong and durable socialist party; they were unable to create an independent labor party in alliance with mainstream unions, as in other English-speaking societies; and they were unable to capture one of the major parties (263). This is to say, following Daniel Bell, that they failed for strategic and specifically political as well as cultural reasons. Yet the overarching explanatory claim made by Lipset and Marks is cultural and sociological. "Our comparative studies lead us to the conclusion," they wrote, "that the American social system is a starting point for explaining the failures of socialism" (265). The dice are loaded against socialism in America; other new world experiences like those of Australia and New Zealand work within different constraints, follow differing, formatively British traditions, and innovate in ways that American socialists generally evade. American foundational influences are German and often marxian rather than Anglo or Fabian, and their results are exclusivist and dogmatic rather than mainstream or pragmatic. Australia and New Zealand were naturally statist, having been founded via the British state or through the impulse to new, cooperative or small holding beginnings. Distinctive elements of American culture—antistatism and individualism—negated the appeal of socialism for the mass of American workers for much of the twentieth century. Americanism begat the American Dream, open in principle to all. America became, in consequence, the only Western democracy without a labor, social democratic, or socialist party (270). Industrial relations and radical politics never quite met as they did in Europe.

Yet for all this, the American model is now becoming more universal, less exceptional. The combined forces of neoliberalism and globalization have meant that labor parties like those in Australia and New Zealand have become more "American," antistatist and individualized, less closely connected to unions, generally less distinct from non–labor parties. New Labor looks more and more American, at least in the Clintonian sense. The postwar boom is conspicuously over, and with it all its attendant forms—postwar statism, social democracy, citizenship à la Marshall, full employment à la Keynes, nuclear families, Pleasantville, and so on. Perhaps the most signal remaining theme from the socialist tradition, alongside the grating inequality that seems to have no effect on those untouched by it, remains the problem of nature, ecology, sustainability, and waste. But then, as Lipset and Marks conclude, what America now plainly lacks is not socialism but anything like a Green Party. Exceptionalism, in this regard, persists (chap. 1).

Size, power, global hegemony—certainly in these senses America is exceptional. But then all experiences in policy and culture are. As Zygmunt Bauman concluded, the idea of exceptionalism remains problematical, connected as it is to American global domination and to the inevitable contrast of Europe, that "old" world that also wants to be a new and different world.[5] In this way the idea of exceptionalism still reflects the incomplete intellectual struggle between the newly established American social sciences of the early twentieth century and the European fathers of sociology, the writers of the classics, whose frame of reference was conventionally the old world rather than the new. Not that this was absolute: Marx knew that the new world was a wild card, that social experiment there would be different in Australia, in California, or in the sense in which the United States would carry forward the Faustian mission of modernism so powerfully anticipated in *The Communist Manifesto*. Weber was deeply impressed by American drive, by Chicago, like a man with his skin peeled off. Durkheim's case for sociology was plainly French but also profoundly taken by the need for modernization. Yet America is not Europe, especially if we focus on California, the fifth largest economy in the world and a rather different place than Boston, New York, or Philadelphia. In this way, America might still be leading rather than exceptional. For if political cultures like those in Australia are traditionally British, patterns of suburban life and culture are Californian.

Victoria de Grazia also tacks off Sombart's question in her major recent book *Irresistable Empire: America's Advance through Twentieth Century Europe*.[6] De Grazia's achievement, from the perspective of this essay, is to explain Fordism and its commercial and advertising regime as co-constituted by transatlantic traffic. Americanism was at work in Europe from the beginning of the twentieth century, which made it less than unalloyed. She tells this as the story of the rise of a great imperium with the outlook of a great emporium (3). The Marshall Plan had begun fifty years earlier as a marketing plan. The Rotary Clubs, for example, were established in Dresden into the 1920s, having first met there in 1905 (27).

The significance of Sombart in this larger story was not that the workers had been bought off by buckets of roast beef and pie but that consumption in America was not mediated by status in the way it was in Europe. Culture was more open in the United States, even as economic inequality was more marked than in Europe (100). Mass marketing fit the mass society. As Hendrik de Man later put it in his book on Americanism, the significant question was less "Why no socialism in America?" than "Why is there socialism in Europe?" (117).

According to de Grazia, it was not only Stalin and Ford but also Hitler and Ford who were connected (125). Porsche visited Detroit, and so on; but Hitler's was plainly a regime of command consumption. In the United States, the hegemony of Fordism gave way to that of Sloanism, the General Motors version, which reintroduced status and model differentiation against the dull uniformity of the model T (135). These influences were indeed global, universal in reach if not always in application.

What does it mean, then, a century after Sombart, to say that America is exceptional? Plainly Sombart imagined America as a case deviating from the European norm, though, as we have seen, he nevertheless persisted in expecting a reversal. After exceptionalism, there would come conformity, as in Marx's scenario in the closing of *Das Kapital*—America would lead, after all, but this time to socialism.

A different view, more sober than that of Sombart, more nuanced in its analysis, comes from the historical sociologist Michael Mann (out of California, of all places). Mann developed an even more exhaustive list of reasons as to why there has been so little socialism historically in America. The nuance of his historical sociology is to place special emphasis on political violence and the role of the state rather than exceptionalism as such. Mann's catalog is exhaustive and demands attention. It is as follows. He counts thirteen answers to Sombart's question:

Individualism
1. *Dominance by small property ownership.* Most colonial settlement was by small farm proprietors who remained central to the Revolution and to the Jeffersonian and Jacksonian movements. The ideology of small property ownership dominated from the beginning. Early America was unsympathetic to "feudalism"; later America, to socialism. . . .
2. *The frontier thesis,* originally proposed by Turner in 1893, argues that the struggle to extend the American frontier in a harsh environment against warlike foes resulted in a rugged individualism hostile to collectivism. As the frontier acquired mythic cultural resonance, it influenced all of the United States, encouraging racial and spatial, not class, struggle.
3. *Moral Protestantism* encouraged individualism. Without a state religion, yet with strong Protestant sects, America encouraged individuals to solve social problems from within their own moral resources.
4. *Mobility* opportunities encouraged individuals to seek personal, not collective, advancement.
5. *Capitalist prosperity* diffused among Americans. They have been reluctant to tamper with private property relations. American workers have been individually materialistic.

Sectionalism
6. *Racism.* Slavery divided the early working class. Segregation survived in the South until after World War II, and united class action of blacks and whites remained difficult everywhere, especially during the mass black migration to the North in the early twentieth century. . . .
7. *Immigration.* Waves of immigrants added ethnic, linguistic, and religious divisions. Older immigrant groups became occupationally entrenched, reinforcing skilled sectionalism with ethnic stratification. Catholic immigration in the late nineteenth century impeded socialism because the church was then engaged in a crusade against socialism. Kraditor (1981)

claims that immigrants were more attached to their ethnicity than their class. Their goal was to create self-sufficient ethnocultural enclaves, not a working-class community. Workers' communities did not reinforce the collective laborer—they undermined him.

8. *Continental diversity.* The size and diversity of America ensured that industrialization differed among regions. Workers in different industries have been spatially segregated from each other and industry has kept moving into nonunionized regions. Workers migrated more, ensuring that hereditary working-class communities did not emerge. National class solidarity never really appeared.

9. *Sectarianism.* American labor was internally divided by factional fighting among groups like the Knights of Labor, the American Federation of Labor, rival socialist parties, syndicalists, the Congress of Industrial Organizations, and the Communist party. Had they fought capitalism more and one another less, the outcome would have differed. . . .

American democracy

10. *Early male democracy.* The United States achieved adult white male democracy by the 1840s—before the working class emerged. It had, in Perlman's (1928: 167) famous words, the "free gift of the ballot." This is an upbeat, approving view of American democracy: Workers could remedy grievances through liberal democracy without recourse to alternative ideologies like socialism. . . .

11. *Federalism.* The U.S. Constitution divides powers between a relatively weak federal government (with a small nonindustrial capital city) and stronger state governments, and among three branches of government—the presidency, two houses of Congress, and a separate judiciary. Workers had to divide their attention among government agencies, and this weakened national class politicization and unity. . . .

12. *The two-party system.* By the time labor emerged, two cross-class parties were institutionalized. Congressional elections were based on large constituencies; presidential elections, on just one national constituency. Emerging third parties, including labor parties, could not advance steadily by first obtaining minority representation in national politics. As labor was not at first strong enough to elect the president or senators, it worked within bourgeois parties that could win elections instead of forming a labor party that could not. The parties, however, were weaker in the federal system than in more centralized polities. This reduced party discipline and made them less responsive to broader class programs.

13. *Repression.* A more cynical view of American democracy emphasizes the extraordinary level of repression, judicial and military, mobilized against American working-class movements.[7]

Mann concluded that the United States represents an extreme case, which became extreme rather than being so from the country's birth. He argued that there were four distinct American political crystallizations—domestic militarism; capitalist liberalism; party democracy; and Federalism—that made the U.S. experience different.[8] The workers' response to these peculiarities was sectionalism rather than exceptionalism: the United States became extreme. This was a politically led process, as Mann concluded in the spirit of Karl Polanyi's *Great Transformation*.

Does capitalism, then, invariably draw out socialism? The short answer is yes, historically, though often the most this means is that socialism persists as a counterculture. The more acute periods of socialist development correspond to the more formative struggles against the establishment and the consolidation of capitalism in its more openly violent historical forms. Perhaps this is the most we can hope for as we enter the new century.

There are other explanations for the marginalization of socialism, and other contributors to the argument. John Kautsky (related to Karl, of course) famously argued that socialism was, ironically in light of Marx's dreams, as much to be explained by feudal heritage as by capitalist disruption of the eighteenth-century calm.[9] The broader question, appropriately for the close of this book, is less "Why no socialism in America?" than "Why so little socialism at all today?" And "Why has socialism become so marginal?"

Michael Mann's broader work offers one way to approach the global impasse. After generating two massive volumes of civilizational sociology in *The Sources of Social Power*, Mann took two significant sidesteps, one to deal with fascism, one with genocide. The twentieth century may, in retrospect, have been the American Century, but it was also what Eric Hobsbawm called *The Age of Extremes*. Most notably, it was the century of totalitarianism, of communism and fascism. The debate about totalitarianism remains unresolved because it is unresolvable. The differences between the German and Soviet experience remain significant, yet the results were appallingly similar, especially viewed at a distance.

Mann's view of fascism is that it was merely the most extreme form of nation-statism, replacing class conflict with claims to ethnic unity.[10] Contrary to the old marxist axiom, then, fascism was less the potential in all of capitalism than the most extreme manifestation of state-organized nationalism. In Mann's definition—shorter than his answer to the question of why is there no socialism in America—there were five key factors: nationalism, statism, transcendence of the present, cleansing (which anticipates ethnic cleansing), and paramilitarism.[11] This specific combination was what served to make fascism historically specific and non-repeatable, though its component parts are still raised and persistent in different ways.

Mann pursued the logic of his own case into the book called *The Dark Side of Democracy: Explaining Ethnic Cleansing*.[12] Across a characteristically broad and comprehensive comparative canvas, the essential claim here is that class conflict and democracy go together, whereas dominant ethnonationalism leads to ethnic cleansing. Democracy, in this view, is dangerous when open to manipulation by *ethnos* rather than *demos*. But is ethnic cleansing really the dark side of democracy? In terms of the concepts used across the essays in the present book, it might look, rather, like the dark side of modernity. Indeed, this is one suggestive shorthand definition of totalitarianism itself—that it was the dark side of modernity in the twentieth century.

Finally, Robin Archer's important study *Why Is There No Labor Party in the United States?* arrives in the center of the present field of analysis.[13] Archer's question is significantly different from Sombart's or Mann's: not Why is there no socialism? but Why is there no labor party? And his point of comparison bears directly on the essays gathered here, for it is the Australian Labor Party.

Archer's argument begins with the fact of political contingency. Both the American and the Australian labor movements were subject to repression in the 1890s; the Australians turned to politics, whereas Gompers and the AFL turned away. These two "most similar cases," America and Australia, take Archer's analysis to a different place than the Sombart comparison of Europe and America, and away from the conventional stories about exceptionalism, roast beef, and apple pie (chap. 1). The path of his argument is fascinating, covering both larger and smaller issues, noting, for example, that the Australians had even more roast beef than the Americans (chap. 1).

On the larger issues, Archer concludes that the weakness of the new unionism in the United States, resulting partly from repression, stood alongside religion and socialist sectarianism as major issues preventing the establishment of an American Labor Party (240–41). The strength of European socialist influences seems to have been a weakness rather than a strength, as Bell had argued earlier.

At the end of the long twentieth century and the beginning of a new one, the irony is not that there was no socialism in America but that the very proposition itself seems counterintuitive. It is not that socialists and radicals have ceased to exist or that the problems that motivate them have disappeared. The point, rather, as Daniel Bell argued in 1952, is that the question was always wrong. Socialists should never presume that their projected desire is built into history as necessity. Socialism remains a necessary utopia. That is a good enough place to end, and to begin.

(2009)

Notes

Introduction

1. Peter Beilharz, *Postmodern Socialism: Romanticism, City and State* (Melbourne: Melbourne University Press, 1994).
2. Ferenc Fehér and Agnes Heller, "Class, Modernity, Democracy," *Theory and Society* 12 (1983).
3. Georg Lukács, "Reification and the Consciousness of the Proletariat," in *History and Class Consciousness* (London: Merlin, 1971).
4. Peter Beilharz, *Trotsky, Trotskyism, and the Transition to Socialism* (London: Croom Helm, 1984).
5. Ferenc Fehér, Agnes Heller, and George Markus, *Dictatorship over Needs* (Oxford: Blackwell, 1983).
6. Zygmunt Bauman, *Europe* (Oxford: Polity, 2004).
7. Johann P. Arnason, *The Future That Failed: Origins and Destinies of the Soviet Model* (London: Routledge, 1993).
8. Johann P. Arnason, *Civilizations in Dispute* (Leiden: Brill, 2003).
9. Johann P. Arnason, "Perspectives and Problems of Critical Marxism in Eastern Europe," Part One, *Thesis Eleven* 4 (1982); Part Two, *Thesis Eleven* 5, no. 6 (1982).
10. Arnason, *The Future That Failed*, 118.
11. Antonio Gramsci, *Selections from the Prison Notebooks* (New York: International, 1971).
12. Terry Smith, *Making the Modern: Industry, Art and Design in America* (Chicago: University of Chicago Press, 1993). On Germany see Mary Nolan, *Visions of Modernity: American Business and the Modernization of Germany* (New York: Oxford University Press, 1994); James W. Ceaser, *Reconstructing America: The Symbol of America in Modern Thought* (New Haven, Conn.: Yale University Press, 1997); Anton Kaes, Martin Jay, and Edward Dimmendberg, eds., *The Weimar Republic Sourcebook* (Berkeley and Los Angeles: University of California Press, 1994).

13. Alan Ball, *Imagining America: Influence and Images in Twentieth Century Russia* (Lanham, Md.: Rowman and Littlefield, 2003).
14. Ibid., 26.
15. Ibid., 30–31.
16. Ibid., 43.
17. Ibid., 58.
18. Ibid., 124.
19. Ibid., 133.
20. Charles Beard and Mary Beard, *The Rise of American Civilization* (New York: Macmillan, 1927); Max Lerner, *America As a Civilization* (New York: Henry Holt, 1957).
21. C. L. R. James, *American Civilization* (Boston: Blackwell, 1993), 13.
22. Ibid., 28.
23. Ibid., 240–41.
24. Peter Beilharz, *Imagining the Antipodes: Theory, Culture and the Visual in the Work of Bernard Smith* (Melbourne: Cambridge University Press, 1997).
25. Peter Beilharz, *Zygmunt Bauman: Dialectic of Modernity* (London: Sage, 2000).
26. Peter Beilharz, "Trotsky, Trotskyism, and the Theory of the Transition to Socialism," Ph.D. dissertation, Monash University, Clayton, Australia, 1983; Beilharz, *Trotsky, Trotskyism, and the Transition to Socialism* (London: Croom Helm, 1987).
27. Peter Beilharz, *Labour's Utopias: Bolshevism, Fabianism, Social Democracy* (London: Routledge, 1992).
28. Peter Beilharz, *Transforming Labor: Labour Tradition and the Labor Decade* (Melbourne: Cambridge University Press, 1994); Beilharz, *Postmodern Socialism*.

1. Socialism

1. Zygmunt Bauman, *Socialism: The Active Utopia* (London: Allen and Unwin, 1976); Zygmunt Bauman, *Memories of Class* (London: Routledge, 1982).
2. Peter Beilharz, *Postmodern Socialism: Romanticism, City and State* (Melbourne: University of Melbourne Press, 1994).
3. Donald Sassoon, *One Hundred Years of Socialism* (London: Tauris, 1996).
4. Alain Touraine, *The Workers Movement* (Cambridge: Cambridge University Press, 1987); Ronald Tiersky, *Ordinary Stalinism* (London: Allen and Unwin, 1983); Alastair Davidson, *The Theory and Practice of Italian Communism* (London: Merlin, 1982); Peter Beilharz, *Transforming Labor* (Melbourne: Cambridge University Press, 1994).
5. Anthony Wright, *Socialisms* (Oxford: Oxford University Press, 1986); Bauman, *Memories of Class*.
6. Alec Nove, *The Economics of Feasible Socialism* (London: Allen and Unwin: 1980).
7. Ferdinand Tönnies, *Community and Association* (London: Routledge, 1974).
8. Peter Beilharz, *Labour's Utopias: Bolshevism, Fabianism, Social Democracy* (London: Routledge, 1992), 7–8.
9. Ibid., 11.
10. Cornelius Castoriadis, *The Imaginary Institution of Society* (Oxford: Polity, 1987); Jean Baudrillard, *The Mirror of Production* (St. Louis: Telos, 1975).
11. Beilharz, *Labour's Utopias*, 4.
12. Ibid.; Manfred Steger, *Selected Writings of Eduard Bernstein* (Atlantic Highlands: Humanities, 1996); Manfred Steger, *The Quest for Evolutionary Socialism: Eduard Bernstein and Social Democracy* (New York: Cambridge University Press, 1997).
13. Beilharz, *Labour's Utopias*, chap. 2; Johann Arnason, *The Experiment That Failed* (London: Routledge, 1993).

14. Beilharz, *Labour's Utopias*, 24.
15. Ibid., 30.
16. Ian Britain, *Fabianism and Culture* (Cambridge: Cambridge University Press, 1982).
17. Martin Wiener, *English Culture and the Decline of the Industrial Spirit* (Cambridge: Cambridge University Press, 1985).
18. Anthony Wright, *G. D. H. Cole and Socialist Democracy* (Oxford: Oxford University Press, 1979).
19. Anthony Wright, *R. H. Tawney* (Manchester: Manchester University Press, 1987).
20. Beilharz, *Labour's Utopias*, chap. 3.
21. Werner Sombart, *The Jews and Modern Capitalism* (New York: Free Press, 1951); Hilaire Belloc, *The Servile State* (London: Constable, 1913).
22. Beilharz, *Labour's Utopias*, 62.
23. Antonio Gramsci, *Selections from the Prison Notebooks* (New York: International, 1971); Alastair Davidson, *Antonio Gramsci* (London: Merlin, 1978).
24. George Lukács, *History and Class Consciousness* (London: Merlin, 1971).
25. Martin Jay, *The Dialectical Imagination* (Boston: Little Brown, 1973); Rolf Wiggershaus, *The Frankfurt School* (Cambridge, Mass.: MIT Press, 1994).
26. François Dosse, *History of Structuralism* (Minneapolis: University of Minnesota Press, 1997).
27. Peter Beilharz, *Trotsky, Trotskyism, and the Transition to Socialism* (London: Croom Helm, 1987).
28. Boris Frankel, *Beyond the State?* (London: Macmillan, 1983); Bob Jessop, *The Capitalist State* (London: Martin Robinson, 1982).
29. Anne Showstack Sassoon, *Gramsci's Politics* (London: Hutchinson, 1987).
30. Andrew Arato and Jean Cohen, *Civil Society and Political Theory* (Cambridge, Mass.: MIT Press, 1992).
31. Ferenc Fehér and Agnes Heller, "Class, Democracy, Modernity," *Theory and Society* 12 (1983).

2. Socialism by the Back Door

1. Quoted by Susan Buck-Morss in *Dialectics of Seeing: Walter Benjamin and the Arcades Project* (Boston: MIT Press, 1989), 336.
2. See Paul Sauer, *The Story of the Beilharz Family* (Sydney: Temple Society, 1988); Paul Sauer, *The Holy Land Called: The Story of the Temple Society* (Melbourne: Temple Society, 1991).
3. Peter Beilharz, "Trotsky, Trotskyism, and the Theory of the Transition to Socialism," Ph.D. thesis, Monash University, Clayton, Australia, 1983; Peter Beilharz, *Trotsky, Trotskyism, and the Transition to Socialism* (London: Croom Helm, 1987).
4. Peter Beilharz, *Labour's Utopias: Bolshevism, Fabianism, Social Democracy* (London: Routledge, 1992).
5. Peter Beilharz, ed., *Social Theory: A Guide to Central Thinkers* (Sydney: Allen and Unwin, 1992); Peter Beilharz, Mark Considine, and Rob Watts, *Arguing about the Welfare State: The Australian Experience* (Sydney: Allen and Unwin, 1992); Peter Beilharz, Gillian Robinson, and John Rundell, eds., *Between Totalitarianism and Postmodernity* (Boston: MIT Press, 1992).
6. Verity Burgmann, "The Strange Death of Labour History," in *Bede Nairn and Labor History*, ed. Bob Carr et al. (Sydney: Pluto, 1991); Raelene Frances and Bruce Scates, "Is Labour History Dead?" *Australian Historical Studies* 25, no. 100 (April 1993): 470–81.

7. Peter Beilharz, *Postmodern Socialism: Romanticism, City and State* (Melbourne: University of Melbourne Press, 1994).
8. Peter Beilharz, *Transforming Labor: Labour Tradition and the Labor Decade in Australia* (Melbourne: Cambridge University Press, 1994).
9. See my "Republicanism and Citizenship," in *The Republicanism Debate*, ed. Wayne Hudson and David Carter (Sydney: Allen and Unwin, 1993), 109–17; Carole Pateman, *Participation and Democratic Theory* (Oxford: Oxford University Press, 1970); Orlando Patterson, *Freedom* (New York: Basic, 1991); and my *Postmodern Socialism*.
10. William Morris, "A Dream of John Ball," in *William Morris*, ed. G. D. H. Cole (Bloomsbury, England: Nonesuch Press, 1934), 214.

3. The Life and Times of Social Democracy

1. Crawford B. Macpherson, *The Life and Times of Liberal Democracy* (Oxford: Oxford University Press, 1977).
2. See, for example, Norman Dennis and Albert H. Halsey, *English Ethical Socialism* (Oxford: Oxford University Press, 1988); cf. my review in *Australian Society* (September 1989).
3. These arguments are detailed more fully in Peter Beilharz, *Labour's Utopias: Bolshevism, Fabianism, Social Democracy* (London and New York: Routledge, 1992).
4. E. Belfort Bax, "Our German-Fabian Convert," in *Marxism and Social Democracy*, ed. H. Tudor and J. M. Tudor (Cambridge: Cambridge University Press, 1988), 61–65; H. Hirsch, *Der "Fabier" Eduard Bernstein* (Bonn: Dietz 1977); see also Roger Fletcher, *From Bernstein to Brandt* (London: Edward Arnold, 1987); H. Kendall Rogers, "Eduard Bernstein Speaks to the Fabians," *International Review of Social History* 28 (1983): 320–338; Thomas Meyer, *Bernstein's Konstruktiver Sozialismus* (Berlin: Dietz, 1977); Horst Heiman and Thomas Meyer, *Bernstein und der Demokratische Sozialismus* (Berlin: Dietz, 1978).
5. Eduard Bernstein, "Möglichkeiten Sozialismus," Bernstein Papers (International Institute for Social History, Amsterdam), E123, n.d., 14.
6. E. Belfort Bax, "Our German Fabian Convert," in *Marxism and Social Democracy*, ed. H. Tudor and J. M. Tudor (Cambridge: Cambridge University Press, 1988), 61–62.
7. Eduard Bernstein, "Among the Philistines," in *Marxism and Social Democracy*, ed. H. Tudor and J. M. Tudor (Cambridge: Cambridge University Press, 1988), 66.
8. Tudor and Tudor, *Marxism and Social Democracy*, 23.
9. See generally Gunther Roth, *The Social Democrats in Imperial Germany* (Totowa, N.J.: Bedminster, 1963); Vernon Lidtke, *The Alternative Culture: Socialist Labour in Imperial Germany* (Oxford: Oxford University Press, 1985); Hans-Josef Steinberg, *Sozialismus und deutsche Sozialdemokratie* (Bonn: Neue Gesellschaft, 1972); Fletcher, *From Bernstein to Brandt*.
10. "Evolutionary Socialism: Interview with Herr Eduard Bernstein," *Jewish Chronicle* 24, no. 11 (1899), available in the Bernstein Papers (International Institute for Social History, Amsterdam), G462, 22.
11. Eduard Bernstein, "The Socialistic Theory of the Bolsheviks . . . ," Bernstein Papers (International Institute for Social History, Amsterdam), A123, n.d.
12. Gugliemo Carchedi, *Class Analysis and Social Research* (Oxford: Blackwell, 1987); H. Müller, *Der Klassenkampf in der deutschen Sozialdemokratie* (Zurich: Magazin, 1892).
13. Carchedi, *Class Analysis and Social Research*, 11.
14. Tudor and Tudor, *Marxism and Social Democracy*, 192f.
15. Ibid., 193, 217.
16. Ibid., 168–69.

17. Ibid., 151.
18. Ibid., 90–97.
19. Ibid., 221, 229f.
20. Ibid., 233, 240.
21. Eduard Bernstein, *Evolutionary Socialism* (New York: Schocken, 1965), 96.
22. Ibid., 143.
23. Ibid., 147f.
24. Ibid., 148.
25. Ibid., 149.
26. Ibid., 148.
27. See generally Dieter Groh, *Negativ Integration und revolutionarer Attentismus* (Frankfurt: Ullstein, 1973).
28. See generally Karl Kautsky, *The Agrarian Question,* 2 vols. (Winchester, England: Zwan, 1988). Some of the antinomies of his position are nicely summarized by the editors, Hamza Alavi and Teodor Shanin, in their introduction.
29. Kautsky, *The Agrarian Question,* vol. 2, 443.
30. Karl Kautsky wrote about Morris in *Der Wahre Jacob* 268 (1896): 231f.
31. On dialectics, see especially Carchedi, *Class Analysis and Social Research.*
32. Karl Kautsky, *Bernstein und das Sozialdemokratische Programme* (Stuttgart: Dietz, 1899).
33. Karl Kautsky, *The Materialist Conception of History,* ed. J. H. Kautsky (New Haven: Yale University Press, 1988), 5–6. This is a labor of scholarship and love, and Kautsky's grandson and the publishers are to be applauded for it.
34. Ibid., 260.
35. Ibid., 28, 38–39, 43.
36. Ibid., 69, 70. Cf. Kautsky, *Agrarian Question,* vol. 2, 329.
37. Ibid., 356.
38. Ibid., 387.
39. Ibid., 395–97.
40. Ibid., 399.
41. Kautsky, *Agrarian Question,* vol. 2, 362.
42. Kautsky, *Materialist Conception,* 410, 419–21.
43. Ibid., 425–26.
44. Ibid., 464.
45. See generally the useful study by Harry Liebersohn, *Fate and Utopia in German Sociology, 1870–1923* (Cambridge, Mass.: MIT Press, 1989).
46. Martin Jay, *Fin de Siècle Socialism* (London: Methuen, 1988).
47. Peter Beilharz, "The Australian Left: Beyond Labourism?" in *Socialist Register 1985/1986* (London: Merlin, 1986); "The Labourist Tradition and the Reforming Imagination," in *Australian Welfare Historical Sociology,* ed. R. Kennedy (Sydney: Macmillan, 1989); "Social Democracy and Social Justice," *Australian and New Zealand Journal of Sociology* 25, no. 1 (1989).
48. See generally Marilyn Lake, "Socialism and Manhood: The Case of William Lane," *Labour History* (Sydney), 50 (1986); *The Limits of Hope: Soldier Settlement in Victoria 1915–1938* (Oxford: Oxford University Press, 1987).
49. Kevin McDonald, "After the Labour Movement," *Thesis Eleven* 20 (1988).
50. C. B. Macpherson, *The Rise and Fall of Economic Justice* (Oxford: Oxford University Press, 1986).
51. Michael Ignatieff, "Citizenship and Moral Narcissism," *Political Quarterly* 60, no. 1 (1989).

52. Beatrice Potter, *The Co-operative Movement in Great Britain* (London: Swan Sonnenschein, 1891), 75.
53. Pierre Rosanvallon, "The Decline of Social Visibility," in *Civil Society and the State*, ed. John Keane (London: Verso, 1988), 218.

4. The Fabian Imagination

1. See John K. Galbraith, *The Culture of Contentment* (New York: Houghton Mifflin, 1992); Rosalind Williams, *Notes on the Underground* (Boston: MIT, 1990).
2. See Anthony Wright, *Socialisms* (Oxford: Oxford University Press, 1980); Peter Beilharz, *Labour's Utopias: Bolshevism, Fabianism, Social Democracy* (London: Routledge, 1992).
3. See Peter Beilharz, *Transforming Labor: Labour Tradition and the Labor Decade* (Melbourne: Cambridge University Press, 1994); *Postmodern Socialism: Romanticism, City and State* (Melbourne: University of Melbourne Press, 1994).
4. For example Richard Kearney, *The Wake of Imagination* (London: Hutchinson, 1988); Martin Jay, *Fin-de-Siècle Socialism* (London: Routledge, 1988); Stjepan G. Mestrovic, *The Coming Fin-de-Siècle* (London: Routledge, 1991).
5. Martin Jay, "The Apocalyptic Imagination and the Inability to Mourn," paper presented at the Thesis Eleven Conference on Reason and Imagination, Melbourne, August 6, 1991.
6. David W. Lovell, "Some Propositions on 'The End of Socialism'?" *History of European Ideas* 19 (1990).
7. Peter Beilharz, "Fabianism and Marxism: Sociology and Political Economy," *Australian Journal of Political Science* 27 (1992).
8. Beilharz, *Labour's Utopias*, chap. l; Peter Beilharz, "Karl Marx," in *Social Theory*, ed. Peter Beilharz (Sydney: Allen and Unwin, 1992).
9. See chapter 3 of this volume.
10. Beilharz, "Fabianism and Marxism."
11. Alan McBriar, *Fabian, Socialism, and English Politics* (Cambridge: Cambridge University Press, 1962); Ian Britain, *Fabianism and Culture* (Cambridge: Cambridge University Press, 1982).
12. Anthony Wright, *G. D. H. Cole and Socialist Democracy* (Oxford: Oxford University Press, 1979). Wright also discusses recent enthusiasms for Tawney in his *R. H. Tawney* (Manchester, England: Manchester University Press, 1987).
13. Paul Hirst, ed., *The Pluralist Theory of the State* (London: Routledge, 1989).
14. Sally Alexander, ed., *Women's Fabian Tracts* (London: Routledge, 1986).
15. Sidney Webb, "The Existence of Evil," Passfield Papers (London School of Economics and Political Science) VI, 1, p. 35.
16. Sidney Webb, "The Ethics of Existence," Passfield Papers (London School of Economics and Political Science) VI, 4, p. 20.
17. Beatrice Potter, *The Co-operative Movement in Great Britain* (London: Swann Sonnenschein, 1891), 35; and see generally Sidney Webb and Beatrice Webb, *The Consumers Cooperative Movement* (London: Longmans, 1921).
18. Beatrice Potter, "The Relation between Co-operation and Trade Unionism," in *Problems of Modern Industry*, ed. Sidney Webb and Beatrice Webb (London: Longmans, 1920), 193.
19. Ibid., 200–201.
20. Sidney Webb and Beatrice Webb, *What Syndicalism Means: An Examination of the Origin and Motives of the Movement with an Analysis of its Proposals for the Control of Industry*, supplement to *The Crusade*, August 1912.

21. Sidney Webb, "The Economic Function of the Middle Class," Passfield Papers (London School of Economics and Political Science) VI, 20.
22. Ibid., 32.
23. Brian L. Crowley, *The Self, the Individual and the Community* (Oxford: Oxford University Press, 1987).
24. Leonard Woolf, "Political Thought and the Webbs," in *The Webbs and Their Work*, ed. M. Cole (London: Penn, 1949).
25. Anthony Giddens, *The Constitution of Society* (Cambridge: Polity, 1984); Cornelius Castoriadis, *The Imaginary Institution of Society* (Cambridge: Polity, 1987).
26. G. D. H. Cole, *Guild Socialism Re-stated* (London: Parsons, 1920), 124.
27. Ibid., 33.
28. Sidney Webb and Beatrice Webb, *A Constitution for the Socialist Commonwealth of Great Britain* (London: Longmans, 1920), 149, 309.
29. Ibid., 51.
30. Edward Pease, *History of the Fabian Society* (London: Fifield, 1916), 215; Beatrice Webb, *Minority Report of the Poor Law Commission*, 2 vols. (London, 1909).
31. Webb, *Minority Report*, vol. 1, 10–11.
32. Ibid., 12.
33. Ibid., 547.
34. Sidney Webb and Beatrice Webb, *The Prevention of Destitution* (London: Longmans, 1911), 33–35.
35. Webb and Webb, *A Constitution*, 196; and see the Webbs' *Methods of Social Study* (Cambridge: Cambridge University Press, 1975).
36. See chapter 3 of this volume; see generally Karl Kautsky, *The Labour Revolution* (London: Allen and Unwin, 1925), and *The Materialist Conception of History* (New Haven: Yale University Press, 1988).
37. See chapter 3 of this volume; Karl Kautsky, *The Dictatorship of the Proletariat* (Ann Arbor: University of Michigan Press, 1971).
38. Webb and Webb, *What Syndicalism Means*, 151.
39. See, for example, Beatrice Webb, *The Wages of Men and Women: Should They Be Equal?* (London: Longman, 1919), 26–27.

5. The Australian Left

1. See further Ralph Miliband, "Socialist Advance in Britain," *Socialist Register 1983* (London: Merlin, 1983). The peculiarly Australian configuration of laborism is detailed by Winton Higgins in "Reconstructing Australian Communism," *Socialist Register 1974* (London: Merlin, 1974), and by P. Love in *Labour and the Money Power* (Melbourne: Melbourne University Press, 1984).
2. Peter Wilenski, "Reform and Its Implementation: The Whitlam Years in Retrospect," in *Labor Essays 1980*, ed. Gareth Evans and John Reeves (Melbourne: Drummond, 1980).
3. Robert Catley and Bruce McFarlane, *Australian Capitalism in Boom and Depression* (Sydney: APCOL, 1981); Brian Head, ed., *State and Economy in Australia* (Melbourne: Oxford University Press, 1983).
4. See especially G. Elliott, "The Social Policy of the New Right," in *Australia and the New Right*, ed. M. Sawer (Sydney: Allen and Unwin 1982).
5. Jim Hagan, *History of the ACTU* (Melbourne: Longman-Cheshire 1981), 452.
6. Liberal Party of Australia (LPA), *Facing the Facts: Report of the Liberal Party Committee of Review* (Sydney: LPA, 1983).

7. See, for example, the references to and quotations from Curtin peppered throughout Bob Hawke, *National Reconciliation: The Speeches of Bob Hawke* (Sydney: Fontana 1984).

8. Herbert C. Coombs, "John Curtin: A Consensus Prime Minister?" *Arena* 69 (1984).

9. Robert Watts, "The Light on the Hill: The Origins of the Australian Welfare State, 1935–1945," doctoral thesis, Melbourne University, Melbourne, 1983; "The ALP and Liberalism 1941–1945," *Thesis Eleven* 7 (1983); "The Origins of the Australian Welfare State," in *Australian Welfare History*, ed. Richard Kennedy (Melbourne: Macmillan 1982).

10. See especially the work of Watts, and see also Tim Rowse, *Australian Liberalism and National Character* (Malmsbury, Australia: Kibble, 1978).

11. This view has been presented in Britain by Barry Hindess in "Bob's Bon Accord," *New Socialist*, January 1985.

12. Australian Labor Party–Australian Council of Trade Unions (ALP-ACTU), *Statement of Accord* (ACTU, Melbourne, n.d.), 1–3.

13. Ibid., 7.

14. Ibid., 4.

15. Ibid., 16.

16. See Australian Government Publishing Service (AGPS), *National Economic Summit Conference: Documents and Proceedings* (Canberra: AGPS 1983), vol. 2, 18–21; Peter Beilharz, "The View from the Summit," *Arena* 64 (1983).

17. AGPS, *National Economic Summit Conference*, 21ff.

18. See, for example, Chilla Bulbeck, "The Accord: The First Two Years," *Thesis Eleven* 14 (1986); and see Gwyneth Singleton, "The Economic Planning Advisory Council," and Randal Stewart, "The Politics of the Accord," in *Politics* 20, no. 1 (1985).

19. See, for example, Paul Keating, "Opportunities for Investment and Corporate Finance in Australia," *Australian Foreign Affairs Record* 56, no. 2 (1985).

20. See, for example, Ted Wheelwright, "The Dollar Is Down, the Debt Is Up and the Government Is Out to Lunch," *Australian Left Review* 92 (1985).

21. "The Strategic Basis Papers" (*National Times*, March 30, 1985) clarified this tendency; and see Bill Hayden, *Uranium, the Joint Facilities, Disarmament, and Peace* (Canberra: AGPS 1984).

22. Wilenski, "Reform and Its Implementation," 43; Peter Beilharz and Patricia Moynihan, "Medibank: Monument or Mausoleum of the Whitlam Government?" *Thesis Eleven* 7 (1983).

23. For detail see, for example, *Tribune* (Melbourne), July 3, 1985.

24. See, for example, Katharine West, *The Revolution in Australian Politics* (Ringwood, Australia: Penguin, 1984); cf. Peter Beilharz and Robert Watts, "The Discovery of Corporatism," *Australian Society*, November 1983.

25. See especially Bob Jessop, "Corporatism, Parliamentarism and Social Democracy," in *Trends toward Corporatist Intermediation*, ed. Phillipe Schmitter and Gerhard Lehmbruch (Beverly Hills, Calif.: Sage, 1979).

26. Pete Steedman, *Full Employment Is Possible: The Accord—A Framework for Economic and Industrial Democracy* (Canberra, June 6, 1984); and see generally Peter Beilharz, "The Left, the Accord, and the Future of Socialism," *Thesis Eleven* 13 (1986): 5–21.

27. Andrew Theophanous, "Back to Basics, Says the Left," *Age* (Melbourne), July 5, 1984.

28. Tim Colebatch, "Cliches, Not Logic, Behind Condemnation of the Left," *Age* (Melbourne), March 9, 1985; Kevin Childs, "The New Socialist Left," *Age* (Melbourne), November 15, 1984. It has been suggested that their hand can be seen in the Victorian ALP

policy document *Social Justice* (*Age* [Melbourne], March 7, 1985). If this is true, there is little to be impressed by: the document is, like the Accord, lacking in any real rigor or adequate mechanisms of implementation.

29. See, for example, Bill Hayden, *The Implications of Democratic Socialism*, Fabian pamphlet 16 (Melbourne), 1968; see also "The Contemporary Implications of Democratic Socialism," in *Labor Essays 1982*, ed. Gareth Evans and John Reeves (Melbourne: Drummond, 1982), and even Bob Hawke, "Fabianism and Labor Policy," in *National Reconciliation: The Speeches of Bob Hawke* (Sydney: Fontana, 1984).

30. See the essays collected in *Labor Essays 1980*, ed. Evans and Reeves, 157.

31. See Love, *Labour and the Money Power*.

32. See Gareth Evans's essays in *Labor Essays 1980* and in B. O'Meagher, *The Socialist Objective* (Sydney: Hale and Iremonger, 1983).

33. Bob Connell, "Towards a Socialist Program," in *The Socialist Objective* (Sydney: Hale and Iremonger, 1983), and *Socialism and Labor: An Australian Strategy* (Sydney: Labor Praxis, 1978). Agnes Heller, *Why We Should Maintain the Socialist Objective* (Kooyong, Australia: ALP, 1982).

34. Ferenc Fehér and A. Heller, "Class, Democracy, Modernity," *Theory and Society* 12 (1983).

35. See, for example, Gareth Evans's essays in *Labor Essays 1980*.

36. Bruce O'Meagher, Introduction to *The Socialist Objective*.

37. Connell, "Towards a Socialist Program."

38. See Rick Kuhn, "Alternative Strategies: Left Nationalism and Revolutionary Marxism," *Journal of Australian Political Economy* 12/13 (1982).

39. See Alastair Davidson, *Antonio Gramsci: The Man, His Ideas* (Sydney: ALR, 1968). Davidson had in fact also introduced Althusser to Australians; see his "Althusser: Marxism Old and New," *Arena* 19 (1969). The young Althusserians were apparently less than taken with Davidson's views; Grant Evans criticized them in *Intervention* 2 (1972), while Winton Higgins overlooked Davidson's contribution in his *Socialist Register* article.

40. See especially Kelvin Rowley, "Pastoral Capitalism," *Intervention* 1 (1972); J. Collins, "Immigrant Workers in Australia," *Intervention* 4 (1974).

41. See, for example, "Beyond Marxism? Interventions after Marx," *Intervention* 17 (1983).

42. See, for example, Tom O'Lincoln, *Into the Mainstream: The Decline of Australian Communism* (Sydney: Stained Wattle, 1985), 143ff.

43. Higgins, "Reconstructing Australian Communism," 179ff.

44. Laurie Carmichael, "A Peoples' Program," *Intervention* 9 (1977), and A. Game and R. Pringle, "Reply to Carmichael," *Intervention* 10 (1978).

45. John Sendy, *The Communist Party: History, Thoughts, and Questions* (Melbourne: CPA History Group, 1978), 28; and see generally his *Comrades Come Rally!* (Melbourne: Nelson, 1978).

46. For example, Bernie Taft, "Marxism Is Open Ended," *Australian Left Review* 83 (1983).

47. Cf. Fehér and Heller, "Class, Democracy, Modernity."

48. *Statement by 23 Members of the Victorian State Committee of the CPA* (Melbourne, April 17, 1984); and see "The CPA Split: Renewal or Dissolution?" *Thesis Eleven* 9 (1984).

49. CPA, *Australian Socialism: A Proposal for Renewal* (Sydney: CPA, 1984).

50. See, for example, Jill Julius Mathews, "Putting Women First," *Australian Left Review* 84 (1983).

51. Laurie Aarons, *A Case for Radical Tax Reform* (Sydney: CPA, 1984).
52. *Socialist Perspectives on Issues for the Eighties: CPA 28th National Congress* (Sydney: CPA, 1984), 5.
53. Socialist Alternative Melbourne Collective, *Make Melbourne Marvellous* (Melbourne: CPA, 1985).
54. Alan Barcan, "The Socialist Left in Australia," APSA (Sydney) Monograph 2, 1960. And see *Fabian Newsletter* (Melbourne) 24, no. 4 (1985).
55. David McKnight, "Rethinking Socialism in the 80s," in *Socialism in Australia: Towards Renewal?* ed. David McKnight (Sydney: D. McKnight, 1985), 3.
56. Ibid., 10.
57. *Australasian Spartacist*, March 1985.
58. See, for example, O'Lincoln, *Into the Mainstream*.
59. See, for example, Denis Freney, *The Socialist Labour League: Moonies of the Left* (Sydney: Denis Freney, 1982); Nick Beams, *A Stalinist Liar Unmasked: A Reply to Denis Freney* (Sydney: Workers News Pamphlet, 1983).
60. *Manifesto of Social Rights* (Sydney: Strawberry Hills, n.d.); Socialist Party of Australia and Socialist Workers Party, *Joint Statement of the Socialist Party of Australia and the Socialist Workers Party* (n.p.: 1984); Anna Pha, *ACTU Policies on Unemployment* (Sydney: SPA, n.d.); Anna Pha and Jack McPhillips, *The Crisis, the Accord and Summit Communique* (Sydney: SPA, n.d.); Socialist Workers Party, *The Struggle for Socialism in the Imperialist Epoch* (Sydney: Pathfinder, 1984).
61. *Joint Statement of the SPA and the SWP*, 9f, 4.
62. See, for example, *Tribune* (Melbourne), May 1, 1985; Ken Cooke, "Confusion in the Peace Ranks," *Age* (Melbourne), May 28, 1985; Ken Mansell, "Making Sense of the NDP Split," *Tribune* (Melbourne), May 29, 1985.
63. *Joint Statement of the SPA and SWP*, 7ff.
64. O'Lincoln, *Into the Mainstream*, 128ff, 154. The debate had other points of significance, signaling as it did both the attraction of the Althusserians to the revolutionary legacy of Trotskyism and the affinity between Deutscher's views and those of the frontist-Eurocommunist lineage.
65. See Mansell, "Making Sense of the NDP Split."
66. Metal Trades Unions, *Policy for Industry Development and More Jobs* (Sydney: Metal Trades Unions, August 1984).
67. Ibid., iii, xvi.
68. Ibid., 197.
69. Ainslie Jolley, *Towards the Regeneration of Australian Manufacturing*, Victorian Chamber of Manufacturers Research (Melbourne) Discussion Paper 14, 1984.
70. *Australasian Spartacist*, March 1985.
71. See, for example, the editorial in *Journal of Australian Political Economy* 17 (1984).
72. Stewart Clegg, Geoff Dow, and Paul Boreham, "From the Politics of Production to the Production of Politics," *Thesis Eleven* 9 (1984); Geoff Dow, "The Case for Corporatism," *Australian Society*, November 1984.
73. Walter Korpi, *The Democratic Class Struggle* (London: Routledge and Kegan Paul, 1984).
74. Winton Higgins and Nixon Apple, "How Limited Is Reformism?" *Theory and Society* 12 (1983).
75. Clegg, Dow, and Boreham, "From the Politics of Production to the Production of Politics," 27.
76. Winton Higgins, "Response to Questionnaire on Social Democracy," *Thesis Eleven* 7 (1983): 134.

77. See, for example, Clegg, Dow and Boreham, "From the Politics of Production to the Production of Politics."
78. Winton Higgins, "Why Do We Need a Left Party?" *Tribune* (Melbourne), August 8, 1984.
79. Julian Triado, "Corporatism, Democracy, and Modernity," *Thesis Eleven* 9 (1984); Beilharz and Watts, "The Discovery of Corporatism"; Beilharz, "The View from the Summit"; Peter Beilharz and Rob Watts, "Tories in Labor Drag?" *Australian Society*, May 1984; Beilharz and Watts, "The Accord and Morals," *Australian Society*, February 1985. Related but different arguments have been put forward by feminists, for whom exclusion is a lived reality. See, inter alia, Danny Blackman, "Women and the Accord," *Australian Left Review* 89 (1984); Ann Game and Rosemary Pringle, "From Here to Fraternity: Women and the Hawke Government," *Scarlet Woman* 17 (1983); Philipa Hall and Barbara Preston, "The Accord: What's in It for Women," *Scarlet Woman* 17 (1983); Ann Game, "Affirmative Action: Liberal Rationality or Challenge to Patriarchy?" *Legal Service Bulletin*, December 1984.
80. Triado, "Corporatism, Democracy, and Modernity," 40.
81. See Hagan, *History of the ACTU*.
82. Stephen Frenkel and Alice Coolican, *Unions against Capitalism?* (Sydney: Allen and Unwin, 1984).
83. Triado, "Corporatism, Democracy, and Modernity," 33.
84. See, for example, Hindess, "Bob's Bon Accord"; R. Curtain, "Abstaining and Complaining," *Australian Society*, March 1985; Mark Burford, "Interpreting Socialism," *Australian Society*, March 1984.
85. Alastair Davidson, *The Communist Party of Australia* (Stanford, Calif.: Hoover, 1969), 183.
86. See the survey in Melbourne Revolutionary Marxists, *A Call for the Revolutionary Regroupment of the Australian Left* (Melbourne: Melbourne Revolutionary Marxists, September 1975 (http://wordpress.com/tag/melbourne-revolutionary-marxists/). On the meanderings of Maoism see, for example, Ted Hill, *Reflections on Communism in Australia* (Melbourne: CPA-ML, 1983); J. Herouvim, "Politics of the Revolving Door—The CPA (ML)," *Melbourne Journal of Politics* 15 (1983–84).
87. Barcan, "The Socialist Left in Australia."
88. See, inter alia, Terry Irving, "Radical Political Science," in *Surveys of Australian Political Science*, ed. Don Aitken (Sydney: Allen and Unwin, 1985); Diane Austin, *Australian Sociologies* (Sydney: Allen and Unwin, 1984).
89. See, for example, *Interventions beyond Marx*; cf. Bob Connell, "Marxists and Antimarxists," *Intervention* 18 (1984); and see the Local Consumption series, as well as G. Gill, "Post-Structuralism as Ideology," *Arena* 69 (1984).

6. Australian Laborism, Social Democracy, and Social Justice

1. E. Gough Whitlam was Prime Minister of the reformist Australian Labor Party government between 1972 and 1975. Details of "Whitlam labor" are provided later in the chapter.
2. Peter Beilharz, "The Australian Left: Beyond Labourism?" in *Socialist Register 1985/1986*, ed. Ralph Miliband et al. (London: Merlin, 1989); "The Left, the Accord and the Future of Socialism," *Thesis Eleven* 15 (1986).
3. Frank Castles, *The Working Class and Welfare* (Sydney: Allen and Unwin, 1985).
4. Stuart Macintyre, *Winners and Losers* (Sydney: Allen and Unwin, 1985); Rob Watts, *Foundations of the National Welfare State* (Sydney: Allen and Unwin, 1987).

5. Peter Love, *Labor and the Money Power* (Melbourne: Melbourne University Press, 1985).
6. Peter Beilharz, "Social Democracy and Social Justice," *Australian and New Zealand Journal of Sociology* 23 (1987).
7. Tim Rowse, *Liberalism and Australian National Character* (Malmsbury, Australia: Kibble, 1978).
8. Ralph Miliband, "Socialist Advance in Britain," *Socialist Register* (1983).
9. Noel Butlin, A. Barnard, and J. J. Pincus, *Government and Capitalism* (Sydney: Allen and Unwin, 1982).
10. Stuart Macintyre, "Labour, Capital, and Arbitration 1890–1920," in *State and Economy in Australia*, ed. B. Head (Melbourne: Oxford University Press, 1983).
11. Henry Bourne Higgins, 1851–1929, leading "friend of labor," advocate of arbitration, delivered the controversial Harvester basic wage case in 1907, thus enshrining the principles of New Protection.
12. Macintyre, "Labour, Capital, and Arbitration."
13. Albert Metin, *Socialism without Doctrines* (Sydney: APCOL, 1977).
14. Alfred Deakin, quoted in Robin Gollan, *Radical and Working Class Politics* (Melbourne: Melbourne University Press, 1960), 165.
15. Stuart Macintyre, "Equity in Australian History," in *A Just Society?* ed. P. Troy (Sydney: Allen and Unwin, 1981).
16. H. B. Higgins, *A New Province for Law and Order* (London: Grant Richards, 1922).
17. John Rickard, *H. B. Higgins* (Sydney: Allen and Unwin, 1984).
18. W. K. Hancock, *Australia* (Brisbane: Jacaranda, 1961), 35.
19. C. J. Don, quoted in Gollan, *Radical and Working Class Politics*, 69.
20. William Roylance, quoted in J. Philipp, "1890: Turning Point in Labour History? in *Historical Studies: Selected Articles, Second Series* (Melbourne: Melbourne University Press, 1967), 130.
21. Hancock, *Australia*.
22. Love, *Labour and the Money Power*.
23. Ben Chifley, *Things Worth Fighting For* (Melbourne: ALP, 1952), 65.
24. Ibid., 65.
25. Rob Watts, "Revising the Revisionists: The ALP and Liberalism 1941–1945," *Thesis Eleven* 7 (1983).
26. Marc Robinson, "Labour and Market Forces: Labor Party Views on the Economic Role of Government from the 1940's to the 1970's," *Journal of Australian Studies* 20 (1987): 92.
27. The ALP "split" occurred in 1955. The result of anticommunist agitation led by B. A. Santamaria's Catholic Action Movement, it produced the right-wing Democratic Labor Party (DLP), which was the main third party until the 1970s. The DLP combined anticommunism with laborist welfare policies and helped for twenty years to keep the ALP from office, none of which has prevented the right from regenerating within the ALP since the 1980s.
28. Stuart Macintyre, "The Short History of Social Democracy in Australia," *Thesis Eleven* 15 (1985).
29. Gough Whitlam, *The Whitlam Government 1972–1975* (Ringwood, Australia: Penguin, 1985).
30. Gough Whitlam, *On Australia's Constitution* (Camberwell, Australia: Widescope, 1977), 199.
31. Ibid., 200–201, 178, 265.

32. Ibid., 61.
33. James Walter, *The Leader: A Political Biography of Gough Whitlam* (St. Lucia: University of Queensland Press, 1980), 117.
34. Robinson, "Labour and Market Forces."
35. Whitlam, *The Whitlam Government*, 743.
36. Gregory Elliot, "The Social Policy of the New Right," in *Australia and the New Right,* ed. M. Sawer (Sydney: Allen and Unwin, 1982).
37. Paul Keating, "How We Kept the Faith for Labor," *Age* (Melbourne), March 27, 1987.
38. Frank Castles, "Australia and Sweden: The Politics of Economic Vulnerability," *Thesis Eleven* 16 (1987).
39. Peter Beilharz, "Reading Politics: Social Theory and Social Policy," *Australian and New Zealand Journal of Sociology* 23 (1989).
40. Robert J. Hawke, *National Reconciliation: The Speeches of Bob Hawke* (Sydney: Fontana, 1984).
41. Australian Council of Trade Unions (ACTU)–Trade Development Commission (TDC), *Australia Reconstructed* (Canberra: AGPS, 1987).
42. Peter Beilharz, "Political Unionism: The Way Ahead?" *Arena* 82 (1988).
43. Peter Beilharz and Rob Watts, "The Discourse of Labourism," *Arena* 77 (1987).

7. The End of Australian Communism

1. Frank Hardy, *Journey into the Future* (Melbourne: Australasian Book Society, 1952), 11.
2. Ibid., 31.
3. Ibid., 119.
4. Leon Trotsky, *The Revolution Betrayed* (New York: Pathfinder, 1972), 14.
5. Hardy, *Journey into the Future,* 257.
6. Ibid., 264.
7. Ibid., 273.
8. See, for example, Socialist Party of Australia (SPA) and Socialist Workers Party (SWP), *Joint Statement of the Socialist Party of Australia and the Socialist Workers Party* (Sydney: SPA and SWP, 1984).
9. See my "Elegies of Australian Communism," *Australian Historical Studies* 92 (1989).
10. C. M. H. Clark, *Meeting Soviet Man* (Melbourne: Angus and Robertson, 1960), 1.
11. Ibid., chap. 10.
12. Ibid., 117.
13. The standard history of the CPA is Alastair Davidson, *The Communist Party of Australia* (Stanford, Calif.: Hoover, 1969). A new history of the CPA is being prepared by Stuart Macintyre and Andrew Wells. See also Tom O'Lincoln, *Into the Mainstream: The Decline of Australian Communism* (Sydney: Stained Wattle Press, 1985); Peter Beilharz, "Australia," in *Yearbook on International Communist Affairs* (Stanford, Calif.: Hoover, 1976); W. Higgins, "Reconstructing Australian Communism," *Socialist Register* (London: Merlin, 1974); Peter Beilharz, "The Australian Left: Beyond Labourism?" *Socialist Register* (London: Merlin, 1985/1986). On the 1984 split, see, for example, A. Gouley and P. Hind, "The CPA Split: Renewal or Dissolution?" *Thesis Eleven* 9 (1984). An exceptional cultural analysis can be found in Andrew Metcalfe, *For Freedom and Dignity* (Sydney: Allen and Unwin, 1988).
14. See, for example, W. G. K. Duncan, ed., *National Economic Planning* (Sydney: Angus and Robertson/AIPS, 1934).

15. See, generally, Anne Curthoys and John Merritt, eds., *Australia's First Cold War*, 2 vols. (Sydney: Allen and Unwin, 1984 and 1986); Bernice Morris, *Between the Lines* (Melbourne: Sybylla, 1988).
16. Jean Baudrillard, *America* (London: Verso, 1988), 98.
17. See Victor S. Clarke, *The Labour Movement in Australasia: A Study in Social Democracy* (New York: Burt Franklin, 1906); Albert Metin, *Socialism without Doctrines* (Sydney: APCOL, 1977); Jurgen Tampke, *Wunderbar Country: Germans Look at Australia, 1850–1914* (Sydney: Hale and Iremonger, 1982); A. G. Austin, ed., *The Webbs' Australian Diary 1898* (Melbourne: Pitman, 1965).
18. See, generally, Stephen Garton, *Out of Luck: Poor Australians and Welfare* (Sydney: Allen and Unwin, 1990); Peter Beilharz, Mark Considine, and Rob Watts, *Arguing about the Welfare State: The Australian Experience* (Sydney: Allen and Unwin, 1994).

8. Between Totalitarianism and Postmodernity

1. Jacques Derrida, *Spectres of Marx* (London: Routledge, 1994).
2. Steven Seidman, *Liberalism and the Origins of European Social Theory* (Berkeley: University of California Press, 1983).
3. Peter Beilharz, Gillian Robinson, and John Rundell, eds., *Between Totalitarianism and Postmodernity: A Thesis Eleven Reader* (Cambridge, Mass.: MIT Press, 1992).
4. Zygmunt Bauman, "A Sociological Theory of Postmodernity," in ibid.
5. Alain Touraine, "Is Sociology Still the Study of Society?" in ibid.
6. Peter Beilharz, *Transforming Labor—Labour Tradition and the Labor Decade in Australia* (Melbourne: Cambridge University Press, 1994).
7. Alain Touraine, *The Workers' Movement* (Cambridge: Cambridge University Press, 1987).
8. Zygmunt Bauman, *Memories of Class* (London: Routledge, 1983); Craig Calhoun, *The Question of Class Struggle* (Oxford: Blackwell, 1982).
9. Peter Beilharz, Mark Considine, and Rob Watts, *Arguing about the Welfare State: The Australian Experience* (Sydney: Allen and Unwin, 1992).
10. Peter Beilharz, *Postmodern Socialism: Romanticism, City and State* (Melbourne: Melbourne University Press, 1994).
11. Marshall Berman, *All That Is Solid Melts into Air* (New York: Simon and Schuster, 1984).

9. Socialism after Communism

1. Peter Beilharz, *Postmodern Socialism* (Melbourne: Melbourne University Press, 1994).
2. See generally Roberto Michels, *Political Parties* (London: Jarrold, 1915), and see Peter Beilharz, *Labour's Utopias: Bolshevism, Fabianism, Social Democracy* (London: Routledge, 1992). More specifically, see Gunther Roth, *The Social Democrats in Imperial Germany* (Totowa, N.J.: Bedminster, 1963), and Vernon Lidtke, *The Alternative Culture: Socialist Labour in Imperial Germany* (Oxford: Oxford University Press, 1985).
3. See, for example, Ernesto Laclau and Chantal Mouffe, *Hegemony and Socialist Strategy* (London: Verso, 1985).
4. Karl Marx, *Capital*, vol. 1 (Moscow: Progress 1970); Beilharz, *Labour's Utopias*, chap. 1.
5. Vladimir I. Lenin, *State and Revolution* (Moscow: Progress, 1970); Beilharz, *Labour's Utopias*, chap. 2.

6. Jean Cohen and Andrew Arato, *Civil Society and Political Theory* (Cambridge, Mass.: MIT Press, 1992); John Keane, *Democracy and Civil Society* (London: Verso, 1988).
7. Leonard Trelawney Hobhouse, *Liberalism* (London: Oxford University Press, 1942), 123, 127. In sociology, of course, the very idea of personality is necessarily social.
8. Hobhouse, *Liberalism*, 133, and see L. T. Hobhouse, *Metaphysical Theory of the State* (London: Allen and Unwin, 1918).
9. John Stuart Mill, *Principles of Political Economy*, books 4 and 5 (Harmondsworth, England: Penguin, 1970), 129, 133, 364–67. Beatrice Webb and Sidney Webb, *Industrial Democracy* (London: B. and S. Webb, 1913), and *The Consumers' Co-operative Movement* (London: Longman, 1921); Sally Alexander, ed., *Women's Fabian Tracts* (London: Routledge, 1986).
10. See Beilharz, *Labour's Utopias*, chap. 5.
11. Richard Henry Tawney, *Equality* (London: Unwin, 1964), 173.
12. G. D. H. Cole, *Guild Socialism Re-stated* (London: Parsons, 1920); Paul Hirst, ed., *The Pluralist Theory of the State* (London: Routledge, 1989).
13. Peter Beilharz, "Negation and Ambivalence: Marx, Simmel and Bolshevism on Money," *Thesis Eleven* 47 (1996).
14. Zygmunt Bauman, *Memories of Class* (London: Routledge, 1982); E. P. Thompson, *The Making of the English Working Class* (London: Gollancz, 1962); Craig Calhoun, *The Question of Class Struggle* (Oxford: Blackwell, 1982).
15. Axel Honneth, *Critique of Power* (Cambridge, Mass.: MIT Press, 1991).
16. Richard Rorty, *Contingency, Irony, Solidarity* (Cambridge: Cambridge University Press, 1989).
17. Mill, *Principles of Political Economy;* John Maynard Keynes, *The General Theory of Employment Interest and Money* (London: Macmillan, 1936), chap. 24; William Beveridge, *Full Employment in a Free Society* (London: Allen and Unwin, 1944), 37.
18. See Peter Beilharz, *Postmodern Socialism: Romanticism, City and State* (Melbourne: Melbourne University Press, 1994).

10. Socialism in Europe

1. Donald Sassoon, *One Hundred Years of Socialism* (London and New York: I. B. Tauris, 1996).
2. Johann P. Arnason, *The Future That Failed* (London: Routledge, 1993); *Nation and Modernity* (Rejkjavik: NSU, 1996).
3. Peter Beilharz, *Labour's Utopias: Bolshevism, Fabianism, Social Democracy* (London: Routledge, 1992).
4. Peter Beilharz, Mark Considine, and Rob Watts, *Arguing about the Welfare State: The Australian Experience* (Sydney: Allen and Unwin, 1992).
5. Otto Schuddekopf, *Linke Leute von rechts* (Berlin: Kohlhammer, 1960).
6. Zeev Sternhell, *The Birth of Fascist Ideology, From Cultural Rebellion to Political Revolution* (Princeton, N.J.: Princeton University Press, 1994).
7. Jeffrey Herf, *Reactionary Modernism* (New York: Cambridge University Press, 1989).
8. Oswald Spengler, *Preussentum und Sozialismus* (Munich: Beck, 1919).
9. Sassoon, *One Hundred Years of Socialism*, 96.
10. Zygmunt Bauman, *Memories of Class* (London: Routledge, 1982); Craig Calhoun, *The Question of Class Struggle* (Oxford: Blackwell, 1982).
11. Peter Beilharz, *Imagining the Antipodes* (Melbourne: Cambridge University Press, 1997).

12. Peter Beilharz, *Postmodern Socialism* (Melbourne: Melbourne University Press, 1994).
13. Peter Beilharz, *Transforming Labor* (Melbourne: Cambridge University Press, 1994).
14. Alain Touraine, *L'Apres socialisme* (Paris: Grasset, 1983), 1.
15. Sassoon, *One Hundred Years of Socialism*, 747.
16. Ibid.
17. Peter Beilharz, *Trotsky, Trotskyism, and the Transition to Socialism* (London: Croom Helm, 1987).
18. Michael Mann, "As the Twentieth Century Ages," *New Left Review* 214 (November 1995).
19. Sassoon, *One Hundred Years of Socialism*, 757.
20. Ibid.
21. Orlando Patterson, *Freedom* (New York: Basic Books, 1991).

11. Intellectuals and Utopians

1. Zygmunt Bauman, *Socialism: The Active Utopia* (London: Allen and Unwin, 1916), 9. Subsequent references to this book will be cited in the text using page numbers only.
2. Émile Durkheim, *Socialism* (London: Routledge 1959; first published 1894/95).
3. See Cornelius Castoriadis, *Devant la Guerre* (Paris: Fayard, 1981).
4. See Peter Beilharz, *Labour's Utopias: Bolshevism, Fabianism, Social Democracy* (London: Routledge, 1992), and *Postmodern Socialism* (Melbourne: Melbourne University Press, 1994).
5. Zygmunt Bauman, *Legislators and Interpreters: On Modernity, Post-Modernity and Intellectuals* (Oxford: Polity, 1987). Subsequent references to this book will be cited in the text using page numbers only.
6. See also Beilharz, *Trotsky, Trotskyism, and the Transition to Socialism* (London: Croom Helm, 1987) and *Labour's Utopias*.

12. Modernity and Communism

1. Zygmunt Bauman, *Modernity and the Holocaust* (Oxford: Polity, 1989).
2. Peter Beilharz, *Zygmunt Bauman: Dialectic of Modernity* (London: Sage, 2000).
3. Zygmunt Bauman, *Legislators and Interpreters* (Oxford: Polity, 1987).
4. See Beilharz, *Zygmunt Bauman*.
5. Zygmunt Bauman, *Modernity and Ambivalence* (Oxford: Polity, 1991).
6. Leszek Kolakowski, "A Pleading for Revolution: A Rejoinder to Z. Bauman," *Archives Europeenes de Sociologie* 12 (1971); Zygmunt Bauman, "Twenty Years After: Crisis of Soviet Type Societies," *Problems of Communism* 20, no. 6 (1971).
7. Julian Hochfeld, "Poland and Britain: Two Concepts of Socialism," *International Affairs* 1 (1957).
8. Zygmunt Bauman, "Stalin and the Peasant Revolution: A Case Study in the Dialectics of Master and Slave," Leeds Occasional Papers in Sociology 19 (Leeds University, Leeds, England), 1985.
9. Ibid., 21. Emphasis in the original.
10. Ibid., 50. Emphasis in the original.
11. Zygmunt Bauman, "Dictatorship over Needs," *Telos* 60 (1984): 263, reprinted in *The Bauman Reader*, ed. Peter Beilharz (Boston: Blackwell, 2001).
12. Zygmunt Bauman, "The Age of Camps," in *Postmodern Ethics* (Oxford: Polity, 1995), reprinted in *The Bauman Reader*, ed. Peter Beilharz (Boston: Blackwell, 2001).

13. Zygmunt Bauman, "Economic Growth, Social Structure, Elite Formation: The Case of Poland," *International Social Science Journal* 5, no. 16 (1964).
14. Zygmunt Bauman, "Officialdom and Class: Bases of Inequality in Socialist Societies," in *The Social Analysis of Class Structure*, ed. Frank Parkin (London: Tavistock, 1974), 129.
15. Ibid., 132.
16. Ibid., 137–39.
17. Ibid., 140.
18. Ibid., 144.
19. Ibid., 147.
20. Zygmunt Bauman, "The Second Generation of Socialism," in *Political Opposition in One Party States*, ed. L. Schapiro (London: Macmillan, 1972), 224.
21. Ibid., 226–27.
22. Ibid., 228–29.
23. Zygmunt Bauman, "Social Dissent in the East European Political System," *Archives Europeene de Sociologie* 12, no. 1 (1971): 46.
24. Zygmunt Bauman, "On the Maturation of Socialism," *Telos* 47 (1981).
25. Ibid., 51.
26. Ibid., 53.
27. Zygmunt Bauman, "Poland: On Its Own," *Telos* 79 (1989): 47.
28. Ibid., 63.
29. Zygmunt Bauman, "Communism: A Postmortem," in *Intimations of Postmodernity* (London: Routledge, 1992).
30. Ibid.
31. Ibid., 171.
32. Zygmunt Bauman, "Assimilation into Exile: The Jew As a Polish Writer," in *Exile and Creativity: Signposts, Travellers, Outsiders, Backward Glances*, ed. S. Suleiman (Durham, N.C.: Duke University Press, 1996).
33. Ibid., 335.
34. Ibid., 337.

13. Looking Back

I write this essay with thanks to David Lovell for friendship over a distance for a very long time. This essay revisits my own thinking in *Labour's Utopias* (1992) and *Postmodern Socialism* (1994) and uses my 2002 work at Harvard in the Houghton Library as William Dean Howells Fellow in American Literature, 1860–1920, where I worked on the Bellamy papers. My thanks to the Houghton Library and to Bernard Bailyn and Daniel Bell for their support in getting me there. Thanks, finally, to George Ritzer for poking me hard about my insistence that Marx was more romantic than futurist. Further resolution of these matters awaits another study.

1. Peter Beilharz, *Labour's Utopias: Bolshevism, Fabianism, Social Democracy* (London: Routledge, 1992), chap. 1.
2. Peter Beilharz, *Postmodern Socialism: Romanticism, City and State* (Melbourne: Melbourne University Press, 1994), chap. 3.
3. Monika Langer, "The Notion of Expression in Marx," *Thesis Eleven* 8 (1984).
4. See Beilharz, *Labour's Utopias*, chap. 1.
5. Karl Marx, *Grundrisse* (Harmondsworth, England: Penguin, 1973 [1857–58]), 704–5.

6. Karl Marx, *Capital*, vol. 3 (Moscow: Progress Publishers, 1971 [1895], 820.
7. Beilharz, *Labour's Utopias*, chap. 1.
8. Ibid., chap. 2.
9. Peter Beilharz, *Trotsky, Trotskyism, and the Transition to Socialism* (London: Croom Helm, 1987).
10. Edward Morgan, "The Philosophy of Edward Bellamy," Bellamy Papers (Houghton Library, Harvard University, Cambridge, Mass.), 1940, 10.
11. Beilharz, *Labour's Utopias*.
12. Peter Beilharz, "Edward Bellamy: Looking Back at American Socialism in the Nineteenth Century," paper delivered to the Annual Proceedings of the American Sociological Association, Atlanta, August 2003.
13. Patrick Riley, ed., *Fenélon, Telemachus* (Cambridge: Cambridge University Press, 1994), xvii; Beilharz, "Edward Bellamy."
14. Edward Bellamy, "The Religion of Solidarity," Bellamy Papers (Houghton Library, Harvard University, Cambridge, Mass.), 1869, 12.
15. Edward Bellamy, *Dr. Heidenhoff's Process* (New York: Appleton, 1880).
16. Franklin Rosemont, ed., *Edward Bellamy: Apparitions of Things to Come* (Chicago: Charles Kerr, 1990).
17. John C. Thomas, *Alternative America: Henry George, Edward Bellamy, Henry Demarest Lloyd and the Adversary Tradition* (Cambridge, Mass.: Harvard University, Belknap Press, 1983).
18. Leo Marx, *The Machine in the Garden: Technology and the Pastoral Ideal in America* (New York: Oxford, 1964).
19. Ibid., 215.
20. Ibid., 226.

14. Socialism and America

1. Werner Sombart, *Why Is There No Socialism in the United States?* (White Plains, New York: M. E. Sharpe, 1976), xix–xxii; and see generally Jürgen Backhaus, *Werner Sombart*, 3 vols. (Marburg, Germany: Metropolis, 1996). With thanks to Sian Supski.
2. Sombart, *Why Is There No Socialism in the United States?* 3. Subsequent references to this book will be cited in the text using page numbers only.
3. Ibid.; Daniel Bell, *Marxian Socialism in the United States* (Ithaca, N.Y.: Cornell University Press, 1996), xxxix. Subsequent references to this book will be cited in the text using page numbers only.
4. Seymour Martin Lipset and Gary Marks, *It Didn't Happen Here: Why Socialism Failed in the United States* (New York: Norton, 2000). Subsequent references to this book will be cited in the text using page numbers only.
5. Zygmunt Bauman, *Europe: An Unfinished Adventure* (Oxford: Polity, 2004).
6. Victoria de Grazia, *Irresistible Empire: America's Advance through Twentieth Century Europe* (Cambridge, Mass.: Harvard University, Belknap Press, 2005). Subsequent references to this book will be cited in the text using page numbers only.
7. Michael Mann, *The Sources of Social Power* (New York: Cambridge University Press, 1993).
8. Ibid., 644–54.
9. John Kautsky, *Social Democracy and the Aristocracy* (New Brunswick, Canada: Transaction, 2002).
10. Michael Mann, *Fascists* (Cambridge: Cambridge University Press, 2004).

11. Ibid., 15–16.

12. Michael Mann, *The Dark Side of Democracy: Explaining Ethnic Cleansing* (New York: Cambridge University Press, 2005).

13. Robin Archer, *Why Is There No Labor Party in the United States?* (Princeton, N.J.: Princeton University Press, 2007). Subsequent references to this book will be cited in the text using page numbers only.

Publication History

Chapter 1 was first published in *Handbook of Social Theory,* ed. Barry Smart and George Ritzer (London: Sage, 2003).

Chapter 2 first appeared in *Labour Histories,* ed. Bain Attwood, Monash Publications in History 17 (Clayton, Australia: Monash University, 1994).

Chapter 3 was first published in *Thesis Eleven* 26, no. 1 (1990): 78–94.

Chapter 4 first appeared in *History of European Ideas* 19 (1994): 1–3, 285–91.

Chapter 5 was first published in *The Socialist Register* (London: Merlin Press, 1985–86).

Chapter 6 was first published in *Social Justice* 16, no. 3 (1989): 15–29.

Chapter 7 was first published in *Thesis Eleven* 27 (1990): 54–62.

Chapter 8 was published in *Political Theory Newsletter* 7 (1995): 571–79.

Chapter 9 was published in *European Legacy* 1, no. 2 (1996): 538–44.

Chapter 10 first appeared in *International Journal of Politics, Culture, and Society* 11, no. 1 (1997).

Chapter 11 is from Peter Beilharz, *Zygmunt Bauman: Dialectic of Modernity* (London: Sage Publications, 2000).

Chapter 12 comes from *Thesis Eleven* 70 (2002): 88–99.

Chapter 13 was originally published in *European Legacy* 9, no. 5 (2004): 597–604.

Index

Accord, the, 54–69, 77
Althusserianism, 60–61
Australian Council of Trade Unions (ACTU), 51–71
Australian Labor Party (ALP), 21, 51–72

Bauman, Zygmunt, 97–98, 112, 142–78
Bellamy, Edward, 183–86, 188
Benjamin, Walter, 17, 22
Bernstein, Eduard, 29, 30–34
Bolshevism, 5–21, 108, 121–28, 137, 148, 167–69
British Labor Party, 135

Calwell, Arthur, 80
Capital, 2–6, 12, 20, 35, 43, 108, 191–96
capitalism: Zygmunt Bauman, 164; Karl Marx, 4–5; socialism, 1, 138–41, 198; United States, 190–91
Catholicism, 90–92
Chifley government, 78–80
cities, 103–4
communism: Australian, 87–94; Zygmunt Bauman, 167–78; Catholicism, 90–92; Eurocommunism, 117; marxism, 136–37; modernity, 119, 167–78; socialism, 107–15; Soviet Union, 169–71. *See also* Communist Party of Australia
Communist Manifesto, The, 5–6
Communist Party of Australia (CPA), 24, 51, 58–63, 69–70, 88–89. *See also* communism
critical theory, 14–15, 112–13
culture, 1
Curtin government, 54, 78–79

Das Kapital. See Capital
Durkheim, Émile, 3, 22, 44
dystopias, 142, 149, 165

Eastern Europe modernity, 171–75
Enlightenment, 27, 129, 152–56
Eurocommunism, 117

Fabianism, 9–11, 21, 42–49; Australian laborism, 74; Australian Labor Party, 59; Eduard Bernstein, 30; British laborism, 120; Gough Whitlam, 54
fascism, 122–23, 132, 137
feminism, 132
Frankfurt School, 168
Fraser government, 51–53

German Social Democratic Party (SPD), 6–7, 13–14, 108, 120–22
Gramsci, Antonio, 5, 12–14, 19–20, 32, 108–9, 118–24, 147–48

Hardy, Frank, 87–88
Hawke government, 51–65, 68–71
hermeneutics, 153–54
Higgins, Henry Bourne, 77–78

intellectuals, 142–66
interpreters. *See Legislators and Interpreters*
Italian Communist Party (PCI), 117

Jacobinism, 144

Kautsky, Karl, 7, 29, 34–40, 108

laborism, 50–86; Accord, the, 58–69; Australian, 52–54, 69–80; Hawke government, 54–58; social democracy, 71–75; Whitlam government, 80–84. *See also* Fabianism; labor movement
labor movement: Australian New Labor, 50–71; communism, 90; marxism, 22–26; socialism, 120. *See also* laborism; social democracy
left. *See* communism; laborism; marxism
Legislators and Interpreters, 151–65
Lenin, Vladimir, 7–11, 147–51
liberal democracy. *See* social democracy
liberalism, 28, 74–75, 107–15
Lovell, David, 43

Macpherson, C. B., 27–29
Mann, Michael, 196–99
Manuscripts, 4
Marx, Karl, 2–6, 137–38, 179–83
marxism: Althusserian, 60–61; in Australia, 102–4; author's perspective, 22; Bolshevism, 148; collapse, 15; communism, 136–37; Fabianism, 43; as ideology, 6, 106; Karl Kautsky, 34–40; David Lovell, 43; without modernity, 138; postmodernity, 95–97; Jean-Jacques Rousseau, 3; socialism, 1–16, 108–9; sociology, 99–100; totalitarianism, 95–97; utopianism, 109; Max Weber, 38
Menzies government, 79

modernity: Edward Bellamy, 188; Eduard Bernstein, 30; cities, 104; communism, 119, 167–78; contemporary marxism, 22; Eastern Europe, 171–78; "end" of, 23; Antonio Gramsci, 13; Karl Kautsky, 36; without marxism, 138; postmodernity, 23, 152–53; social democracy, 27–41; socialism, 1–16, 27–42, 113, 126–32, 146; Soviet Union, 169–71; Alain Touraine, 98

New Prince, 144–47

order, 145, 150
Owen, Robert, 45

pluralism, 107, 112
Polish modernity, 171–78
politics, 149
postmodernism, 23, 43. *See also* postmodernity
postmodernity, 95–106; Zygmunt Bauman, 157–58; modernity, 23, 152–65

romanticism, 1, 10–12, 43
Rousseau, Jean-Jacques, 3, 6, 109
Russian Revolution, 93

Sassoon, Donald, 116–41
self-reflexivity, 142
Simmel, Georg, 3, 22
social democracy, 27–41, 132–38; Eduard Bernstein, 30–34; definition, 28; Fabianism, 43; Karl Kautsky, 34–40; laborism, 71–75; marxism, 111; significance, 39; Werner Sombart, 189–90; utopianism, 28–29; Whitlam government, 54. *See also* laborism; socialism
Social Democratic Party (SPD), 30–32
socialism: alter ego of modernity, 42; Edward Bellamy, 183–86; Eduard Bernstein, 31–34; Bolshevism, 9; as capitalism by default, 127; after communism, 107–15; as counterculture of capitalism, 1, 138–41, 170; definition, 110; European, 116–41; Fabianism, 42; French, 135; and French Revolution, 117; goals, 146; labor

movement, 120; liberalism, 28, 107–15; Karl Marx, 179–83; marxism, 1–16; modernity, 1–16, 27–41, 126–32, 146; romanticism, 1, 10–12; as social theory, 1–16; United States, 14, 189–200; utopianism, 142–51, 200. *See also* social democracy
Socialist Party of America (SPA), 192
Socialist Party of Australia (SPA), 64
Socialist Workers Party (SWP), 64
sociology: cities, 103–4; historical, 100–103; marxism, 99–100; self-reflexivity, 142; Alain Touraine, 98–99
Solidarity movement, 175–77
Sombart, Werner, 189–96
Soviet Union, 169–71

Thesis Eleven, 19–20, 39, 66, 96–97, 105
Tönnies, Ferdinand, 3, 22, 145–46

totalitarianism, 95–106, 167–78
Touraine, Alain, 97–99
Trotsky, Leon, 8–11, 19
Trotskyism, 19–20

United States, 14, 189–200
utopianism, 4, 142–66; Zygmunt Bauman, 143–44; Edward Bellamy, 183–86; Eduard Bernstein, 29; communist, 93; Jacobinism, 144; Karl Kautsky, 29; Karl Marx, 4–5, 137–38, 180–83; Robert Owen, 45; reformist, 21; socialism, 29, 142–51, 200; Sidney Webb, 45–48

Webb, Sidney and Beatrice, 43–48
Weber, Max, 3, 6, 22, 37–38; Fabianism, 44; Russian Revolution, 93
Whitlam, Gough, 54
Whitlam government, 50–53, 80–84

Contradictions
(continued from page ii)

10 Giovanni Arrighi and Beverly J. Silver, *Chaos and Governance in the Modern World System*

9 François Dosse, *History of Structuralism, Volume 2. The Sign Sets: 1967–Present*

8 François Dosse, *History of Structuralism, Volume 1. The Rising Sign, 1945–1966*

7 Patricia Hill Collins, *Fighting Words: Black Women and the Search for Justice*

6 Craig Calhoun and John McGowan, editors, *Hannah Arendt and the Meaning of Politics*

5 Gérard Noiriel, *The French Melting Pot: Immigration, Citizenship, and National Identity*

4 John C. Torpey, *Intellectuals, Socialism, and Dissent: The East German Opposition and Its Legacy*

3 T. M. S. Evens, *Two Kinds of Rationality: Kibbutz, Democracy, and Generational Conflict*

2 Micheline R. Ishay, *Internationalism and Its Betrayal*

1 Johan Heilbron, *The Rise of Social Theory*

PETER BEILHARZ is professor of sociology at La Trobe University in Australia. His other books include *Postmodern Socialism: Romanticism, City, and State*.